This Abled Body

Society of Biblical Literature

Semeia Studies

Number 55

THIS ABLED BODY
Rethinking Disabilities in Biblical Studies

edited by
Hector Avalos, Sarah J. Melcher, and Jeremy Schipper

This Abled Body
Rethinking Disabilities in Biblical Studies

edited by
Hector Avalos
Sarah J. Melcher
Jeremy Schipper

Society of Biblical Literature
Atlanta

THIS ABLED BODY
Rethinking Disabilities in Biblical Studies

Copyright © 2007 by the Society of Biblical Literature

Drawing on page 85 by Richard Parkinson from John F. Nunn, *Ancient Egyptian Medicine* (London: British Museum, 1996). Copyright © Richard Parkinson. Used by permission.

Library of Congress Cataloging-in-Publication Data

This abled body : rethinking disabilities in biblical studies / edited by Hector Avalos, Sarah J. Melcher, and Jeremy Schipper.
        p.   cm. — (Society of Biblical Literature semeia studies ; v. 55)
Includes bibliographical references.
ISBN 978-1-58983-186-5 (pbk. : alk. paper)
    1. People with disabilities—Biblical teaching. 2. People with disabilities—Mediterranean Region—History. I. Avalos, Hector. II. Melcher, Sarah J. III. Schipper, Jeremy.

BS680.A25A25 2007
220.8'305908—dc22   2007035805

14 13 12 11 10 09 08 07   5 4 3 2 1

Printed in the United States of America on acid-free, recycled paper conforming to ANSI/NISO Z39.48-1992 (R1997) and ISO 9706:1994 standards for paper permanence.

Contents

Abbreviations

AAR	American Academy of Religion
AB	Anchor Bible
ABD	*Anchor Bible Dictionary.* Edited by D. N. Freedman. 6 vols. New York, 1992
AfO	Archiv für Orientforschung
AHB	*Ancient History Bulletin*
AIA	Archaeological Institute of America
AJA	*American Journal of Archaeology*
ANET	*Ancient Near Eastern Texts Relating to the Old Testament.* Edited by J. B. Pritchard. 3rd ed. Princeton, 1969
AOAT	*Alter Orient und Altes Testament*
ARM	Archives royales de Mari
ASOR	American Schools of Oriental Research
BAGD	Bauer, W., W. F. Arndt, F. W. Gingrich, and F. W. Danker. *Greek-English Lexicon of the New Testament and Other Early Christian Literature.* 2nd ed. Chicago, 1979
BAR	*Biblical Archaeology Review*
BAS	Biblical Archaeology Society
BASOR	*Bulletin of the American Schools of Oriental Research*
BHS	*Biblia hebraica stuttgartensia*
BLB	Blue Letter Bible. www.blueletterbible.org
BR	*Bible Review*
BS	*Bibliotheca Sacra*
BT	*The Bible Translator*
CAD	*The Assyrian Dictionary of the Oriental Institute of the University of Chicago.* Chicago, 1956–
CANE	*Civilizations of the Ancient Near East.* Edited by Jack Sasson. 4 vols. New York, 1995
CBQ	*Catholic Biblical Quarterly*
CEV	Contemporary English Version
COS	*The Context of Scripture.* Edited by W. W. Hallo. 3 vols. Leiden, 1997–
DSS	Dead Sea Scrolls
DtrH	The Deuteronomistic History
FCB	Feminist Companion to the Bible
GNB	Good News Bible
HSM	*Harvard Semitic Monographs*

HSS	*Harvard Semitic Studies*
HTR	*Harvard Theological Review*
IDB	*The Interpreter's Dictionary of the Bible.* Edited by G. A. Buttrick. 4 vols. Nashville, 1962
IEJ	*Israel Exploration Journal*
JAAR	*Journal of the American Academy of Religion*
JAOS	*Journal of the American Oriental Society*
JARCE	*Journal of the American Research Center in Egypt*
JBL	*Journal of Biblical Literature*
JCS	*Journal of Cuneiform Studies*
JECS	*Journal of Early Christian Studies*
JFSR	*Journal of Feminist Studies in Religion*
JNES	*Journal of Near Eastern Studies*
JRAS	*Journal of the Royal Asiatic Society*
JSNT	*Journal for the Study of the New Testament*
JSOT	*Journal for the Study of the Old Testament*
JSOTSup	*Journal for the Study of the Old Testament: Supplement Series*
JSP	*Journal for the Study of the Pseudepigrapha*
KMT	*KMT: A Modern Journal of Ancient Egypt*
KTU	*Die Keilalphabetischen Texte aus Ugarit.* Edited by Manfred Dietrich. Münster, 1995
LÄ	*Lexikon der Ägyptologie.* Edited by W. Helck, E. Otto, and W. Westendorf. Wiesbaden, 1972
LCL	Loeb Classical Library
LXX	Septuagint
MT	Masoretic Text
NAB	New American Bible
NEA	*Near Eastern Archaeology*
NIBCOT	New International Commentary on the Old Testament
NIGTC	*New International Greek Testament Commentary*
NIV	New International Version
NRSV	New Revised Standard Version
NT	New Testament
NTS	*New Testament Studies*
OBO	Orbis Biblicus et Orientalis
OEANE	*Oxford Encyclopedia of Archaeology in the Near East.* Edited by E. Meyers. New York, 1997.
OT	Old Testament
OTL	Old Testament Library
PMLA	*Publications of the Modern Language Association*
RA	*Revue d'Assyriologie et d'archéologie orientale*
RelSRev	*Religious Studies Review*
RlA	*Reallexikon der Assyriologie.* Edited by Erich Ebeling et al. Berlin, 1928–
RSV	Revised Standard Version
SANE	*Sources from the Ancient Near East*
SBL	Society of Biblical Literature
TCS	*Texts from Cuneiform Sources*

TDNT	*Theological Dictionary of the New Testament.* Edited by G. Kittel and G. Friedrich. Translated by G. W. Bromiley. 10 vols. Grand Rapids, 1964–1976
TLOT	*Theological Lexicon of the Old Testament.* Edited by E. Jenni, with assistance from C. Westermann. Translated by M. E. Biddle. 3 vols. Peabody, MA, 1997
TUAT	*Texte aus der Umwelt des Alten Testaments*
VT	*Vetus Testamentum*
VTSup	*Supplements to Vetus Testamentum*
WAW	Writings from the Ancient World
ZAW	*Zeitschrift für die alttestamentliche Wissenschaft*
ZDMG	*Zeitschrift der deutschen morgendländischen Gesellschaft*
ZDVP	*Zeitschrift des deutschen Pälastina-Vereins*

Introduction

Hector Avalos
Sarah J. Melcher
Jeremy Schipper

How manifold are Thy works, O Lord! All those which Thou hast made
in wisdom (Ps. 104:24), David meant: Thou hast made all in wisdom,
and hast made well, except for madness. And David said to the Holy
One, blessed be He: "Master of the Universe, what profit is there for the
world in madness? . . . is this beautiful in Thine eyes?"
　　　　　　　—Midrash on Psalm 34 (Braude 1959:408–9)

David's question to God understands disabilities as a great unsolved mystery. Essentially, he asks why certain disabilities exist. How one responds to such a question depends largely on the discourse in which the question is framed. For example, the Midrash on Psalm 34 frames the question within a theological discourse. According to this midrash, when the Philistines capture David, God grants him a temporary cognitive disability. Thus, the Philistines no longer perceive David as a political threat and decide to release him (1 Sam 21:10–22:1a). Through this experience, the rabbis suggest, God shows David how a disability is not a divine oversight within God's created order. Rather, when framed within this theological discourse, disability becomes a means of divine deliverance for David.

Yet if the same question were framed within the medical discourses common in contemporary Western culture, disability may represent a biological condition confined to the boundaries of an individual's body rather than one part of a divine master plan. On the other hand, social-scientific discourses may understand disability as resulting from social responses to certain physical or cognitive differences among humans.

Disability studies foregrounds an awareness of how the particular discourse(s) one uses (including theological, medical, social-scientific discourses, and so on) influences the way in which one conceptualizes the term "disability." This approach draws on the tools of various disciplines

1

to examine how social, literary, and institutional discourses produce and represent a conception of disability. Through the innovative perspective of disability scholarship, "disability" does not simply describe a set of biological conditions, but emerges as a complex product of social, institutional, environmental and biological discourses. Such scholarship opens up the study of disability as a subject of critical inquiry (Snyder et al. 2002:3). It promotes the need for critical theorization of disability just as scholars in the humanities and social sciences have critically theorized race, gender, sexuality, and other identity markers.

A History of Disability Studies in Biblical Studies

The burgeoning field of disability studies as an academic discipline has emerged within the humanities and social sciences only in the last few decades. Although disability scholarship routinely makes passing and often generalized references to the role of the Bible and Near Eastern literature in the cultural production and reception of disability, biblical scholars are just beginning to contribute to this growing body of scholarship. With the essays in this volume, biblical scholars make a significant contribution to this exciting field of inquiry. They provide both greater exegetical and theoretical rigor to the study of disability in the Bible and the ancient Near East.

   As an academic discipline, disability studies arose mainly within the social sciences and the humanities. Influenced by neo-Marxist theories and political activist organizations, disability studies emerged in the British social sciences in the 1980s. Indeed, social sciences continue to dominate disability studies in Great Britain. During the 1990s, North American disability studies developed within the humanities. Currently, North American disability studies focus more on the humanities. Nonetheless, biblical scholarship in both Europe and North America has only begun to engage the wider field of disability studies within the present decade. As several fine histories of the rise of disability studies in general exist (Albrecht, Seelman, and Bury; Lennard J. Davis; Stiker), we have limited this review of disabilities studies to its emergence within biblical studies.

   Prior to the rise of disability studies, the study of disability within biblical studies focused on medical diagnosis. This focus is easily illustrated by reference works, which measure the status of the field. For example, in the article "Lame" in *The Interpreter's Dictionary of the Bible* (1962), Roland K. Harrison tells us that the man in Acts 3:2 suffered from "weakness of the astragalus and metatarsus bones of the foot." The person healed at Lystra (Acts 14:8) probably "suffered from some form of cyllosis." Along similar lines, when 1 Kgs 15:23 notes that King Asa was "diseased in his feet," diagnosis of this disease proves to be the dominant interpretative issue for this verse among recent commentators. The recent publication of *Diagnoses in Assyrian and Babylonian Medicine* by JoAnn Scurlock and Burton R.

Andersen shows that such diagnostic approaches have not disappeared. Scurlock and Andersen's massive tome purports to provide precise diagnoses ranging from Parkinson's disease (336–37) to conditions related to individual "cranial nerves" (299–302).

However, increasingly replacing these diagnostic approaches are those interested in how illnesses were experienced by the people and represented in the literature of the ancient Near East. Such an approach is exemplified in works by Avalos (1995a, 1999), Raphael (2004, 2007, forthcoming), Melcher (1998, 2004), and Schipper (2006). In general, such scholars study how socio-religious frameworks interact with health care and with the valuation of persons. The construction of the differential valuation of persons, based on presumed or real mental and physical features and "abilities," is at the root of what we call "Disability Studies."

Within academic biblical and religious studies per se, we may point to Monday, November 20, 1995, as a landmark event. It was on that day that the first session of the "Religion and Disability Studies Consultation" was held at the American Academy of Religion/Society of Biblical Literature (AAR/SBL) Annual Meeting in Philadelphia. The theme of the session was "People with Disabilities and Religious Constructions of Theodicy and Tragedy."

Nine years later, at the 2004 Annual Meeting in San Antonio, we had the debut session of the Biblical Scholarship and Disabilities Consultation within the SBL. The theme there was "The Blind, the Deaf, and the Lame: Biblical Representations of Disability." Over the next few years, this consultation provided a venue for scholars and students to discuss and develop their research on matters of disability within biblical and cognate literature. A number of the contributors to this volume have actively participated in this unit in recent years. In fact, the idea for this volume was first proposed by Gerald O. West during our session at the 2004 AAR/SBL meeting. Its editors and contributors were chosen through informal conversations that began at this meeting. At the time of this volume's publication, the SBL sponsors a unit at its annual meeting entitled "Disability Studies and Healthcare in the Bible and Near East." This new unit grew out of and remains indebted to the earlier Biblical Scholarship and Disabilities Consultation.

Methods and Perspectives

Informed by recent developments in critical disability theory, this collection of essays interrogates the use of the conceptual category "disability" in biblical and other Near Eastern texts and in scholarly interpretations of these texts. The literary and cultural "meanings" of disability in antiquity are still often assumed to be rather stable and transparent by interpreters of the Bible and other Near Eastern texts. The following essays examine how conceptions of disability become a means of narrating, interpreting, and organizing human life in the ancient world and ask how these conceptions contribute to a continuum of attitudes, still reflected in the present, toward the body and persons with disabilities. This volume helps recast disability as a complex mode of interpreting human difference, not unlike gender, race, or sexuality. The approach taken in the volume is not so much a method of criticism as an interrogation of various literary and cultural poetics within ancient texts as well as various scholarly interpretative assumptions regarding disability within the academy.

The essays in this volume employ diverse approaches to biblical criticism including source criticism, the study of comparative Near Eastern literature and cultures, and newer literary and cultural interpretative methods. Writing from a range of scholarly specializations within biblical criticism, the authors explore both methodological issues regarding the study of disability in the ancient world and specific texts related to physical and cognitive disabilities. The diversity of approaches within this collection demonstrates that there is no one way to do disability studies within the humanities or social sciences, even within the sub-category of biblical criticism. Instead, as with feminist criticism, the method of disability study depends on the particular background and specialization of the researcher. Furthermore, the following essays do not present a unified understanding of how the Bible and other Near Eastern texts and cultures from antiquity understand and represent disability. As with many incipient areas of inquiry, differing approaches develop very rapidly. The differentiation in such approaches to disabilities in the Bible is rooted in the diversity of pre-existing approaches to biblical studies, which range from rhetorical criticism to ideological criticism of texts.

If one focuses on the "purpose" of the study of disabilities in the Bible, one can identify at least three approaches that are already evident in the short history of disability studies in biblical studies: (1) redemptionist; (2) rejectionist; (3) historicist (Avalos 2007a). Each of these approaches may stand independently in any scholar's work. However, scholars may also combine, in varying proportions, at least some of these approaches.

A "redemptionist" approach seeks to redeem the biblical text, despite any negative stance on disabilities, by recontextualizing it for modern application. When the biblical text is not viewed as bearing negative attitudes, a redemptionist approach seeks to rescue the text from the misinterpretations of modern scholars with normate views (for a discussion of the term "normate," see the essay by Kerry H. Wynn in this volume). Alternatively phrased, a redemptionist approach seeks to "rescue" the Bible from itself or from any modern misperception. As such, it is part of a longer tradition that has emerged in other liberationist approaches to scriptures from marginalized minorities and feminist critics.

An opposing approach may be described as "rejectionist" because it would argue that the Bible has negative portrayals of disability that should be rejected in modern society. The aim of such an approach is not to re-contextualize, but to repudiate. Such an approach is illustrated by John M. Hull, an unsighted biblical scholar, in his *In the Beginning There Was Darkness: A Blind Person's Conversations with the Bible*, where he frequently criticizes biblical authors for their negative portrayals of the blind. A variant of the rejectionist approach is perhaps best termed a "post-scripturalist approach," which argues that we should not use any ancient text at all, whether it has positive or negative portrayals of disability, to provide normative values today (Avalos 2007b).

A third approach may be called "historicist," because it undertakes historical examinations of disabilities in the Bible and its subsequent interpretation, sometimes in comparison with neighboring ancient cultures, without any overt interest in the consequences of the conclusions for modern application (e.g., Avalos 1995a; Raphael, forthcoming). Such historical interests may involve the study of the socio-literary contexts of texts that pertain to disability studies. They may examine the dynamic relationship between writers and texts and the cultures to which they belong in an effort to "map out" the ideological landscape encoded in imagery of disability. Both writers and texts remain subject to the way disability has been previously represented in their culture, but they are not completely dependent on it either. Thus, disability images provide a window into a dynamic interchange between culture, author, text, and audience (Schipper 2006; Mitchell and Snyder 2000: 27).[1] In general, the following essays reflect, but are not limited to, one or more of these three approaches.

Scope and Organization

The contributors to this volume do not all share one definition of disability in antiquity. Furthermore, they read these texts with a variety of ideological, social, and theological commitments. For example, some understand the Bible as a sacred text that holds religious authority in their lives. Others do not. Some choose to self-identify as disabled or as a family member of a disabled person and suggest that such disclosures remain critical to an understanding of the positions that their essays express. Others do not. There is also a range of opinions regarding the ideologies or theologies, if any, encoded within images of disability in a given biblical or cognate text.

We have divided the volume into three main categories. Part One focuses on issues of methodology. The essays by Neal H. Walls and Nicole Kelley discuss conceptions of disability within ancient Near Eastern and Greco-Roman cultures. These cultures provided the historical matrix for

---

1. We are not alluding to the negative type of "historicism" critiqued by Karl Popper (Popper). We might be more in accord with the "new historicism" (see Gallagher and Greenblatt).

much of the Bible and its cognate literature. The essays throughout this volume often assume some awareness of these cultures. Hector Avalos considers matters of "criticism" in relation to the study of disability in antiquity, while Carole R. Fontaine and Thomas Hentrich discuss biblical representations of disability in relation to the social construction of femininity and masculinity.

The essays in Part Two provide both overviews and close readings of selected biblical texts dealing with issues of disability. Kerry H. Wynn focuses on certain Yahwistic narratives in the Pentateuch, while Jeremy Schipper and Sarah J. Melcher focus on images of disability in the Deuteronomistic History and the Latter Prophets. Turning to the New Testament, Holly Joan Toensing provides a close reading of Mark 5:1–20, and Martin Albl relates Paul's treatment of disability to his proclamation of the gospel.

Part Three contains brief response pieces to the essays in Parts One and Two. Bruce C. Birch is a Hebrew Bible scholar who has written extensively on the books of Samuel as well as biblical ethics. Janet Lees is a speech therapist, pastoral minister, and socially committed biblical scholar who works with people with communication difficulties in the United Kingdom (2007a, 2007b). David T. Mitchell has written extensively on issues of disability in the humanities (1997, 2000, 2005, forthcoming). He has served as president of the Society of Disability Studies and director of the University of Illinois at Chicago's doctoral program in disability studies, which was the first Ph.D. program of its kind. All three respondents are involved in disability scholarship or activism in various capacities and put their work into conversation with selected essays in this volume. The inclusion of these responses aims to situate the work done in this volume within the larger fields of biblical and disability studies.

At this point we turn more specifically to the following essays to indicate for the reader why these essays and their authors were selected. Part One begins with a study of some of the earliest textual references to disability in Walls's "The Origins of the Disabled Body: Disability in Ancient Mesopotamia." Walls has worked extensively in myth and in representations of people and the divine in ancient Mesopotamian literature (1992, 2001, 2005). Adopting Martha L. Edward's community model of disability (1997:35), Walls undertakes a groundbreaking exploration of representations of disability. He introduces relevant data on disability in ancient Mesopotamian texts, provides bibliographic information on cuneiform sources, and discusses a Sumerian myth about the introduction of persons with disabilities into the world.

Kelley's essay, "Deformity and Disability in Greece and Rome," examines deformity and disability in ancient Greek and Roman sources. She draws on her strong expertise in classical literature, including works of the Greco-Roman period (2006). This author uses two mythological portrayals of deformed and disabled persons to explore the relationship between disability and the divine, the use of deformed and disabled persons as entertainment for the non-disabled, the treatment of congenitally deformed infants, the career prospects for the disabled, disability as punishment by the gods, and special compensatory abilities associated with certain disabled individuals.

In chapter 3, "Introducing Sensory Criticism in Biblical Studies: Audiocentricity and Visiocentricity," Avalos, who has devoted much of his career to the study of health care in the ancient Near East (1995a, 1995b, 1995c, 1998, 1999, 2007a), introduces us to what he calls "sensory criticism," which "would center on how different books, corpora, genres, and traditions value the natural senses, including, but not restricted to, the five natural senses usually identified in Western cultures" (p. 47). He uses "sensory criticism" to demonstrate how the Deuteronomistic History is audiocentric insofar as it privileges hearing over seeing in evaluating information about the world and the divine. In contrast, Avalos argues, Job is visiocentric, in privileging seeing over hearing.

In chapter 4, "'Be Men, O Philistines!' (1 Samuel 4:9): Iconographic Representations and Reflections on Female Gender as Disability in the Ancient World," Fontaine turns to art history in order to uncover data supporting the idea "that in ancient patriarchal societies, the low-status disabled female sits at the very bottom of the ladder of cultural preferences" (p. 62). A prolific contributor to biblical scholarship, this author has published in the area of disability in the Bible, feminist approaches to biblical scholarship, and artistic representation in the ancient Near East (1993, 1996, 2005). Particularly fascinating here is Fontaine's discussion of how gender and disability conventions in art and literature are used to depict enemies and foreigners in a state of greatly reduced status.

Chapter 5, "Masculinity and Disability in the Bible," by Hentrich, builds on the insight from disability studies that disability narratives tend to be composed in gendered terms, with disability modulating gender-based expectations of individuals. Hentrich asks the question of how disability affects a man's relationship with God and pursues an answer by looking at the role of priests in ancient Israel. In addition, Hentrich addresses two distinct aspects of masculinity and disability in the Bible: the predominantly masculine portrayal of YHWH and the general aspect of illness and disability in the Bible. The author uses his established skill in redaction-critical approaches to re-create the distinctive stages of composition for various passages as he explores the interrelationship of disability and masculinity in these locations (2000).

Part Two of this collection begins with Wynn's essay, "The Normate Hermeneutic and Interpretations of Disability within the Yahwistic Narratives." Wynn chooses in his essay to focus on contemporary interpretation of the Yahwistic narratives. Informed by Rosemary Garland Thomson's concept of the "normate" (1997), Wynn argues that "contemporary interpretation of disability within the narratives attributed to the Yahwist shows that a 'normate hermeneutic' dominates modern biblical thought" (p. 92). The author describes a "normate hermeneutic" as "the means by which scripture is interpreted so that it complies with and reinforces the socially constructed norms" (p. 92). The author has previously published on the translation of disability terms in the Bible (2001).

Schipper examines in chapter 7 the way images of disability are used in texts that recount key transitions in ancient Israelite leadership. In his essay, "Disabling Israelite Leadership: 2 Samuel 6:23 and Other Images of Disability in the Deuteronomistic History," Schipper tests the theory that images of disability in this corpus function to provide "ideological commentary on the state of national leadership" (p. 104). He examines the relationship of disability images to David's solidification of power. The author has published widely in the nascent field of disability in the Bible, including his very recent book, *Disability Studies and the Hebrew Bible: Figuring Mephibosheth in the David Story* (2006), as well as several journal articles related to disability in the Bible (2004, 2005a, 2005b).

Chapter 8, "With Whom Do the Disabled Associate? Metaphorical Interplay in the Latter Prophets," studies the interaction of metaphors of physical impairment with other prophetic metaphors in order to explore how these metaphors communicate the prophets' theological conceptions of divine sovereignty. Melcher's essay examines three areas: the role of metaphors of impairment within a prophetic emphasis on healing; the use of prophetic metaphors of impairment to depict moral deficiency; and a prophetic resource for a disability liberation ethic. Looking at how metaphors interact within prophetic passages may aid in fleshing out the broader discourse in which metaphors of impairment function. Melcher has published numerous articles on representations of the body in the Bible, with particular emphasis on sexual practice and disability (1996, 1998, 2002, 2003, 2004, Dille and Melcher, forthcoming).

In chapter 9, " 'Living among the Tombs': Society, Mental Illness, and Self-Destruction in Mark 5:1–20," Toensing reveals her motivations in studying this well-known biblical passage. She does so, in part, because of the experience related to her brother's struggle with mental illness and his eventual suicide. As Toensing points out, the passage has played a role in the stigmatization of the mentally ill, particularly through the association of mental illness with a spiritual cause:

> Interpreting the demoniac story of Mark 5 using the lens of Disability Studies gives readers an opportunity not only to understand how such texts may contribute to this stigmatization, but also to explore the textual resources for changing those perceptions or for thinking differently about the theory of a spiritual cause for mental illness. (p. 133)

She places the biblical text in dialogue with the modern experience of mental illness, investigating the response of communities to the mentally ill, including the community in Mark 5:1–20. The author not only brings personal life experience to her study, but previous work in innovative, feminist approaches to biblical texts (1995, 1997, 2005).

Paul's view of disability is central to his proclamation of the gospel, according to Martin Albl's essay, " 'For Whenever I Am Weak, Then I Am Strong': Disability in Paul's Epistles" (chapter 10). Albl draws upon two modern definitions of disability from the field of disability studies (cf. Wassermann: 219–22) to explore three major facets of Paul's message in the authentically Pauline epistles: "(1) Paul's general understanding of disability; (2) Paul's view of disability in the context of his gospel message; and (3) analysis of Paul's personal experience with disability as related in Gal 4:13–14 and 2 Cor 12:1–10" (p. 146). Previous to this essay, Albl has contributed an article about the health care system reflected in the Letter of James (2002), as well as important monographs about early Christian testimonia (1999) and Pseudo-Gregory of Nyssa's *Testimonies against the Jews* (2004).

As stated above, the brief response pieces by Birch, Lees, and Mitchell follow the essays in Parts One and Two. They engage selected topics and themes that emerge from the previous essays.

Conclusion

The claim of novelty decorates the advertisements of most publishers and authors. *This Abled Body* is the brainchild of necessity, which is the mother of invention. As we, the editors, worked on our own individual projects, we saw the need for a more coherent articulation of the expanding and diversifying approaches we were witnessing in disability studies. No previous work, either as a monograph or as an edited anthology, has attempted to integrate disability studies with biblical studies in a manner that addresses general theoretical issues with specific applications in biblical and Near Eastern texts. As such, our volume is situated within the venerable tradition of *Semeia*, which is devoted to experimental approaches in biblical studies.

But our ambition is larger than the Bible. We seek to place the Bible within a larger corpus of texts, ancient and modern, which, for better or for worse, is part of our literary, social, and religious heritage. We aim to bring biblical studies into conversation with the wider field of disability studies and with the humanities and social sciences. To this end, the volume includes responses from established disability activists and academics working in the social sciences and humanities. We hope the volume marks the beginning of an interdisciplinary dialogue that is critical for understanding the role of disability in the human experience.

Essays

Part One
Rethinking Disabilities in Ancient Texts

1

The Origins of the Disabled Body

Disability in Ancient Mesopotamia

Neal H. Walls

Since historical records from ancient Mesopotamia and Egypt provide our earliest written references to people with disabilities, it is appropriate to begin a "rethinking" of disability in biblical studies within this larger context.[1] Unfortunately, scholars of the ancient Near East have only begun to approach the representation of disability in ancient sources, and progress has been minimal.[2] What little work has been done has usually assumed a medical model of disability or discussed medical aspects of textual depictions. Although there are sporadic references in ancient Mesopotamian and Egyptian records to persons with physical or cognitive disabilities (as defined by modern constructs), there are very few sources that actually shed much light on the ancient concept of disability or social attitudes toward people with disabilities.[3] The geographical and temporal expanse

---

1. I would like to thank Mary Foskett for sharing her insights into this topic. Hector Avalos, Raymond Westbrook, and JoAnn Scurlock generously answered my questions on cuneiform sources. Unless otherwise noted, all translations from Akkadian are the author's, whose normalizations follow Huehnergard (2000).

2. In contrast to the study of Hellenistic and Graeco-Roman culture, there are no published books on disability in ancient Mesopotamia and few studies of "the body" (e.g., Asher-Greve 1998). The only direct treatment of disability in Mesopotamia is a chapter by Elena Cassin (1987). She concludes her discussion of *kudurru* phrases by stating that they reflect a taxonomy of the marginal or "other" in contrast to the healthy or the norm (1987:93), but her argument is not particularly cogent. For a fuller consideration of available resources, see now the annotated bibliography by M. Miles on the web at http://cirrie.buffalo.edu/bibliography/mideast/historicalantiquity.html.

3. For ancient Egypt, see Dasen (1993:99–103) on "physical minorities," including disabled people (cf. Jeffreys and Tait 2000; Nunn 1996). Weeks (1995) notes the Egyptian pictorial representation of many pathological physiologies—such as

of the ancient Near East precludes concise summaries of ancient social constructs. What might be documented for one century in one location does
not necessarily hold true for other places or times. The mass of textual data
through which scholars must comb to establish even basic social facts for
the ancient world further complicates general overviews or conclusions
about the representations of disability in the ancient literature.

Chapter 25 of The Instruction of *Amenemope* provides an extremely
rare expression of ancient attitudes toward people with disabilities.

> Do not laugh at a blind man,
> Nor tease a dwarf,
> Nor cause hardship for the lame.
> Don't tease a man who is in the hand of the god [i.e., ill or insane],
> Nor be angry with him for his failings.
> Man is clay and straw,
> The god is his builder.
> He tears down, he builds up daily. (Lichtheim 1997:121)

This Egyptian wisdom text explains that men are made poor or elevated as
chiefs at the whim of the gods. Even with its explicit reference to disabled
humans, however, such proverbial concern for the fragility of life and the
ephemeral quality of human achievement provides little information about
actual social attitudes toward people with disabilities in the ancient Near
East. Similarly, the first tablet (of 107 tablets) of the Mesopotamian omen
series *Šumma Ālu* (see Sally M. Freedman 1998) recognizes certain physical
anomalies, deformities, or disabilities. Lines 85–98 of this tablet include
observations of types of people who might be seen in a city, including
lame men and women, "idiots," deaf men, and blind men (see Sally M.
Freedman 1998:33). Yet this simple list of persons with recognizable medical conditions tells us almost nothing about social attitudes toward them
as individuals or as an identifiable social category. There is no correlation
between the negative or positive association of the observed person with
a good or bad omen, for example, so one cannot assume that the presence
of people with disabilities augured good or ill.

Given the expanse of ancient Near Eastern history and the difficulties
of reconstructing ancient ideologies of "disability," therefore, the present
chapter limits its focus to the representation of people with disabilities in
ancient Mesopotamian textual sources. My goal is to introduce relevant
data on disability in ancient Mesopotamia, to provide bibliographic references for the cuneiform evidence, and to present one Sumerian myth that
accounts for the origin of people with disabilities. Rather than a "rethinking" of the complex issue, this essay offers only an initial approach to the
rhetorical representation of disability in ancient Babylonian literature; this

---

people with club feet, hunchbacks, hernias, and achondroplastic dwarfism—and
provides a useful description of each of the available medical papyri.

chapter remains more of a prolegomena than a reconsideration of previous scholarly constructs.

Ancient sources for identifying and defining "disability" in Mesopotamia include medical, magical, and omen texts, as well as rare references in letters and literary texts. There recently have been extensive publications of Mesopotamian medical and magical texts.[4] The most important cuneiform sources for ancient medicine include therapeutic texts that derive from the Old Babylonian tradition, the diagnostic and prognostic series of forty tablets called "the symptoms" (*sakikku*; see now Heessel 2000), the omen series *Šumma Izbu* on anomalous births (see Leichty 1970), and the *Alamdimmû* or "physiognomic omen texts" (see Böck 2000). These texts provide the vocabulary for what ancient Mesopotamians recognized as medical conditions apart from the norm (i.e., Akkadian terms often translated as "cripple," "blind," etc.). Unfortunately, the medical model for identifying forms of disability in an ancient culture proves too limited an approach to reconstruct ancient social concepts.

In this essay I assume a community model of disability, in which disability is defined or measured by one's capacity to fulfill socially prescribed tasks or functions rather than by medical or physical criteria (see Martha Lynn Edwards 1997:35). Disability, whether physical or cognitive, is thus a relative and socially constructed category that rests upon a particular society's expectations. For example, while the loss of a hand could lead to "the impairment of major life functions" (as the Americans with Disabilities Act of 1990 characterizes a disability) for an ancient singer, it would perhaps not qualify as a professional "disability" in Mesopotamian ideology (cf. Mitchell and Snyder 1997:2). Indeed, a Sumerian proverb compares a "scribe without a hand" to a "singer without a voice" as examples of people unable to perform their professional duties (Alster 1997:53). A community or social model of disability may allow for a more subtle or nuanced analysis of textual representations of disability in our ancient sources, but this conceptual approach also highlights the difficulties of reconstructing ancient ideology from the meager historical sources available to modern scholars.

As Martha Lynn Edwards (1997:43–44) points out in her studies of disability in ancient Greece, information about disabled people in the ancient Near East is often difficult to uncover precisely because they were integrated into society in productive ways. Conversely, those individuals who suffered from truly debilitating conditions are unlikely to appear in the public or literary records. In his study of health care in the ancient world, Hector Avalos concludes, "Mesopotamia exhibits a long tradition

---

4. See the bibliographies in Abusch (2002), Biggs (2005), Farber (1995), Scurlock (2005; 2006), and Scurlock and Andersen (2005). Interested readers should also consult the *RlA* and *LÄ* for particular terms and topics concerning medicine and disability in the ancient Near East. I was unable to consult the recently published book *Disease in Babylonia* (Finkel and Geller 2007).

in which individual households, not a state institution or the temple, bore direct responsibility for the long-term care of the ill" (1995a:176). Similarly, Raymond Westbrook (1998:242) explains that the ancient Mesopotamian family system was designed to provide support for non-productive persons, such as children, the sick, and the elderly. This familial responsibility was based on the social obligations of honor and shame. In the prologue to his laws, for example, Lipit-Ishtar proclaims, "I made the father support his children, I made the child support his father" (Roth 1997:25). No law exists, however, in any Mesopotamian legal text that actually requires a man to care for his parents (see Stol and Vleeming 1998).

When the social institution of family support was lacking, the elderly and destitute could seek public support from the temple system. Avalos (1995a:176–77) concurs with I. J. Gelb's description of the Mesopotamian temple as a place for "widows, orphans, old people, especially old women, sterile and childless women, cripples, especially blind and deaf persons," among others (Gelb 1972:10), who would function as working servants in household tasks such as milling and weaving. Gelb's (1972) discussion of the personnel associated with the temple in Sumerian sources from the third millennium B.C.E. includes rations lists of temple workers in the *arua* institution. Although he focuses on the economic motivation in giving people into temple service, Gelb's research also notes various people with disabilities. He mentions one Pre-Sargonic text, for example, that lists 180 blind men (IGI.NU.DU$_8$) among 723 women, 1,741 children or babies, and more than 600 (healthy) men in temple service (1972:4).

Rather than begin with the medical or historical evidence for disabled people in ancient Mesopotamia, therefore, this essay begins with the literary genre of creation myth. As poetic and rhetorical expressions of the human condition, mythological texts may provide useful insights into the ancient construction of physical normality, abnormality, and disability. I return to the Mesopotamian evidence for forms of disability after an examination of the origin of disabled people in the Sumerian mythological imagination.

Creating the Disabled Body: Enki and Ninmah

Ancient Mesopotamian myths of creation describe humanity as laborers who were created to serve the gods and relieve them of their labors. Through the onerous work of digging canals, growing grain, and brewing beer, humans provide the daily sacrificial meals and ritual clothing of the gods. Tablet VI of the Babylonian Creation Epic (*Enuma Elish*), for example, reports that when Ea created humankind "he imposed the toil of the gods (on man) and released the gods from it" so that they might be at rest. Similarly, in the first tablet of the Old Babylonian myth of Atrahasis, the gods call upon "the midwife of the gods, wise Mami," to form humans:

Create a human being [*lullû*] that he may bear the yoke,

> Let him bear the yoke, the task of Enlil,
> Let man [*awīlum*] assume the drudgery of the gods. (trans.
>   Benjamin J. Foster 1995:58)

Mami creates mortals with the aid of her consort, Enki (also called Ea), from divine flesh, blood, and spittle, as well as clay. Humans are a hardy and fertile stock, built for manual labor as the expendable servants of the deities. The myth of Atrahasis explains that the gods may attempt to exterminate their pesky creatures if they become too rambunctious and noisy, thus disturbing the divine leisure, but after the Deluge the gods recognize the importance of humans in the created order as those who feed, clothe, and tend to the divine needs.

Since humans were created to be laborers, it is not surprising that the only Mesopotamian anthropogony to include disabled humans does so within the context of assigning them productive work within society. Older than the Akkadian myths of Atrahasis and *Enuma Elish,* the Sumerian myth of Enki and Ninmah describes the creation of humanity in a playful tale that also explains the origin of normal and abnormal human forms.[5] The first half of the myth narrates the traditional creation of humans as laborers and the assignment of their fate in service of the gods. Thorkild Jacobsen (1987:151) describes this section as a myth about Enki and his mother, Namma, who fashions humans along with the "ovary goddesses" before their fate is assigned by Namma and Ninmah, the midwife goddess. The latter half of the text, which concerns us here, describes the divine banquet at which the deities are celebrating their success in establishing a life of leisure for themselves within the new cosmic order. After much celebration, the inebriated goddess Ninmah boasts, "Man's body can be either good or bad and whether I make a fate good or bad depends on my will." Jacobsen (1987:152) describes Ninmah as a "goddess of gestation and birth, the numinous power of the uterus to expand, shape, and mature the embryo," who determines a human's fate by the manner in which she shapes them in the womb. Enki claims that he can counterbalance any form that Ninmah creates, and the contest begins.

The first man fashioned from clay by Ninmah "could not bend his outstretched weak hands," and Enki appoints him as "a servant to the king." The second man is blind, and Enki decrees his fate, "allotting to him the

---

5. On this difficult Sumerian myth, see the most recent translation, transliteration, and bibliography in the Electronic Text Corpus of Sumerian Literature (ETCSL) on the web at http://www-etcsl.orient.ox.ac.uk/. It is listed as 1.1.2, Enki and Ninmah. Recent translations in print include Jacob Klein (1997) and Willem H. P. Römer (1993:386–401), as well as the useful discussions of Jacobsen (1987:151–66), Bottéro and Kramer (1989:188–98), Kramer and Maier (1989:31–37), and Stol (2000:109–10). Many of the text's final thirty lines remain lost or obscure. Unless otherwise noted, all translations of Enki and Ninmah follow the online ETCSL version.

musical arts." Although the text is broken, it appears that Enki assigns him a court function. The third man is "one with both feet broken, one with paralyzed feet," whom Enki sets as a silversmith. A variant text describes the third being as a "moron" or "idiot" (LIL), who also serves as a courtier, according to Jacobsen (1987:160). The Sumerian terminology is imprecise, so this word may refer to a deaf person rather than one with a cognitive disability. The fourth created being is incontinent, dripping either urine or semen, and Enki's actions regarding him remain obscure.

The fifth person in Ninmah's challenge to Enki is a "woman who could not give birth," whom Enki places either in the service of the queen or as a weaver in the Women's House. It is unclear whether her occupation takes place within the royal harem, the queen's household, or the "Women's Quarter" (see Jacob Klein 1997:518). Regardless, this infertile woman has gainful employment in either the textile industry or in attendance on the queen rather than adopting the normative social role of a wife and mother in a husband's house. The Old Babylonian creation myth Atrahasis, which describes the creation of humanity to relieve the gods of their hard labors in Tablet I, concludes in Tablet III with new initiatives to limit human population. Although the text is broken, it appears that Enki and his consort, here called Nintu, establish new categories of people, including the "woman who gives birth yet does not give birth (successfully)," as translated by Stephanie Dalley (1991:35; cf. Benjamin R. Foster 1995:76). In addition to these infertile women, the institution of celibate priestesses (ugbatu, entu, and egiṣītu) and the creation of baby-killing demons will help to control population growth. Apart from these infertile women, there are no descriptions of disabled bodies in the (admittedly broken) text of Atrahasis.

The sixth human created in the Sumerian myth of Enki and Ninmah is "one with neither a penis nor a vagina on its body," to whom Enki assigns the role of a eunuch from Nippur (see Jacob Klein 1997:518) "to stand before the king." This asexual creature parallels the infertile woman in the previous line of the Sumerian myth. The reference may denote men who become eunuchs through castration as well as those born without external sexual organs. Such a surgical procedure, or physical mutilation, did not constitute an economic disability in the sense that it actually qualified a man to work in powerful and influential governmental positions, especially in the Neo-Assyrian period (see Grayson 1995).[6]

In each of these six cases Enki provides a social position and productive economic role for Ninmah's purposefully malformed children. Indeed,

---

6. On eunuchs, see also the Middle Assyrian Palace Decrees (in Roth 1997:195–209) for examples of castration for service in the palace and royal harems. See also Tougher (2002). Various cult actors and devotees of Ishtar (assinnu, kurgarrû, kulu'u) may also have been eunuchs (see Nissinen 1998:28–36, with notes). Hermaphrodites were also recognized in Mesopotamian texts, such as šumma Izbu omens (see Scurlock and Andersen 2005:404–5).

some of these people are given advanced technical skills (silversmith) or powerful positions at court rather than menial tasks to earn their bread. When it is Enki's turn to fashion a human for Ninmah to accommodate, he apparently introduces a new mode of creation by placing semen within the womb of a woman, who is to give birth to the new being; it appears that the myth contrasts the original mode of human production from clay with sexual procreation (contra Jacob Klein 1997:517). This innovation has the effect of creating the first human infant, who is called Umul ("its day is far off"). Although earlier interpretations suggest that Umul is a very old man, many Sumerologists now argue that Umul is either a vulnerable newborn infant, a premature infant, or "miscarried" fetus (see Rivkah Harris 2000:11; Kilmer 1976; Stol 2000:110). The myth states that Umul's head, eyes, neck, lungs, heart, and bowels are "afflicted." This portion of the narrative concludes, "With its hand and its lolling head it could not put bread into its mouth; its spine and head were dislocated. The weak hips and the shaky feet could not carry (?) it on the field—Enki fashioned it in this way." After inspecting the misshapen and helpless creature, Ninmah in exasperation proclaims, "The man you have fashioned is neither alive nor dead. He cannot support himself (?)." Stol (2000:110) translates the last phrase of Ninmah's complaint, "I cannot take care of it" (cf. Jacobsen 1987:163). Enki responds to Ninmah's inability to find a social role for Umul by repeating his own success in decreeing a fate and "giving bread" to each of her creatures. The text unfortunately becomes fragmentary at this point, but the myth apparently concludes with an acknowledgment of both sexes' contribution to the birth of healthy infants (see Stol 2000:109–10).

For all of its textual difficulties, the Sumerian myth of Enki and Ninmah is clear in its rhetorical attempt to incorporate people with a range of disabilities into the larger social structure. The Sumerian text recognizes the non-normative medical condition of these persons, but it does not categorize them as "disabled" or unemployable. Rather than naming "disability" as a means to exclude some persons from city life, this myth recognizes an "otherness" to each of Ninmah's children. Each becomes a functioning member within the social organization, and many are given technical skills and high social status consistent with their abilities. The text thus presupposes a community model of disability. While Ninmah's new creations are assigned gainful employment in order to earn their bread, Umul, as a fetus or (premature) newborn, has no such productive role to play. Rather than contribute to society, he must have all of his most basic needs supplied by others in order to survive. The text of Enki and Ninmah thus distinguishes between those humans with physical or functional abnormalities who are integrated into their community in economically productive ways and those humans (represented by Umul) who are unfit for productive labor of any kind.

The Limits of Disability: Infanticide and Euthanasia

Bendt Alster (1997:203) translates a remarkable Sumerian proverb: "A man whose knees are paralyzed, Nintu has not conceived him, as they say." The metaphor of divine conception by the birth-goddess (here called Nintu instead of Ninmah) is reminiscent of the Western metaphor of humans being created in the image of God (Gen 1:27), but the proverb seems to humorously contradict the myth of Enki and Ninmah by identifying disabled people as "children of a lesser god(dess)." Yet one must also consider the more serious question of whether severely deformed newborns were recognized as fully human beings in ancient Mesopotamia. If Umul is indeed a miscarried fetus or premature baby, as many Sumerologists now argue, then the myth of Enki and Ninmah raises the question of how ancient Mesopotamians actually treated infants born with severe disabilities.[7] Akkadian literature appears to represent the stillborn infant (*kūbu*) and the ominous malformed fetus (*izbu*) as distinct from a healthy newborn.[8] In what contexts might a newborn child be rejected as either less than fully human or too much of a liability for society to tolerate? An answer to this question may provide insight into the limits of "disability" as a social construction in ancient Mesopotamia.

In contrast to ancient Greece (e.g., Dasen 1993:205–10), there is no evidence for the common practice of exposure or infanticide of disabled or deformed infants in the ancient Near East. Mesopotamian legal codes contain no reference to infanticide, although they do address abortion and accidental miscarriage.[9] Cuneiform documents suggest that it was not un-

---

7. See Rivkah Harris (2000:7–16) for an excellent overview of earlier research on infancy in Mesopotamia. See Stol (2000) for an extended treatment of related topics.

8. For malformed or anomalous miscarriages and births see the convenient survey of Stol (2000:158–70), with references to earlier literature. An incantation against the "scarlet demon," Samana, seems to identify the (human) *izbu* and *kūbu* as stillborn infants: "(Just an) an anomaly [*izbu*] never saw his fellow man, / (Just as) a premature child [*kūbu*] never sucked its mother's milk, / Let Samana never return, let it never seize its prey!" (Finkel 1998:95–96). The Akkadian term for a stillborn fetus, *kūbu*, is usually written with the determinative for a divine being (see Rivkah Harris 2000:9), perhaps because their spirits may haunt the living. Their spirits were also provided with a comfortable existence in the netherworld in Mesopotamian myth (see George 1999:189). See also Rivkah Harris (2000:15–16 with notes) on the burial of stillborn infants and children under the floors of houses.

9. See Stol (2000:39–48) for a convenient overview of abortion in ancient Mesopotamia. In addition to the monetary damages (and possible execution) if one accidentally causes a woman to miscarry, note the Middle Assyrian Law (A §53): "If a woman [*sinniltu*] aborts her fetus by her own action and they then prove the charges against her and find her guilty, they shall impale her, they shall not bury her. If she dies as a result of aborting her fetus, they shall impale

common for (wealthy) people to adopt infants who had been "abandoned in the street or at the city well" by their parents (see Malul 1990:104–5). The ancient rhetoric describes these children as being adopted "from the street," "found in a well," or "snatched from the dog's mouth" (see Malul 1990; Rivkah Harris 2000:15). This legal terminology of abandonment precludes the birth parents from laying claim to the child at a later time. Rivkah Harris (2000:15) describes the exposure of "children with deformities" and refers to Malul (1990) and others, but she apparently conflates the financial motivation to give a child up for adoption with the exposure of deformed infants. I remain unaware of any evidence of adoptions of unhealthy or disabled children in cuneiform sources.

There are, however, two references to the practice of infanticide in the so-called diagnostic handbook (sakikku) from ancient Mesopotamia.[10] The first reference describes a child born with a disease, the "spawn of Shulpaea," which puts the entire household at risk of being "scattered." JoAnn Scurlock and Burton Andersen (2005:332) identify the disease as one of a usually fatal group, collectively referred to as "floppy baby syndrome" (i.e., Werdnig-Hoffman disease and Prader-Willi syndrome), in which extremely poor muscle tone results from a disease of the central nervous system and peripheral nerves. If the infant is born with this condition, then "you throw him alive [balṭussu] into the river and his evil will be carried away." Scurlock and Andersen (2005:332) explain, "Throwing the baby into the river (also the preferred method of disposal of malformed stillbirths [izbū]) dispatched it to the netherworld from which its spirit (zaqīqu) might eventually return for another try at life." Marten Stol (2000:145, 165–66) also explains that Babylonians disposed of ominous "malformed births" (izbū) by throwing their bodies into the river as part of the apotropaic namburbi ritual to avert a portended evil (see Caplice 1974:11; Maul 1994:336–43).[11]

The diagnostic handbook's second example of infanticide prescribes burial alive as a reaction to the birth of an infant with a form of Hunting-

---

her, they shall not bury her" (Roth 1997:174; cf. Stol 2000:41). The denial of burial suggests the heinous nature of the crime in ancient Assyrian thought. The Middle Assyrian Laws also includes provisions for persons who (accidentally) cause a woman to miscarry (A §50–53; see Roth 1997:173–74).

10. Scurlock and Andersen (2005:332, 335, 336) describe four references to the practice of euthanasia in Mesopotamian medical texts. Their index includes a fifth example on page 326, which Dr. Scurlock (in a personal communication) explains as a reference to 13.221. This text describes a one- or two-month-old infant with "falling spell(s)," which the authors suggest is caused by meningitis. They avoid the term "infanticide" for the cases involving infants because they believe this is a form of euthanasia or eugenics.

11. On the role of rivers as a symbolic means of expelling evil substances, see also Avalos (1995a:182–84). Caplice (1974:11) and Scurlock and Andersen (2005:332) imply that the namburbi ritual was performed on stillborn or dead humans and animals, not on living human infants with minor abnormalities.

ton's disease, as identified by Scurlock and Andersen (2005:336). The sign of this disease is that the infant, "from the moment he is born, wails, twists, and is continually rigid."[12] The text stipulates that "in order that the house of his father not be scattered, you lay him to rest as if he were a stillborn child [*kīma* *ᵈkūbi tušnālšū-ma*] and the evil will be carried away (with him)." These two texts thus prescribe treatment of the afflicted infants in accordance with the disposal of malformed (*izbū*) and developmentally normal (*kūbū*) stillborn infants, as though they were not fully human.

Scurlock and Andersen (2005:335–36) also present two cases of euthanasia involving adults from a Neo-Assyrian diagnostic text from Sultantepe (see also Stol 1993:96). They identify "the spawn of Shulpaea" in these two passages as Huntington's disease. The first case reads: "As its sign, (it portends) destruction of the house of the father. His father and mother will bear his punishment. In order for it not to approach (them) you bury him alive in the earth [*balṭussu ina erṣeti teqebberšu*]; its evil will be dispelled." In the second case, the delirious patient announces the impending death of his family members. The prescription calls for the man to be burned alive: "In his illness, you burn him with fire" (*ina murṣīšu ina išāti taqalīšu*). Burning the victim alive appears to be an attempt to annihilate the disease along with the victim's spirit so that neither would return to plague the living.[13] Scurlock and Andersen (2005:335) explain, "As with floppy baby syndrome, this action was apparently taken because it was considered to be a hopeless situation and because of a fear that the rest of the family" would be affected. They (2005:335–36) continue, "This approach to a medical problem is in such striking contrast to the often intensive and exhaustive treatment used to cure or ameliorate other medical problems that it demands an explanation. It would appear that the *āšipu* recognized that the disease was passed on to descendants, and was attempting to prevent it by practicing eugenics."[14] Here the afflicted individual (certainly recog-

---

12. Scurlock and Andersen do not translate the name of this disease (ᵈLUGAL .ÙR.RA), but see Stol (1993:16–19) for his discussion of Lugal-urra, "Lord of the Roof," whom he identifies as the demon of epilepsy.

13. The belief that burning annihilates a person's spirit is reflected in the Sumerian text of Gilgamesh and the Netherworld, in which the spirits of the burned do not exist in the netherworld (see George 1999:189). Abusch (2002:67–76, 229–30) describes the significance of burning as a means to destroy the victim in his discussion of witches. He notes the common opinion that burning deprives the witch of a burial and of a resting place in the netherworld. On the other hand, note the existence of malevolent ghosts "of someone who was burned to death" that afflict a patient (see Scurlock 2006:5–6 with references). Burning is a rare punishment in legal codes, such as the Laws of Hammurabi §110 and §157 (see Roth 1997:101, 111).

14. Avalos (1995a:142–72) surveys the roles of the *āšipu* and the *asû* as "healing consultants" or therapists. See also Scurlock (2005:304–6), who refers to the

nized as a fully human member of society) is sacrificed for the good of the family and its descendants, according to the logic of the text.

These four cases may help to establish the limits of incorporating people with disabilities into the social structure. The medical tradition stipulates infanticide or euthanasia in the case of select terminal diseases or genetic neurological disorders, while other terminal and hereditary cases receive no treatment. Another text from the diagnostic handbook describes a child afflicted by cerebral palsy, according to Scurlock and Andersen (2005:331): "If an infant of one, two, three, (and then) four years writhes in contortion so that he is unable to get up and stand, he is unable to eat bread, (and) his mouth is 'seized' so that he is unable to talk, 'spawn' of Shulpaea; he will not straighten up." Contrary to the two references to infanticide quoted above, this medical text, among many others, indicates that some children with severe disabilities were given extensive care and survived for many years (e.g., in Scurlock and Andersen 2005:332). Indeed, such long-term care for disabled family members was probably the norm. Infanticide was most likely either an uncommon practice (reserved for very particular circumstances) or a private matter (among midwives, for example) that was not socially recognized or publicly acknowledged in ancient Mesopotamian literature.

In summary, the myth of Enki and Ninmah conveys the positive image of incorporating persons with disabilities into the larger society and giving them skills for productive labor. The Sumerian myth lists disabled people with impairments of the hands and legs, blindness, deafness or mental disability, and incontinence, as well as infertile women and eunuchs. I assume that the fragmentary conclusion to the myth also advocates for the long-term care of Umul, as the first infant, although this interpretation is not certain. On the other extreme, there is evidence for infanticide or euthanasia for those humans so far outside of the norm (e.g., with certain neurological disorders) that they were perceived as a danger to society. We next turn to an examination of the available evidence to see whether other cuneiform sources agree with the Sumerian myth's representation of the social inclusion of people with disabilities, and whether other forms of disability could also lead to the exclusion of people from society.

Identifying Disability in Mesopotamia

As Robert Biggs points out (1995:1912), a good description of the ideal, healthy life in ancient Mesopotamia is provided by the autobiographical account of Adad-guppi, the mother of King Nabonidus of Babylon (ruled 555–539 B.C.E.), who claims to have attained 104 years of age (see Longman 1991:97–103, 225–28). After praising the moon-god Sin for granting

---

asû as the pharmacist and the āšipu as the physician, contrary to earlier usages that tend to describe the former as a physician and the latter as a sorcerer.

her happiness and a good reputation, she writes: "He (Sin) kept me alive and well. My eyesight is clear and my mind is excellent. My hands and my feet are healthy. Well-chosen are my words; food and drink still agree with me. My flesh is vital; my mind is joyful" (Longman 1991:102). Adad-guppi boasts that she has seen four generations of her offspring and lived to a ripe old age in this fictional autobiography. She seems to have avoided even the common parasitic diseases endemic to ancient (and modern) Iraq (see Kinnier Wilson 1967a:194–96). This is indeed a good example of a full life in good health.[15]

On the other hand, the Poem of the Righteous Sufferer (*ludlul bēl nēmeqi*) describes the loss of good health and the acquisition of disabilities through a debilitating illness (see Benjamin R. Foster 1997). Abandoned by his personal god, the poem's narrator loses his powerful position and his influential friends. In Tablet II of the Babylonian poem, the man describes numerous disabilities brought on by an evil vapor, a malignant specter, and a demon. He experiences a loss of vision and hearing; he complains of numbness, paralysis, extreme weight loss, and incontinence.

> I took to bed, confined, going out was exhaustion,
> My house turned into my prison.
> My flesh was a shackle, my arms being useless,
> My person was a fetter, my feet having given way.
> My afflictions were grievous, the blow was severe! (Benjamin R.
>   Foster 1997:489)

The final two tablets of the text narrate his eventual healing by a divine emissary, the return of his physical strength and health, and his praise of Marduk for delivering him from his suffering.

These two texts provide a rare window into ancient Near Eastern attitudes toward good health, illness, and disability, but they nevertheless raise more questions than they answer. These and other texts do not appear to distinguish among disease, affliction, and "disability." The people of ancient Mesopotamia were aware of the natural and infectious quality of many diseases (see Scurlock and Andersen 2005:13–25). Instructions for the treatment of a sick princess in a letter from the Old Babylonian archive at Mari (ARM 10 129) provide the clearest evidence of the ancient appreciation of natural contagion: "Now give stern orders that nobody is to drink from the cup from which she drinks; nobody is to sit on the seat on which she sits; nobody is to lie on the bed on which she lies; and many

---

15. Various Akkadian words and phrases refer to "well-bring" or "good health," such as the nouns (and related verbs) *balāṭu* and *šalāmu*, the adjectives *balṭu* and *šalmu* (*CAD* s.v.v.), and the phrase *ṭūb šīrī* (*CAD* s.v. *šīru*). To cite just one example, a letter to Esarhaddon contains a prayer for the "mental and physical well-being" (*ṭūb libbīšunu u ṭūb šīrīšunu*) of the king's grandchildren, as translated by Parpola (1970:136–37).

women are not to mingle with her. That disease is contagious!" (simmum šū
muštaḫḫiz) (see Scurlock and Andersen 2005:17 with references). Yet Mesopotamian sources clearly show that the primary cause of sickness and
disability was understood to be magical or supernatural intervention, in
modern terms (see Scurlock 2005:307–9). The diagnosis for many illnesses
was the "hand" of a god, the influence of a ghost or demon, or the mali-
cious intent of a sorcerer (e.g., Avalos 1995a:128–42; Scurlock 2006:73–78)
Thus, fate, divine intention, or demonic activity was often responsible for
one's health in Mesopotamian thought.

The assumption of divine intervention, perhaps as punishment for
some hidden sin, also led to a social stigma associated with chronic illness,
lengthy diseases, or other misfortune (Avalos 1995a:177–79). A very rare
diagnosis of the cause of a birth defect in Šumma Izbu (I 69), for example,
explains, "If a woman gives birth to an ecstatic [maḫḫu], male or female, she
has been impregnated in the street by a sinful man" (see Stol 2000:166–67;
cf. Scurlock and Andersen 2005:334). A Standard Babylonian commentary
on this text identifies the "sinful man" (ša arnam īšû) as one suffering from
leprosy (garbānu) or dropsy (malê mê). Dropsy (agannutillû or malê mê, "one
full of water") is identified in cuneiform texts as an incurable divine punishment for sin, and those who died from the disease were perhaps left
unburied (see references in van der Toorn 1985:75–76). As a condition that
required the expulsion of the sufferer from society, leprosy or a similar
skin disease (i.e., garābu and saḫaršubbû) was frequently invoked in curses
as divine punishment for sin.[16] One colorful malediction reads, "May Sin,
luminary of the heavens, clothe him in intractable leprosy [saḫaršubba lā
tebâ] like a garment, so that like a wild onager he may run about cease-
lessly on the outskirts of his city!" (Slanski 2003:222–26).[17] Scurlock and
Andersen (2005:218–19) quote an Old Babylonian physiognomic omen
that explains that if a man has a skin disease called pūṣu ("white spots")
with "points," "that man is rejected by his god; he is rejected by mankind."
Forbidden to "tread the square of his city," the leper in ancient texts must
abandon his house and "roam the desert like the wild ass and the gazelle"
or be restricted to a leper colony (see van der Toorn 1985:74–75). The leper
is ostracized from society even in the netherworld (see George 1999:188).

---

16. On leprosy (Hansen's disease) and other skin conditions (esp. garābu and
saḫaršubbû), see Kinnier Wilson (1966:49–50), van der Toorn (1985:72–75), and
Scurlock and Andersen (2005:70–73, 208–41, 722–24). Van der Toorn (1985:73)
concludes that this skin disease was "one of the most unambiguous sanctions" for
human sin in Mesopotamian thought. See the remarks of Avalos (1995a:18–20;
1995b) and Heessel (2004) on the problems with making precise diagnoses from
these texts.

17. See Slanski (2003:71–73, 222) for similar Akkadian curses; see Parker
(1997:74) for an Ugaritic example. Stol (1993:127–30) discusses the symbolic relationship among the moon, epilepsy, and leprosy in cuneiform literature.

Whatever their pathology, these skin diseases, understood as divine punishment for sin, constitute a disability or impurity that causes one to be expelled from the city and excluded from ancient Mesopotamian society.

A disability, cultic impurity, or even a blemish might bar a person from entering the sacred precincts of the temple. Babylonian texts record a number of physical conditions that disqualify a man from serving as a diviner or priest (see van der Toorn 1985:29–30, 169). A late version of this tradition, in a text edited by Wilfred G. Lambert (1998), requires that the *bārû*-priest be of a particular familial descent and "flawless in body and limbs" (*ina gatti u ina minâtīšu šuklulu*) (lines 27–28). The diviner may not have "squinting eyes, chipped teeth, a cut-off finger, [or] a ruptured(?) testicle" (*zaqtu īnī ḫesir šinnī nakpi ubāni iška* DIR.KUR.RA); he may not have leprosy (*saḫaršubbû*) or be a eunuch (*pilpilānu*) (lines 30–33), among other conditions (Lambert 1998:144, 149, 152) (cf. Lev 21:16–23). These impurities or blemishes do not constitute "disabilities" in the modern sense, but they were sufficient deviations from the norm to disqualify a man from the priesthood.

A chronic and debilitating illness, on the other hand, did not create a stigma sufficient to disqualify King Esarhaddon from the Assyrian throne. Letters to Esarhaddon describe his health problems and provide an interesting insight into ancient medical practices (see Parpola 1983:230–36). In letter 180 the king complains, "My arms and legs are without strength! I cannot open my eyes! I am worn out and lie prostrate" because "this fever lingers inside my very bones" (see Parpola 1970:132–33; 1983:172). Simo Parpola writes, "The texts make it clear that the disease in question must have been *chronic*, with *acute* fits at irregular intervals" (1983:231). The letters indicate that the attacks must have begun before Esarhaddon was thirty-five and that the condition worsened as the king aged. Parpola explains, "Esarhaddon was at times so ill that he could and would not take care of his administrative responsibilities but deferred them temporarily to his son" (1983:235–36), who acted as co-regent. Although earlier scholars have diagnosed Esarhaddon's condition as chronic rheumatism, Parpola (1983:231–32) tentatively identifies the disease as systemic lupus erythematosus. Esarhaddon's chronic illness constitutes a serious disability and cultic impurity, yet it did not disqualify him from kingship; it was apparently not regarded as the mark of a heinous sin.

Mesopotamian legal texts identify a few diseases that would constitute a recognized disability, including leprosy (noted above), epilepsy (*bennu*), and grand mal seizures (*antašubbû*) (see Stol 1993; Scurlock and Andersen 2005:83–84, 208–41; contra Avalos 1995b). Stol (1993:146) explains that epilepsy and leprosy are often paired in ancient sources because both "illnesses evoked an uncanny feelings of disgust, a disgust mixed with awe" (cf. Stol 1993:127–30). The Old Babylonian Laws of Hammurabi (§278) states that recently purchased slaves could be returned for a full refund if they were found to suffer from epilepsy (*bennu*) (Roth 1997:132; Stol 1993:132–38). Two examples from Mesopotamian legal codes also stipulate that a man must support a "disabled" wife. The Sumerian Laws of Lipit-Ishtar (ca. 1930 B.C.E.) proclaims: "If a man's first-ranking wife loses her attractiveness or becomes a paralytic, she will not be evicted from the house; however, her husband may marry a healthy wife, and the second wife shall support the first-ranking wife" (§28; Roth 1997:31–32). A textual variant reads, "[H]e shall support (both) the second wife and the first-ranking wife" (Roth 1997: 35). Similarly, §148 from the Laws of Hammurabi (ca. 1750 B.C.E) stipulates, "If a man marries a woman, and later *la'bum*-disease seizes her and he decides to marry another woman, he may marry; he will not divorce his wife whom *la'bum*-disease has seized. She shall reside in quarters that he constructs and he shall continue to support her as long as she lives" (Roth 1997:109). *La'bum* (or *li'bu*) likely refers to an infectious skin disease (Roth 1997:141; cf. Scurlock and Andersen 2005:29–32, 482–83 and s.v. in index). These afflictions seem to bar their sufferers from fulfilling their expected social or professional roles.

Similarly, a married woman's inability to conceive or bear children was perceived as a dysfunction or disability throughout ancient Near Eastern societies. The Sumerian myth of Enki and Ninmah includes infertile women among its list of non-normative humans, and Atrahasis introduces infertile women to restrain human population growth after the flood. Mythological texts represent infertile women as disabled or defective, in one sense or another, because the cultural presumption was that a woman's normative social role was as wife and mother. According to the Sumerian myth of Gilgamesh and the Netherworld, barren women and eunuchs could look forward to a dreary existence in the netherworld. The eunuch is propped up in the corner "like a useless stick" (cf. Isa 56:4 for a eunuch as a "withered tree"), and the barren woman is cast aside like a defective pot; "no man takes pleasure in her" (see George 1999:188). Male sexual dysfunction was also a medical and psychological problem for ancient men, as attested by the "potency incantations" (ŠÀ.ZI.GA; see Biggs 1967).

In attempting to outline the concept of disability in ancient Mesopotamia, one is reminded of the biblical references to "the blind and the lame" as a rhetorical reference to the disabled. In fact, there is a surprising paucity of literary references to "the blind and the lame" in cuneiform literature, even though visual and mobility impairments are included in Enki and Ninmah's list of disabled humans. Ancient Mesopotamian curses certainly seem to equate the loss of vision with a devastating disability, and certain criminals and prisoners of war were punished with blindness and put to hard labor (see Marcus 1980). Blind men, however, are listed as workers in numerous cuneiform economic texts. In addition to being temple singers as described in Sumerian myth and temple records, visually impaired men worked as basket-weavers, gardeners, millers, and cattle men (see Farber 1985:222–23; Gelb 1972).[18] Even though visual impairment is a serious limitation of life functions, it did not disqualify people from forms of productive labor. Cuneiform texts also refer to people with mobility impairments in a similar manner. Alster (1997:18) translates a Sumerian proverb, "In the city of the lame, the halt are couriers" (see also Hallo 1969). This proverb seems to be the Mesopotamian version of a familiar type: "In the land of the blind, the one-eyed man is king."[19] A metaphorical statement in the Erra Epic (IV 11) describes a world turned upside down: "The cripple (ḫašḫāšu) will overtake the swift-footed" (see *CAD* 2.181; cf. Watson 1979). A bilingual text from Ugarit provides a similar Akkadian proverb from an older collection: "The son of a lame man (mār ḫummuri) catches up with the son of a runner" (see Alster 2005:325–26).

Mesopotamian documents also represent certain categories of people as legally incompetent or not liable for their actions, including people with cognitive or developmental disabilities (e.g., *saklu, sakku, sukkuku, ulālu*) (see Cassin 1987:85–89, 92; Slanski 2003:25–26, 34–39, 71–77; cf. Kinnier Wilson 1967b). Unfortunately, these Akkadian words are often ambiguous, referring perhaps to people who could not hear rather than persons with mental retardation or cognitive disability.

In addition to congenital defects or disease, people in ancient Mesopotamia could also suffer an acquired disability through accident or as punishment. The mutilation of prisoners of war as a means of humiliation or perhaps control was not uncommon in ancient Mesopotamia, especially in the Neo-Assyrian period. Textual evidence is available from third-millennium sources (see Gelb 1973) to Diodorus Siculus (17.69.2), who records the story of Alexander the Great encountering eight hundred Greek prisoners of war whom the Persians had mutilated by cutting off their ears, noses, hands, or feet (cf. Lemos 2006; *CAD* 11/1:275 and s.v. *appu*). The cuneiform legal codes also allow for numerous forms of bodily mutilation as punishment for crimes. The Laws of Hammurabi allows for the following punishments: cutting out a tongue (§192), blinding or plucking out an eye (§193, §196), breaking a bone (§197), knocking out a tooth (§200), and the cutting off of a hand (§195, §218, §226, §253), ear (§205, §282), and a woman's breast (§194), among other physical mutilations. Although

---

18. See Farber (1985) for a lexical survey of words for blindness in Akkadian texts, with references to earlier literature (esp. Marcus 1980). See Stol (1986) on forms of visual impairment and Fincke (2000) on eye diseases in ancient Mesopotamia. On blindness in Ugaritic curses, see Parker (1987:15, 74; cf. Watson 1979).

19. Alster (1997:347–48) notes the possibility that the proverb is about "the dwarf" (LUGUD) rather than "the halt" (BA.ZA) but he rejects that interpretation. Additional Sumerian proverbs describing "the lame man" (KUD.KUD.DU) are found in Alster (1997:209, 347–48). While there has been much written about dwarfs in Egypt (see Dasen 1993), I am not familiar with any significant discussion of this topic in cuneiform sources (see Alster 2005:323 n. 3).

most of these punishments would disable the person in some ways, they would not necessarily keep the people from gainful employment within society.[20]

Finally, old age and death may have been perceived as the ultimate disability of the able body in ancient Mesopotamian thought (see Rivkah Harris 2000: passim). The general disability of "old men and women," defined by physical condition rather than by chronological age, is reflected in economic and proverbial texts that equate them with children (see Rivkah Harris 2000:57–58, 64, 72–73, 90–91). The humorous Sumerian text of The Old Man and the Young Girl (Alster 2005:384–90) lampoons the loss of virility in old age (see Harris 2000:28–31; cf. Biggs 1967). An Akkadian text from Sultantepe describes forty years as the prime of life, fifty as a short life, sixty as maturity, seventy as longevity (ūmū arkūtu), eighty as old age (šībūtu), and ninety as extreme old age (littūtu) (see Rivkah Harris 2000:28–31). There is also a Sumerian tradition that the human life span is capped at 120 years, which is the "misfortune" or "bane" (Sumerian NÍG.GIG; Akkadian ikkibu) of humanity (see Jacob Klein 1990; Alster 2005:336–38). As the Old Babylonian epic of Gilgamesh (X iii 4–5) puts it: "When the gods created mankind, death they dispensed to mankind, life they kept for themselves" (George 1999:124). Whether the gods imposed mortality upon humanity from its creation or as a limitation after the flood (Atrahasis III vi 47–50; cf. Gen 6:3) is unclear in Mesopotamian mythology (see Jacob Klein 1990:68–69). Whatever its origin, death and the deterioration of the able body is the natural conclusion to a life of increasing disability and physical limitations. Just as the drunken gods imposed disability upon humans in the Sumerian myth of Enki and Ninmah, so they also withheld immortality from their earthly creatures.

Conclusion

Much work remains to be done to properly investigate the social construction of disability and difference in ancient Near Eastern societies. A careful examination of primary sources (written and iconographic) and the refinement of conceptual approaches to the study of ancient cultures are required for progress in this complex subject. My limited goal in this essay has been to direct the reader to important textual resources from Mesopotamia and to explore the representation of disability in the myth of Enki and Ninmah using a community model of disability.

---

20. The Middle Assyrian Laws includes among its punishments cutting off the ears and noses of thieves (MAL A §5; Roth 1997:156), the finger of a free man's wife who has injured another man's testicles (MAL A §8; Roth 1997:156–57), and the finger and lower lip of a free man who has attempted to sexually assault a free woman (MAL A §9; Roth 1997:157). A man convicted of adultery may be killed, c the aggrieved husband may cut off his wife's nose and then castrate the adulter and lacerate his face (§15; Roth 1997:158).

The Sumerian myth of Enki and Ninmah describes the deliberate creation of humans with abnormal functions or physical disabilities as part of the organization of the world. The myth fancifully portrays the origin of non-normative human bodies, separate from the creation of "able-bodied" workers, as the result of a drunken contest between Enki and Ninmah. The text lists humans with impairments of the hands and legs, blindness, deafness or mental disability, and incontinence, as well as infertile women and eunuchs. All of these non-normative creatures are represented as fully human and qualified for productive work to earn their own bread. Most of the positions seem to carry high status or require technical skill. The helpless Umul, on the other hand, apparently represents those humans, such as infants, who are incapable of productive labor yet worthy of social recognition, according to my reading.

Although the text leaves much room for interpretation, the myth appears to express a community model of disability, in which people's diverse abilities are valued for what they may contribute to society. A medical condition or physical disability, while recognized as deviating from the norm, does not necessarily define the person or disqualify him or her from meaningful work. Enki assigns each of Ninmah's malformed humans a social function consistent with his or her ability to contribute to society. I believe that the myth of Enki and Ninmah thus communicates a social ideology of inclusion for people of differing abilities.

The available data suggest that the attitude represented in the myth of Enki and Ninmah is shared by much of ancient Mesopotamian ideology. Whatever social stigma was attached to physical disease or mental disability, people with abnormal physical or cognitive conditions were assigned jobs as they were able. Administrative texts and ration lists attest to the accommodation of these people as economically productive workers. Medical texts suggest that severely disabled children and adults were cared for at home over long periods of time. Like all societies, ancient Mesopotamia must have had its own, largely unspoken, taxonomy of abnormalities and limits to its inclusive ideology. Yet apart from a very few prescriptions of infanticide or euthanasia and sparse references to the social exclusion of people with leprosy or dropsy, we see little clear evidence for the social rejection of disabled people based upon their physical forms.

2

Deformity and Disability in Greece and Rome

Nicole Kelley

The study of deformity and disability in ancient Greece and Rome raises a number of intriguing questions. How many people in the ancient world were lame, blind, deaf, or otherwise disfigured or disabled? What were the chief causes of deformity and disability in antiquity? What were the most common deformities and disabilities? What kinds of reactions were provoked by deformed and disabled persons, and what political, social, and economic positions did they occupy? As the parent of a disabled child, I am particularly interested in issues surrounding congenitally acquired abnormalities: How many deformities and disabilities were the result of the circumstances of gestation or birth, and how did Greeks and Romans respond to the birth of defective infants?

Any attempt to answer such questions, however, must quickly come to terms with the nature of the ancient sources available to us. It is quite likely that deformity and disability were overwhelmingly common occurrences in the ancient world. The pervasiveness of malnutrition, disease, and interbreeding—all major causes of birth defects—suggests that many infants may have been born with congenital abnormalities. Postnatally acquired deformities were even more common. Many people were disfigured by participation in combat, sporting events, or the acquisition of viral and bacterial diseases and the like; even something as minor as a broken arm or leg was likely to result in permanent deformity or disability. In light of the prevalence of congenital and acquired deformities and disabilities, we might expect to find a wide range of materials dealing with the topic, but in fact such texts and artifacts are relatively few and far between.

In addition, much of the evidence that we do have is anecdotal or idiosyncratic, belongs to a wide variety of historical periods and literary genres, and does not lend itself well to statistical inquiry. How are we to treat, for instance, references to lameness and blindness in the epic poetry of Homer? Do they correspond in any meaningful sense to the incidence of lame and blind individuals in the eighth century B.C.E.? Can such references be considered alongside the later writings of Aristotle, to allow for the construction of a "Greek portrait" of deformity and disability? Could they fruitfully be paired with the writings of Roman authors such as Tacitus or Horace? Do they accurately reflect either the real-life experience of the deformed and disabled, or common attitudes toward them? Even a cursory glance at such questions reveals that the topic of the present essay is fraught with methodological and practical difficulties.

Several excellent monographs, essays, and articles have dealt with deformity and disability in Greco-Roman culture. Robert Garland's 1995 monograph, *The Eye of the Beholder: Deformity and Disability in the Graeco-Roman World*, for instance, is a landmark study of many aspects of deformity, disability, and teratology. The same could be said of *The Staff of Oedipus* by Martha L. Rose (née Edwards), whose work is rather heavily influenced by the contemporary conversations of disability studies. In the pages that follow, I first summarize some of the more important methodological considerations that can be gleaned from this previous scholarship. In the second half of the essay, rather than attempt a comprehensive study like Garland's, or an *apologia* for the disabled as Rose does, I have used mythological portrayals of two deformed and disabled persons as starting points for discussion of several important issues connected to the study of disability in ancient Greece and Rome. First, the lame fire-god Hephaestus offers us insight into the connection between disability and the divine as well as the use of deformed and disabled persons as entertainment for the non-disabled. Hephaestus's story also allows for discussion of the treatment of congenitally deformed infants and the economic and career prospects of the disabled. Second, the story of the blind prophet Teiresias introduces the topics of disability as punishment by the gods and the special abilities attributed to certain disabled individuals.

Methodological Considerations

In addition to the general methodological difficulties posed by a corpus of materials spanning many centuries, geographical locales, and literary genres, there are three specific definitional problems that need to be considered: the terminology associated with deformity and disability in Greek and Latin sources; the cross-cultural definition of deformity and disability; and the complex relationship between deformity and disability.

Terminology

This essay employs the terms—and hence the categories—*deformity* and *disability*, modern designations for which there are no Greek or Latin equivalents (Rose: 11). This is due at least in part to the fact that the classificatory scheme "disabled"/"nondisabled" did not exist for Greeks and Romans. In modern Western parlance it is common to speak of disabled individuals as belonging to a separate and identifiable group, but this was not the case in the ancient world (Martha Lynn Edwards 1995:166).

Rose argues that "the Greeks did not perceive a category of physical disability in which people were a priori banned from carrying out certain roles and compartmentalized into others" (2). Garland seems to suggest a different interpretation when he states that a legendary connection between Hephaestus and the Cyclopes provides "implicit acknowledgement of the natural kinship that exists between all disabled persons, irrespective of the precise nature of their disability" (Garland 1995:63). The absence of a category of physical disability does not mean, however, that the Greeks did not categorize certain groups of people with bodily handicaps, such as the "maimed" (Martha Lynn Edwards 1995:162), or that their well-known concepts of beauty and symmetry did not result in the negative valuation of deformed and disabled bodies on aesthetic grounds (Rose: 36).

Although the Greeks and Romans lacked our modern categories, they did have a rather extensive vocabulary of terms that described various aspects of physical deformity and disability. This, too, is problematic, due in part to the fact that physical handicaps and abnormalities were considered to be outside of the ambit of scientific medicine. Physical handicaps fell outside the medical sphere because "a Hippocratic practitioner's recognition of an incurable case was part of his art" (Martha Lynn Edwards 1995:13; cf., e.g., von Staden: 75–112). According to Edwards, the result is that "the vocabulary for physical disability appears vague, at best, to the modern eye. Most of the terms are generic, even interchangeable, taking on specific meaning only in the individual contexts in which they were used" (1995:12; cf. Vlahogiannis: 15, Grmek: 2). Some of the more common terms related to disability clearly illustrate the level of abstraction at work: "maimed" (πηρός/mancus), "mutilated" (κολοβός/curtus), "ugliness" (αἴσχος/deformitas), "weakness" (ἀσθενεία/infirmitas), and "lameness in the leg" (χωλός/tardipes). In addition, there are more specific terms such as clubfoot (κυλλοί).[1] The overall terminological imprecision makes the exact identification of specific bodily handicaps difficult if not impossible in many cases.

What Is Disability?

Deformity and disability are, as Robert Garland argues, in the eye of the beholder. Some would take this notion to the extreme, contending that disability is entirely a cultural construct that has no intrinsic meaning

---

1. For a catalog of bodily handicaps in Greek literature, complete with expl
nations of each term's semantic domain, see Martha Lynn Edwards 1995:11–4~

(Martha Lynn Edwards 1995:4). It seems to me more defensible to follow
Garland in arguing that "any judgement upon what constitutes a normal
morphology is influenced by the salient characteristics and distinctive aesthetic viewpoint of the society seeking to establish the definition" (Garland
1995:5). In other words, some aspects of deformity and disability may be
culturally contingent, and analyses of ancient Greco-Roman notions of
disability must take this into account. According to Rose, Greeks lacked
an exact classification of physical disability. Instead, the estimation of an
individual's physical (dis)ability depended on how well he or she was able
to meet the demands of family and civic life (Edwards 1995:9; cf. Rose: 3;
Vlahogiannis: 18).

And it would be remiss to discuss the culturally contingent nature of
deformity and disability without mentioning recent scholarship that employs the vocabulary of postmodernity to challenge the entire concept
of disability as a normative discourse. As Rosemarie Garland Thomson
puts it, "[T]he meanings attributed to extraordinary bodies reside not in
inherent physical flaws, but in social relationships in which one group is
legitimated by possessing valued physical characteristics and maintains
its ascendancy and its self-identity by systematically imposing the role
of cultural or corporeal inferiority on others" (Thomson 1997:7). In other
words, disability is not so much an objective reality as the product of discursive practices (broadly construed) that marginalize, exclude, and limit
those whose bodies have certain physical traits. Thomson's point is an important one, but for the purposes of this essay I have retained, somewhat
hesitantly, the use of the terms *deformed* and *disabled*. Although these terms
and categories were not employed by ancient Greeks and Romans, they
nevertheless capture something of the Greco-Roman notion that physically extraordinary individuals fell short of bodily or aesthetic ideals.

Deformity and Disability

If it is difficult or impossible to map our modern notions of disability onto
ancient Greece and Rome, it is no less complicated to determine the relation between deformity and disability. On the one hand, some situations
suggest that deformity and disability are rather discrete domains. A blind
or deaf person is disabled, but generally (except in cases involving the
physical loss of one or both eyes, for example) not physically deformed.
A polydactylic person may be physically deformed, but not disabled. On
the other hand, as Robert Garland notes, "[N]o absolute distinction exists
between a deformity, which we may define as a deviation from normal
appearance, and a disability, which, whether or not it is the result of a
deformity, produces a malfunction" (Garland 1995:5). Indeed, some situations reveal how these two categories are closely interrelated. Some
physical deformities, such as the absence of an eye, result in disabilities
such as blindness. Physical disability and deformity can be inseparable in

other ways as well. Individuals with cerebral palsy, for example, have difficulties with motor coordination but may also have shorter-than-average arms and legs as a result of their condition. Although it is important to acknowledge that deformity and disability may occupy two distinct spheres, their interrelatedness in general, and in ancient texts in particular, requires that they be treated together in this essay.

Divine Disability: Hephaestus

Hephaestus, the Greek god of fire and artisans, is unlike the other deities in the Homeric pantheon: he performs physical labor, is a cuckold, and must endure the mockery of his divine companions (Hornblower and Spawforth: 682). A "solitary misfit among an unageing population of divine perfect deities," he is also the only major Olympian deity to have a physical handicap (Garland 1995:61). He is described variously as ἀμφιγυήεις ("with both feet crooked"; "lame"); χωλός ("lame"); κυλλοποδίων ("clubfooted"; Hom. *Il.* 8.371, 20.270, 21.331); ἠπεδανός ("weakly"); as well as having ἀραιαί κνήμαι ("slender legs") and being ῥικνὸς πόδας ("withered of foot").[2] According to Apollodorus 3.14.6, Hephaestus pursues Athena while limping, and in *Iliad* 1.600 his awkward gait is the source of much amusement during a banquet on Mount Olympus (see below).

In a mythological world of divine perfection, how do we account for the existence of a lame god? Several explanations have been advanced (see Garland 1995:61–62). Some interpreters have proposed that Hephaestus's role as a magician may explain his defect, since there are many cases in which deformed or disabled persons have special talents (Delcourt 1957:110–36; see also Buxton: 27–30). Others have suggested that Hephaestus is a fire demon, and so he is depicted as deformed for apotropaic reasons (Faraone 1992:134, as cited by Garland 1995:62; Rose: 26). Garland believes that the answer may be more straightforward: "[H]is crippled condition conforms to an authentic social reality, metal-working being one of the few professions available to the lame" (Garland 1995:62). I am inclined to agree with Garland, although it may be that the figure of Hephaestus reflected an even more general social reality: the existence of scores of lame or otherwise disabled persons in the ancient world.

Hephaestus's Birth and Congenital Deformity/Disability

Hephaestus's condition is significant for understanding ancient disabilities in general, but it is particularly relevant for the study of congenital deformity. Although there is some indication that his limp was an acquired disability (Hom. *Il.* 1.590–94), most accounts suggest that Hephaestus was

---

2. For a discussion of these terms and their meanings see Bazopoulou-Kyrkanidou: 146–49.

born with deformed feet (Garland 1995:62–63). In the *Odyssey*, when Aphrodite and Ares are caught in their adulterous act by Hephaestus's trap, the cuckolded husband tells Zeus, "Aphrodite, daughter of Zeus, scorns me for that I am lame and loves destructive Ares because he is comely and strong of limb whereas I was born misshapen. Yet for this is none other to blame but my two parents—would they had never begotten me!" (Hom. *Od.* 8.308–312; translation by Murray). In the *Homeric Hymn to Pythian Apollo* 316–18, Hephaestus's mother, Hera, states: "But my son Hephaestus whom I bare was weakly among all the blessed gods and shrivelled of foot, a shame and a disgrace to me in heaven, whom I myself took in my hands and cast out so that he fell in the great sea" (translation by Evelyn-White). In these instances, the testimonies of Hephaestus and his mother make it clear that his lameness is the result of a congenital abnormality. Though these accounts are obviously mythological in nature, they do point us toward an interesting set of issues: What attitudes did the Greeks and Romans have toward congenitally deformed infants, and what did they do with them?[4]

There are four relevant passages in Greek literature, three of which clearly refer to idealized rather than everyday, "real-life" situations (Rose: 31–34). Book five of the *Republic* (460c) describes Plato's utopian state, in which the offspring of the good are reared, while "the offspring of the inferior, and any of those of the other sort who are born defective (ἀνάπηρον γίγνηται), they will properly dispose of in secret (ἐν ἀπορρήτῳ τε καὶ ἀδήλῳ κατακρύψουσιν), so that no one will know what has become of them" (translation by Shorey). The term κατακρύπτω may be understood as a

---

3. There are two different versions of Hephaestus's conception, the first in Hesiod's *Theogony* 927–28 and the second in Homer's *Odyssey* 8.312. Both are mentioned in Apollodorus, *The Library* 1.3.5 (Bazopoulou-Kyrkanidou 145). In Hesiod's version Hera conceives Hephaestus without the help of Zeus, which makes his birth somewhat parallel to that of Athena and may have been intended either to explain Hephaestus's imperfect condition or to "avoid insulting Zeus by making him the father of a cripple" (Garland 1995:62).

4. For a detailed look at some of the major causes of congenital deformity, see Martha Lynn Edwards 1996:80–82. Patterson 1995 addresses the problem of exposure and infanticide in greater detail. A more general discussion of the abandonment and exposure of children in Western cultures can be found in Boswell 1988. It does appear that, broadly speaking, Greeks and Romans responded differently to abnormal births. In the ancient world such births functioned as a type of divination, although there is no evidence to suggest that ancient Greeks kept official records of these events or attempted to expiate them (Garland 1995:65). Romans, by contrast, kept annual records of such events (see, e.g., the writings of Livy), which they regarded as "a sign that the sacred *pax deorum* or 'covenant with the gods' had been broken" (Garland 1995:67). On prodigies in Greece and Rome, see Bloch 1963 and Delcourt 1938.

euphemistic reference to the practice of exposure, or it may refer to the concealment of the ἀνάπηροι ("maimed," "mutilated"; Viljoen: 65). This reference suggests that the abandonment or exposure of infants was *not* the normal practice in Plato's day (Viljoen: 63; Rose: 34). The same is true of Aristotle's *Politics* 1335b, where the vision of the ideal state includes the following recommendation about raising infants with abnormalities: "As to exposing or rearing the children born, let there be a law that no deformed child (πεπηρωμένον) shall be reared" (translation by Rackham).

Plutarch's *Lycurgus* 16.1 tells of the Spartan practice of examining infants to determine whether they might be worth rearing. The elders inspected each child: infants who were "sound and strong of body" (εὐπαγὲς . . . καὶ ῥωμαλέον) were ordered to be raised, while "low-born and misshapen" (ἀγεννὲς καὶ ἄμορφον) infants were deposited at a place called the Apothetae, a chasm beneath Mount Taygetus. This first- or second-century C.E. account claims to describe historical conditions in ancient Sparta, and as a result it may appear to provide us with a slightly more accurate picture of one culture's practices in dealing with congenitally deformed infants. It must be said, however, that Plutarch's narrative describes not the current state of affairs in Sparta but an idealized past (Rose: 34), and as such it cannot be used with any more confidence than the utopian visions of Plato and Aristotle.

Soranus's *Gynecology* 2.10, written in the second century C.E., provides the most explicit set of criteria for determining an infant's fitness. A baby worth rearing should have a mother who experienced a healthy pregnancy, a suitable gestational age, and a vigorous cry. It should, moreover, be "perfect in all its parts, members and senses," with every body part properly moving and appropriately sized. "And by conditions contrary to those mentioned, the infant not worth rearing is recognized" (translation by Temkin 1956; Rose: 33). With the exception of Soranus's account, these passages offer us very little information about the exposure of deformed infants in ancient Greece. Plato's and Aristotle's idealized portraits strongly suggest that some Greeks decided to raise their congenitally abnormal infants, although the terminology these authors use to describe such defects is extremely vague and tells us little about what would have been perceived as deformity or disability worthy of exposure (Amundsen: 11; Rose: 33).

Let's return for a moment to the declaration of Hera in the *Homeric Hymn to Pythian Apollo* 316–18. Recall her declaration that Hephaestus "was weakly among all the blessed gods and shriveled of foot, a shame and a disgrace to me in heaven, whom I myself took in my hands and cast out so that he fell in the great sea." Hera's revulsion at her son's physical state, in other words, caused her to cast him out of the heavens. According to Garland, her response ought to be understood as typical: "Hera's rejection of her son duplicates the response of a very average Greek mother to the discovery that she had given birth to a cripple" (1995:63). But perhaps the situation is not so clear, as Vlahogiannis (23) suggests: "Did Greeks identify with Hera's disgust and revulsion as common to their own behaviour, or did they recognise it as expressions of a past time?" Rose rejects the idea that the abandonment, exposure, or killing of deformed infants may have been the norm. Although she admits that physical deformities may have been viewed as "blemishes" (42), she questions the extent to which modern assumptions about congenitally deformed infants can be used to interpret ancient evidence:

> In the ancient world, one would not have been shocked to deliver a baby with some anomaly or other. Childbirth was not a medical occasion, abnormal babies were not pathologized, and in fact the health and illness of infants and children were not of medical interest. A deformed baby was not necessarily seen as inferior, unattractive, or in need of medical care: these assumptions are formed by modern medical and cultural values. (Rose: 36)

Garland may be right in asserting that most parents in ancient Greece would have responded much like Hera to the birth of a physically abnormal infant—with revulsion that led to abandonment, exposure, or infanticide. Soranus's instructions, if they reflected a consensus about normal physical characteristics determining the value of infants or if they were followed by others, support this conclusion. But Rose's caution is important: although they may have posed an aesthetic problem for some, we should not assume that deformed infants necessarily would have been rejected as medically fragile or economically burdensome.

The status of congenitally deformed infants is not much clearer in the case of ancient Rome. Let's briefly examine two extant texts that are relevant to our discussion. The first is from Dionysius of Halicarnassus (2.15), who reports that "Romulus ordered all the inhabitants of the city to bring up all their male descendants and not to kill (that is, allow to die) any child before the age of three, unless the child was deformed or monstrous (ἀνάπηρον ἢ τέρας), in which case it was to be put to death immediately after birth. He did not stand in the way of such children being exposed on condition that the parents had first shown them to five neighbours" (cited by den Boer: 98; slightly modified). This passage indicates a familial rather than civic responsibility for the elimination of deformed children and depicts exposure as an option rather than a requirement (den Boer: 99). Did such a law ever exist? It is difficult to believe that a historical reality might lie behind this description of an idealized past (see Garland 1995:16). If anything, like its Greek counterparts, the passage may suggest that some parents of deformed children in ancient Rome did not resort to the practice of exposure.

A fifth-century B.C.E. Roman law, recorded in a code known as the Twelve Tables and referred to in a treatise by Cicero (*Laws* 3.19), makes the killing of deformed children a requirement. Quintus mentions the law in the process of speaking about the legal power of the people's tribune, which came about as the result of civil discord: "[A]fter it had been quickly killed, as the twelve tables direct terribly deformed infants shall be killed, it was soon revived again, somehow or other, and at its second birth was even more hideous and abominable than before" (cited by den Boer: 99; cf. Seneca *Con.* 10.4.16). As Garland points out, however, we have no evidence that parents who chose to raise a deformed child were ever prosecuted under such laws (1995:17). We do, however, have evidence that some congenitally abnormal infants were raised, as the famous example of the emperor Claudius (Suetonius *Claudius* 3.2) and the case of the congenitally mute Quintus Pedius (Pliny *Natural History* 35.21) demonstrate.

The Deformed and Disabled as Entertainment

Claudius's experience as it is represented in the extant literature suggests that the deformed and disabled were not necessarily embraced by their families or communities. His mother referred to him as a monster, and his sister Livilla hoped that Romans could avoid the cruel fate of having him as their emperor (Suetonius *Claudius* 3.2; Garland 1995:41). In fact, there is evidence that many people with physical abnormalities sometimes experienced mockery and derision. In his treatise *On Oratory* 2.239, Cicero states that "in deformity [*deformitatis*] and bodily disfigurement [*corporis vitiorum*] there is good material for making jokes," although he does concede that "one has to know the limit" of this kind of humor (Garland 1994:75). Returning to the example of Hephaestus, it is evident that the Homeric epics reflect this real-life attitude in depicting the exploits of their mythological characters (Rose 48). In a scene that occurs at the end of *Iliad* 1, Hephaestus attempts to defuse tension between Zeus and Hera by playing the part of the wine steward at an Olympian feast. The gods respond to his action with laughter: "But among the blessed immortals uncontrollable laughter went up as they saw Hephaistos bustling about the palace" (Hom. *Il.* 1.599–600; translation by Lattimore). According to Walter Burkert (168) and Christopher G. Brown (287), because Hephaestus intended to provoke this laughter, it should be understood as a genial and light-hearted moment: the gods laugh with Hephaestus rather than at him. Garland, however, suggests that the gods' laughter may be "merely an incidental consequence of [Hephaestus's] wine-pouring" (Garland 1995:79). In other words, Hephaestus's dinner companions may be mocking him: laughing at him, not with him. In either interpretation, the lame god's disability is the source of amusement for others.

In both Greece and Rome, drinking parties similar to Hephaestus's Olympian feast offered occasions for the mockery of deformed and disabled persons (Garland 1994:73). Greek vase paintings, for example, depict "hunchbacks, cripples, dwarfs and obese women" performing a entertainers, and Horace relates a story about two deformed men trading insults at a *convivium* for the entertainment of onlookers (*Sat.* 1.5.50–70; Garland 1995:84–85).[5] According to Lampridius, the emperor Elagabalus was known to extend dinner invitations to "eight bald men or eight one-eyed men or eight gout-sufferers or eight deaf men . . . in order to arouse laughter" (*Heliogab.* 29.3, as cited by Garland 1995:85–86).

Of course, the mockery of such individuals also took place outside of convivial settings. Homer gives us the example of Thersites, who is described in most unflattering terms: "This was the ugliest man who came beneath Ilion. He was bandy-legged and went lame of one foot, with shoulders stooped and drawn together over his chest, and above this his skull went up to a point with the wool grown sparsely upon it" (*Iliad* 2.217–19; translation by Lattimore). The flawed physical characteristics of Thersites are, in this account, indicative of his overall character and suggestive of the influence of physiognomy in the ancient world: he has the audacity to criticize Agamemnon (*Iliad* 2.225–42) and is roundly beaten by Odysseus. This causes the entire army to erupt into laughter (*Iliad* 2.270) at Thersites' expense.

In late republican and early imperial Rome, deformed individuals emerged as a form of personal entertainment. As Carlin A. Barton puts it, "The dwarf and the giant, the hunchback and the living skeleton ceased being prodigies and became pets; they ceased being destroyed and expiated and became objects of the attention and cultivation of every class" (86). Augustus's granddaughter Julia, for example, retained a dwarf named Cinopas as a pet according to Pliny (*Natural History* 7.74–75). Plutarch comments on the existence of a "monster market" in Rome (*Moralia* 520c), and Longinus reports that the demand for *distorti* is so great that some children are being deliberately deformed, presumably to increase their market value (*De sublimitate* 44.5; Barton: 86).

Economic and Career Prospects of the Deformed and Disabled

Although Hephaestus is perhaps mocked by his dinner companions, it is also true that his works are held in great esteem. He is "a cunning blacksmith whose professional skills are highly admired and secretly feared, and whose social skills should not be underrated" (Hornblower and Spawforth: 682). For instance, Hephaestus's τέχνη is evident in a pair of gold and silver dogs that he made to guard the home of Alcinous (Hom. *Od.* 7.91–93) and in a mixing bowl that is the prized possession of the Spartan king Menelaus (Hom. *Od.* 4.617; Newton 14). Hephaestus's traditional epithets

---

5. For a more comprehensive study of the representation of such individuals in Graeco-Roman art, see Stevenson 1975. I am grateful to the editors of the current volume for their helpful suggestions and corrections, all of which have greatly improved the current essay.

include κλυτόμητις ("famous for skill"; Hom. *Hymn.* 20.1) and κλυτοτέχνης ("famous for art"; *Il.* 1.571, 18.143; *Od.* 8.286; Newton: 14 n. 11).

He is a mythological figure rather than a real person, but Hephaestus' reputation for his skills as an artisan is indicative of an economic reality in the ancient world: physically handicapped people were "involved in a wide range of economic activities" (Rose: 40). Artisans, in particular, are often reported to have had some form of physical impairment: we know of a tailor who limped (Alciphron, *Letters of Farmers* 24.1) and a lame peddler (Aristophanes, "Anagyrus" frag. 57 *PCG*; Rose: 40). It is difficult to know whether such people acquired their disability before or after they began their trade (Rose: 40). In addition, many terra-cotta figurines and vase paintings depict deformed persons, notably dwarfs and hunchbacks, as entertainers, which suggests that such individuals must have held positions as singers, dancers, and the like (Garland 1995:32–33). Deformities and disabilities did not prevent people from serving in the military (Hom. *Il.* 2.216–19; Plutarch *Mor.* 234e, 241e, 331b; Demosthenes *On the Crown* 67; Rose: 44). Blind persons, moreover, often appear in both mythological and "historical" literature as prophets, poets, and musicians (Dio Chrysostom, *Or.* 36.10–11; Hom. *Od.* 8.62–70; Pausanias 7.5.7), although surely these occupations were available only to a very few (Garland 1995:34). Nevertheless, it is important to note that these literary representations of blind people as prophets, poets, and musicians do not imply that other professions were closed to those with limited sight or blindness (Rose: 91). Although the political status of the disabled in ancient Greece and Rome is difficult to discern (Garland 1995:31–32), the above examples suggest that their economic outlook was not necessarily bleak or characterized by utter dependence on family and friends (Rose: 39).

Disability as Punishment: Teiresias

If the god Hephaestus allowed us to explore congenital deformity, the mockery of deformed and disabled persons, and the socio-economic status of the disabled, the blind Theban prophet Teiresias opens a new window onto yet another set of issues. After a brief look at blindness in the ancient world, I turn to two interrelated issues: blindness as punishment, and the compensatory powers sometimes awarded to the blind.

There are at least two different explanations for the cause of Teiresias's loss of sight, both of which revolve around the notion that he was blinded as a punishment from the gods. In Callimachus's fifth *Hymn*, Teiresias is blinded because he sees Athena bathing. He receives the gift of prophecy as compensation after his mother Chariclo intercedes on his behalf. In another version of the myth attributed to Hesiod and reported by Apollodorus (3.6.7), Teiresias is blinded by Hera:

> There was a Theban seer called Teiresias. Hesiod says that he witnessed two snakes copulating on Mount Kyllene and when he wounded them

he became a woman from a man, but when he observed the same snakes copulating again he turned into a man. This is because Hera and Zeus had been arguing about whether women or men derived more pleasure from sexual intercourse, and had questioned him. Teiresias had replied that if you think of sexual pleasure as consisting of nineteen parts, men enjoy nine parts and women ten. For this Hera blinded him but Zeus granted him the gift of prophecy. (cited by Garland 1995:100–101)

Once again we are dealing with a mythological account, in which the actions of gods and goddesses take the place of "natural" explanations and in which connections to the real-life experiences of ancient Greeks and Romans are not easy to discern. Before we address two of the more specific issues introduced by Teiresias's blinding, we need to look more generally at blindness in the ancient Greek and Roman world.

Blindness in Ancient Greece and Rome

Blindness is the most frequently mentioned physical handicap in ancient Greek texts. One reason for this may be that blindness and sight impairment were widespread in the ancient world (Martha Lynn Edwards 1995:124, 142). Many causes of blindness can, in the modern world, be addressed by medical or surgical intervention or prevented altogether. This was not so in Western antiquity. People were traumatically blinded in battle and in situations where accidental or purposeful damage was done to the eyes. In addition to the numerous mythological narratives in which individuals are blinded as a result of divine or human revenge, there are historical accounts in which people lose their sight as a result of accidental damage to the eyes. Herodotus (1.174), for instance, states that the Cnidians received eye injuries while breaking stones as they dug a trench (Rose: 82), and Julius Caesar's account of the Civil War mentions that four centurions in a single cohort were blinded in one battle (*On the Civil War* 3.53; Garland 1995:23).

More commonly, people lost their vision as the result of contagious disease, heredity, vitamin-A deficiency, and old age (Rose: 84–86). For example, Hippocratic authors (*On Vision* 9.4–5) and Galen (10.990) recorded observations about cataracts, and Aristotle noted that blind parents sometimes give birth to blind babies (*History of Animals* 585b; Rose: 84). Galen (12.766–77) lists well over one hundred eye pathologies, which should not be surprising in an age without vision-correction devices, vaccinations, or antibiotics (Rose: 85).

Blindness as Divine Punishment

Such examples give us an idea of the natural causes of human blindness that were prevalent in ancient Greece and Rome. At the same time, from a very early stage it is common to find blindness presented as a punishment from the gods (Rose: 81). Such punishment can, in Greek myths, be the result of a person's transgressions against the gods or other mortals. Several individuals are blinded because they look upon a god or a representation of a god, or because they enter a space ordinarily off-limits to humans. As we have just seen in Callimachus's account, Teiresias is blinded because he sees Athena bathing, even though he does so unwillingly. Likewise, Philip of Macedon loses an eye after seeing his wife with the god Ammon (Plut. *Alex.* 3), and one Aipytos is blinded and dies after entering the temple of Poseidon Hippios at Mantineia (Paus. 8.5.4–5, 10.3; Buxton: 30).

Other offenses against the gods were punishable by blindness as well (see Buxton: 30–32). Lycurgus, for instance, is blinded by Zeus because of his persecution of Dionysus: "But the gods who live at their ease were angered with Lykourgos, and the son of Kronos struck him to blindness, nor did he live long afterwards, since he was hated by all the immortals" (Hom. *Il.* 6.138–40; translation by Lattimore). Thamyris was blinded (or maimed, depending on the version) because he tried to compete with the Muses: "[H]e boasted that he would surpass, if the very Muses, daughters of Zeus who holds the aegis, were singing against him, and these in their anger struck him . . ." (Hom. *Il.* 2.597–99; translation by Lattimore). Often this kind of punitive blindness is permanent, but not always: Stesichorus, for example, regains his eyesight after making amends to Helen (Plato, *Phaedrus* 243). In Greek myths, the gods also use blindness to punish offenses committed by mortals against other mortals (Buxton: 32).

Most of these accounts are mythological rather than historical and cannot be assumed to represent directly the lives of blind individuals. They do suggest, however, that blindness is regularly (although perhaps not exclusively) viewed as a punishment and certainly an undesirable fate. At the same time, these mythological accounts often depict the blind as having extraordinary abilities that compensate for their loss of eyesight.

Special Abilities of the Disabled

According to Grmek, the ancient Greeks believed that "loss of sight was linked by a kind of compensation magic to clairvoyance and the gift of poetic creation, song, and enchantment" (25). This is certainly true in the case of Teiresias. He is one of many blind persons represented as having compensatory talents—often the gift of poetry or prophecy—in Greek mythology (Buxton: 27). Although (or perhaps because) he is blind, Teiresias is known for his insight. His vision is compared to that of Apollo (Sophocles, *Oedipus Tyrannus* 284–5). In book ten of the *Odyssey*, the goddess Circe orders Odysseus "to consult with the soul of Teiresias the Theban, the blind prophet, whose senses lay unshaken within him" (Hom. *Od.* 10.492–93; translation by Lattimore; Buxton: 23).

Teiresias is not the only disabled person presented as having remarkable abilities. We have seen that Thamyris was maimed (πηρὸν θέσαν) and made forgetful by the Muses because he boasted that his musical talents rivaled their own (Hom. *Il.* 2.594–600). Hephaestus, although his divine stature surely makes him a special case, also falls into this category: he is a

lame blacksmith known for his artisanal skills. Herodotus (9.93–94) mentions the story of Evenius, who was blinded by his fellow townsmen for
neglecting the sacred sheep of Helios but received the gift of prophecy
as compensation from the gods. Finally, Pausanias (7.5.7) reports that a
blind fisherman named Phormion possessed the ability to have prophetic
dreams, and Apollodorus (1.9.21) mentions Phineus, a blind man who
could foretell the future.

On the one hand, this notion of compensatory gifts is surely related to
the natural tendency of blind persons to develop other powers of sensory
perception. Ancient Greek writers such as Aristotle were certainly aware
of the phenomenon: "the blind remember better, being released from having their faculty of memory engaged with objects of sight" (Aristotle *Eth.
Eud.* 1248b, cited by Buxton: 29). On the other hand, Rose is surely right
in asserting that this common mythological and literary trope had little to
do with the everyday lives of blind Greeks and Romans: "Although myth
shows divine compensation for blindness, I cannot imagine that the average Greek with progressively worsening cataracts would seriously have
been waiting for his ration of clairvoyance and musical talent. Still, blindness was a common enough condition, to which people could and did
adjust" (2003:87).

Even if such portrayals of the disabled as specially talented do not
reflect the everyday experiences of real people, do these accounts reveal
anything about the attitudes of ancient Greeks and Romans toward the
disabled? According to Vlahogiannis, the answer is yes: "On one hand,
heroes and protagonists are marginalised, debased and disempowered by
their disability, and on the other they are protected, empowered and privileged in their unnatural state" (Vlahogiannis: 19–20). The twin themes of
blindness as punishment and a mark of extraordinary talents together reveal that disabled individuals in Greece and Rome appear to have been
regarded with a measure of ambivalence, which no doubt varied according to the time, place, and persons in question.

Conclusion

I have limited this essay to a general overview of deformity and disability
in Greco-Roman culture. Nonetheless, further and more comprehensive
research may address such common disabilities as deafness/hearing loss
and speech disorders, for example (on these see Rose: 50–78), or deal with
the lives of ancient Greek and Roman women, who certainly experienced
disabilities and were by Aristotle's famous judgment merely "deformed"
versions of their male counterparts (*Gen. An.* 4.775a). One emerging ave-
nue for further research is the study of physiognomy, the ancient "science"
that used physical appearance to ascertain an individual's character. The
promise of a new area of research is signaled by the recent publication of
important collections of texts (see, e.g., Swain 2006) and the application

of physiognomy to the study of disability in the ancient world (see, e.g., Parsons 2005 and Albl's contribution to this volume).

All of this suggests that the preceding pages clearly have not exhausted the possibilities for research on deformity and disability in ancient Greco-Roman culture, but instead have merely highlighted some of the more important themes at work. The legend of Hephaestus the lame Olympian god revealed that congenitally deformed infants were not rejected as often as the extant literary evidence might suggest at first glance. Hephaestus's example also highlights the different career options available to the deformed and disabled, who at times were placed in the uncomfortable position of serving as entertainment for others. The story of Teiresias the blind prophet introduced us to the mythological notions of blindness as punishment and as accompaniment to special gifts of perception. Such ideas may not be reflections of the day-to-day life of the average Greek or Roman blind person, but they do underscore a fundamental ambivalence toward the deformed and disabled that surfaces in literary texts.

3

Introducing Sensory Criticism in Biblical Studies

AUDIOCENTRICITY AND VISIOCENTRICITY

Hector Avalos

"Criticism" has a long history in biblical studies. As noted by John H. Hayes and Carl R. Holladay, criticism is "a technical expression used by scholars to denote a field of study which has developed fairly clearly defined principles and techniques" (24–25). More often, the word functions to describe the study of particular features of the Bible. Thus, we have rhetorical criticism, literary criticism, and redaction criticism. All such "criticisms" are value-laden insofar as they select, out of hundreds of possible features, the ones valued for study.

This essay proposes the initiation of a systematic survey of biblical texts that would center on how different books, corpora, genres, and traditions value the natural senses, including, but not restricted to, the five natural senses usually identified in Western cultures. "Sensory criticism" is premised on the idea that concepts and expressions involving the body and its senses are valuable features for study. Since our approach aims to establish itself as a legitimate and systematic approach to biblical texts, then it should be given parity with other approaches labeled as "criticism," including form criticism, textual criticism, or redaction criticism.

As applied to the Bible, sensory criticism would (1) provide a systematic examination of the differential valuation and interaction of the senses in the Bible; (2) furnish a methodological tool to examine texts comparatively inside and outside the biblical corpus; (3) examine how the valuation of the senses is intimately related to the differential valuation of persons that lies at the core of defining disabilities. Sensory criticism, in turn, should be considered part of a much larger endeavor that may be called "corporeal criticism." The latter involves a systematic study of the embodied experience, the study of which is an emerging field in itself (see Bail; Berquist; Stafford).

Since this chapter is intended to be programmatic rather than exhaustive, I have chosen two main case studies to illustrate how sensory criticism could be applied to biblical texts. In particular, the main portion of the essay illustrates the approach by showing how the Deuteronomistic History (DtrH) often is audiocentric in valuing hearing above sight in understanding the world and God's will. Conversely, the book of Job is visiocentric, insofar as it regards vision as superior to, or as a necessary complement of, hearing when perceiving God and his actions in the world.

Making Sense in History

At least from the time of Aristotle's *De Anima*, Western thought has predominantly categorized five senses: (1) sight; (2) hearing; (3) smell; (4) taste; and (5) touch (Durrant). Much of the history of Western philosophy and science has focused on the place of the senses in obtaining knowledge or in the representation of reality (Lindberg). In the twentieth century the rise of new media, particularly film, raised new questions about the differential valuation of the senses in our epistemologies and aesthetic experiences (see Münsterberg; Arnheim; McLuhan; Heyes and Huber).

Within biblical studies, the senses have been studied primarily to provide a philological and theological understanding of how human beings speak of communication and perception. Such studies may be found in standard theological dictionaries such as *TLOT* or *TDNT*, and in the studies by scholars such as Hans-Joachim Kraus and Gerhard Kittel (see Beck for examples in Hinduism). Studies that relate the senses to the differential valuation of human beings, a concept central to disability studies, are at their inception (e.g., Hull).

From a modern bioanthropological perspective, the senses are instruments by which a body gathers and interprets information from the physical environment (Mountcastle: 1–6). All living organisms collect information from the environment and respond to the environment based on that information. Single-cell organisms both receive sensations and respond to them. In multicellular organisms, differentiation developed between the cells receiving stimuli and cells that responded to stimuli. By the time of the arrival of mammals, the reception of environmental stimuli, and the response to those stimuli, were mediated by a highly differentiated and complex nervous system managed by a brain.

Most anthropologists agree that the biological order of primates, to which the human species belongs, originated some sixty-five to fifty-five million years ago (Boaz and Almquist: 142–44). Relative to earlier mammals, primates shifted to a fully frontal positioning of the eyes. Primates also developed color and stereoscopic vision that allowed three-dimensional images to be perceived sharply (Boaz and Almquist: 136–37). The "higher" primates became most active during daylight. Relative to earlier mammals, the senses of smell and taste were reduced among primates (Gilad et al.). In human beings, the right and left ears have developed subtle specialties, and lower frequencies have become the norm (Glendenning).

From an evolutionary perspective, the importance of the hand, in which our sense of touch is centered, in human history rose with the shift among some primates to bipedal locomotion that freed the hand from its earlier weight-bearing function (for managing movement among trees) and allowed further developments of fine motor skills such as those involved in the act of writing (Mountcastle: 27–39).

Within ancient traditions relevant to the Bible, the identification of these five discrete senses is already reflected in the *Testament of Reuben*, which is part of the larger work called the Twelve Patriarchs, and which may date to the Maccabean period (Kee). The *Testament of Reuben* (2:4–6) includes a speech by Reuben, who is lamenting the evil deed of sleeping with his father's concubine, Bilhah (Gen 35:22). In that speech Reuben lists "seven spirits" as follows (Kee: 782):

> First, is the spirit of life, with which man is created as a composite being.
> The second is the spirit of seeing, with which comes desire;
> The third is the spirit of hearing, with which comes instruction;
> The fourth is the spirit of smell, with which is given taste for drawing air and breath;
> The fifth is the spirit of speech, with which comes knowledge;
> The sixth is the spirit of taste for consuming food and drink;
> by it comes strength, because in food is the substance of strength;
> The seventh is the spirit of procreation and intercourse, with which comes sins through fondness for pleasure.

Here we see the five senses usually constructed in modern Western thought. However, the author of this text also saw "procreation and intercourse" and "speech" as part of that broader category of "spirits" (and later also adds "sleep" and "error").

It is difficult to find a common criterion for the classification of all these human features as "spirits" or "senses." Some are classified by their informational function ("instruction," "knowledge"; see also Sir 17:5–7). Taste is understood as an instrument to gain strength rather than as an instrument to analyze chemical compositions of food (a modern bioanthropological view). In addition, the Hebrew word טַעַם, usually translated as "taste," can be used in the sense of judgment or discernment (e.g., 1 Sam 21:14; Prov 11:22). Clearly, some of these "spirits" involve a different categorization of bodily functions, which may reflect categories also found in Stoicism (Kee: 782 n. 2; see also Jager for "speech").

In any case, the *Testament of Reuben* highlights a lesson emphasized by anthropologists such as Diane Ackerman, Constance Classen, Robert

Desjarlais, and Ashley Montagu, who focus on cross-cultural comparisons of how the senses are conceptualized. Their studies amply demonstrate that the Western construction of the senses is not universal in all cultures. Moreover, one should be cautious not to classify all non-Western or non-literate cultures as aural/oral. Non-literate cultures can display a complex interaction of senses, even if one sense might be privileged above others in certain contexts (Classen: 135–38; see also Becking for "touch" and therapy).

The differential privileging of senses can be detected by, among other methods: (1) contrasting expressions of valuation ("hearing is better than seeing"); (2) expressions of antipathy toward particular senses; and (3) narratives about the performance of valued tasks and functions in the absence or diminution of certain senses. Accordingly, I now apply those rudimentary methodological observations in an exploration of how two major works in the Hebrew Bible value the senses in their attempt to obtain information about the world and about God.

Audiocentricity in the Deuteronomistic History

Hearing and seeing are two of the most oft-mentioned senses in the Bible. Hebrew forms of the verb "to hear" (שָׁמַע), for example, are attested about 1,159 times in the Hebrew Bible, ranking forty-fourth overall in a list of the most common words in the Hebrew Bible (*TLOT* 1444). The Hebrew word usually translated "to see" (רָאָה) ranks thirty-seventh with 1,303 occurrences in its active forms (*TLOT* 1444). These "senses" are primarily regarded as conduits of information, whether about human or divine entities.

However, it is clear that biblical authors do not always regard these senses as of equal value, especially in receiving information about the world and about God's will. One illustrative case is found in the so-called Deuteronomistic History (DtrH), which stretches from Deuteronomy through 2 Kings in the Hebrew Bible. As are most corpora in the Bible, DtrH is a contested entity, and scholars still do not agree on the origin, composition, or extent of the corpus (see Richard Nelson; Thomas Römer; Veijola 2002). In any case, one can find repeated instances of audiocentricity, the privileging of hearing, in this corpus. Westermann and Jenni note that the Hebrew root שׁמע is "disproportionately concentrated" in Deuteronomy and Jeremiah (*TLOT* 1375; see also Kraus).

We might begin with the so-called Shema in Deut 6:4, which constitutes a fundamental affirmation about Yahweh in that corpus. Usually, English translations have something similar to this rendition of the NRSV: "Hear, O Israel: The LORD our God is one LORD." However, many scholars have noted that this may be an affirmation that there is only one Yahweh, especially since a number of Hebrew inscriptions apparently indicate the existence of a Yahweh for different localities. "The Yahweh of Samaria" is one example, attested in the Kuntillet 'Ajrud inscriptions dated to Israel's pre-exilic era (Zevit: 390–91). Accordingly, a better translation might be: "Hear, O Israel, Yahweh, our god, is the only Yahweh" (see von Rad: 63).

For our purposes, the instruction emphasizes aurality ("hear") rather than visuality (e.g., as in the imperatives "read" or "see"), a difference for which I discuss explanations below. True enough, the command to "hear" may be part of a formulaic statement found in royal decrees in the Near East. The hearing of royal decrees and covenants was the usual method of communicating information to an audience that was mostly illiterate. Thus, the mere presence of formulaic verbs instructing people to "hear" is not sufficient to show that DtrH is audiocentric.

However, this use of audition in communicating information from, or about, Yahweh is not the only indication that DtrH is audiocentric. Repeatedly, we are told that the Israelites did not see Yahweh, but rather heard him. Deuteronomy 4:12 provides an excellent example:

וידבר יהוה אליכם מתוך האש
קול דברים אתם שׁמעים ותמונה אינכם ראים
זולתי קול:

Then the LORD spoke to you out of the midst of the fire; you heard the sound of words, but saw no form; there was only a voice.

The denial that the Israelites saw any form of Yahweh is repeated in verse 15. This denial, in turn, is directly linked to a warning not to make any visual representations of Yahweh or anything else in the world (vv. 16–19). Furthermore, these passages affirm that the Israelites did not need to see Yahweh to receive correct information about his will and commandments.[1] Hearing was sufficient.

DtrH also shows repeatedly how wrong conclusions based on mere use of sight can be. In 1 Samuel 1, we find a story of Hannah, a barren woman, who came to the temple of Shiloh to petition Yahweh for a child. The narrator indicates that Eli, the priest of the temple, was sitting by a pillar of the temple when Hannah began to pray. The narrator (v. 12) notes that "Eli was watching her mouth" (ועלי שׁמר את־פיה) as she was praying silently. Since Eli could only see her lips move, he concluded that she was drunk (v. 13). The rest of the narrative shows how wrong he was.

If we move to the following chapter, we learn that Eli's perceptiveness is flawed again. In 1 Samuel 2, the sons of Eli, Hophni and Phinehas, are corrupting the worship of Yahweh. They cavort with women at the very door of the sanctuary (v. 22), something that seems evident to everyone but

---

1. All biblical citations follow the NRSV, except as noted. Bail (166) does note that "das Hören der Stimme ist bewusst gegen das Sehen einer Gestalt Gottes abgesetzt." Yet there is no sustained examination of this observation nor extension to the rest of DtrH.

to Eli, who is apparently unable to detect this misbehavior with his sight. Instead, the information about the misbehavior comes through hearing (וישמע את כל־אשר יעשׂון בניו). Note also that Eli's loss of sight is not mentioned until after this episode (1 Sam 3:2). Thus, we are confronted with a very stark juxtaposition: Eli misinterprets the pious worship of Hannah when he relies on his sight, but only hearing provides correct information about his sons' impious worship.

In 1 Sam 9:9 we encounter a very curious note that has long puzzled interpreters. The verse explains that what is now called a prophet in Israel was previously called a "seer" (כי לנביא היום יקרא לפנים הראה). McCarter (1980:177) concludes that it is a redactional note meant to explain why Samuel is called a "seer" and a "man of God" in earlier traditions (see also Birch 1971:59 n. 9). However, McCarter (1980:177) also admits that such a note implies that the author must have thought that נביא had replaced an earlier term. Yet this also seems odd because the later Chronicler routinely uses "seer" when speaking of Samuel and other figures (e.g., 1 Chr 9:22; 26:28; 29:29).

However, if we view at least some of the traditions of DtrH as audiocentric, then the note in 1 Sam 9:9 makes sense. The narrator might also be emphasizing that "seers" should be passé precisely because whoever is responsible for this part of DtrH wants to ensure readers understand that aurality is privileged over visuality. The preferred term, נביא, is more closely associated with aurality/orality. According to Daniel Fleming, its etymology is best understood as "'one who invokes' the name of Yahweh" (224).

And it is not long after this curious note that we witness the antipathy toward the use of vision to make crucial decisions. In 1 Sam 10:17–24, which is apparently part of at least two different traditions about Saul's selection (McCarter 1980:195), Samuel uses lots to obtain information about Yahweh's decision. Saul hides himself among some equipment, but is finally identified. Saul is posed in front of the crowd, which immediately sees that he is taller than anyone else. Samuel and the crowd apparently link his height directly to his selection, and the people do not hesitate to declare him king. However, the subsequent narration tells us that such a selection, based on appearance, was doomed from the start.

The antipathy toward the use of sight continues in 1 Sam 16, in which Samuel is instructed to search for a replacement for Saul. Samuel approaches Jesse, and his sons begin to parade before the prophet. But Samuel, relying on the appearance of Eliab, the oldest son, mistakenly concludes that this is the person whom Yahweh has chosen. Yahweh issues the following correction in 1 Sam 16:7 (RSV):

> Do not look on his appearance or on the height of his stature, because I have rejected him; for the LORD sees not as man sees; man looks on the outward appearance, but the LORD looks on the heart.

The allusion to looking at the heart ties this mode of perception directly back to the Saul episode and to the Hannah episode, in which the narrator tells us that Hannah was praying "in her heart" (1 Sam 1:13).

Another narrative that clearly shows the superiority of hearing over seeing is in the story of Ahijah, the unsighted prophet of Shiloh, in 1 Kgs 14. This narrative begins when Abijah, the son of Jeroboam, king of Israel, falls ill. Jeroboam instructs his wife as follows (1 Kgs 14:2–6; RSV):

> 2: And Jerobo'am said to his wife, "Arise, and disguise yourself, that it be not known that you are the wife of Jerobo'am, and go to Shiloh; behold, Ahi'jah the prophet is there, who said of me that I should be king over this people.

> 3: Take with you ten loaves, some cakes, and a jar of honey, and go to him; he will tell you what shall happen to the child."

> 4: Jerobo'am's wife did so; she arose, and went to Shiloh, and came to the house of Ahi'jah. Now Ahi'jah could not see, for his eyes were dim because of his age.

> 5: And the LORD said to Ahi'jah, "Behold, the wife of Jerobo'am is coming to inquire of you concerning her son; for he is sick. Thus and thus shall you say to her." When she came, she pretended to be another woman.

> 6: But when Ahi'jah heard the sound of her feet, as she came in at the door, he said, "Come in, wife of Jerobo'am; why do you pretend to be another? For I am charged with heavy tidings for you."

The narrator includes at least three features that signal the superiority of hearing. First, he tells us explicitly that Ahijah is unsighted. Second, the narrator lets the reader know that Ahijah can still recognize and understand Yahweh's communications without the aid of sight. Third, Ahijah can still recognize, solely through hearing, Jeroboam's wife despite the fact that she has disguised her appearance. Indeed, sight is not needed at all for the correct perception of either divine or human entities (see also Hull: 21–24).

The mode of perception is an issue in 1 Kgs 19, in which the prophet Elijah flees to Horeb after learning that Jezebel, the wife of the evil king Ahab, plans to kill him. Elijah finds himself in a cave when he hears Yahweh speaking to him (v. 9). Yahweh instructs Elijah to go to the mouth of the cave to witness the presence of Yahweh. Elijah sees a great wind breaking rocks, but the narrator tells us that Yahweh is not in that wind (v. 11). Then, an earthquake arrives, but Yahweh is not in the earthquake (v. 11). A fire appears, but Yahweh is not in the fire (v. 12). Finally, there is a very faint voice or sound (קול דממה דקה), which is identified as Yahweh's communication mode (v. 13). Again, hearing is privileged over dramatic audiovisual theophanies.

Concluding that DtrH is audiocentric does not mean that other expla-

nations are excluded. Certainly, the narrative about Elijah could also be
motivated by the author's attempt to differentiate Yahweh's mode of revelation from those used by Canaanite storm gods, such as Baal or Hadad.
Likewise, I acknowledge that other parts of DtrH do seem to value vision, as in the case in which a narrator views positively the fact that Moses
maintained his eyesight until his death (Deut 34:7). But even in Deut 34:7,
we may be speaking of how unique Moses was in his ability to be such a
great leader despite his great eyesight (for another view, see also Schipper
in this volume). In any case, the emphasis that hearing is superior to vision is repeated sufficiently to believe that it is more than a coincidence in
DtrH.

The reasons for audiocentricity are more difficult to find, but cross-
cultural studies can provide some possible explanations. Classen (106–20)
observes that Andean cultures were largely dependent on orality to convey
information. When the Spaniards arrived with their graphocentric traditions, some Andean cultures resisted the use of writing and the authority
with which the Europeans treated writings, including the Bible.

If DtrH reflects an effort to resist Assyrian or Babylonian imperialism,
then the emphasis on orality might be part of that resistance. Both Assyrian and Babylonian empires projected power through visual means, not
just oral means (Porter 1993, 2003; cf. Ellenius). The emphasis on orality,
therefore, might have served a similar purpose of resisting religious traditions that emphasized the use of icons and vision in communicating and in
imposing their hegemony. And countering the fear of such icons is exactly
what we find in Jer 10:5: "Their idols are like scarecrows in a cucumber field,
and they cannot speak; they have to be carried, for they cannot walk. Be not
afraid of them, for they cannot do evil, neither is it in them to do good."

We certainly have many other indications that arguments against
icons centered on their lack of sense, as in Ps 115:

2: Why should the nations say, "Where is their God?"

3: Our God is in the heavens; he does whatever he pleases.

4: Their idols are silver and gold, the work of men's hands.

5: They have mouths, but do not speak; eyes, but do not see.

6: They have ears, but do not hear; noses, but do not smell.

7: They have hands, but do not feel; feet, but do not walk; and they
do not make a sound in their throat.

As in the *Testament of Reuben*, we recognize a similar list of "senses," including speech, vision, hearing, smell, and touch, which form the criteria of
existence and life itself. The question posed in Ps 115:2 is similar to that
found in the Rabshakeh's taunting speech to the besieged Jerusalemites
in 2 Kgs 18:34.

Likewise, the dangers of relying on texts, which are visual representations of speech, was known to other biblical authors (see Schaper). Note, for example, that Jeremiah (8:8), who has been credited with the author- ship of DtrH (Friedman), complains: "How can you say, 'We are wise, and the law of the LORD is with us?' But, behold, the false pen of the scribes has made it into a lie." It is also in Jeremiah (31:33) that we find the idea that the law will one day not be written in some exterior medium, which would require vision to read it. Instead, the law will be written in the heart, which assures that it will be followed better than ever before.

Visiocentricity in Job

We need not belabor the point that Job is an extremely difficult book to interpret. The vocabulary and syntax are often obscure, and the date of composition and social context are heavily disputed (Clines 1989; Habel; Pope). However, the valuation of vision and hearing is relatively less dif- ficult to study. Some interpreters have noted how often themes relating to vision are mentioned in Job. As Anathea Portier-Young comments, "Imag- ery of light and darkness, sight and blindness, pervades the book of Job" (17). However, most interpreters still overlook how Job's visiocentricity, its privileging of vision, compares or contrasts to that of other works in the Bible.

To understand the relationship between audition and vision in Job, it is perhaps best to begin in Job 42:5, near the end of the book, where we find a remarkable statement:

> I had heard of thee by the hearing of the ear, but now my eye sees thee

לשמע־אזן שמעתיך

ועתה עיני ראתך

Clearly, Job regards this as an advance over what he had experienced be- fore. Job tells us that before this point, he had not "seen" God, but only "heard" of him by the ear. We realize that while the last chapter of Job includes an epilogue that most scholars do not regard as original, the verse (5) at issue here is not regarded as part of that epilogue by some scholars (Greenberg 1987:299; Zuckerman: 25).

If it is the case that Job regards "seeing" God as an advance over, or cul- mination of, his previous experience with Yahweh, then it is reasonable to expect to find some indications that just hearing Yahweh or hearing about Yahweh was not providing Job with sufficient satisfaction. And in earlier chapters, Job does tell us that his yearning for visual perception of Yahweh was unfulfilled. He says in Job 9:11: "Lo, he passes by me, and I see him not; he moves on, but I do not perceive him." In his negational statement ("I see him not"/ולא אראה), he uses the same verb for "see" that is used in the affirmation in Job 42:5. In Job 9:11, however, it is paired with a verb translated as "understand" or "perceive" (בין).

In Job 19:25–27, Job is quite adamant about hoping that he will see God regardless of his physical state:

> 25: For I know that my Redeemer lives, and at last he will stand upon the earth;
>
> 26: and after my skin has been thus destroyed, then from my flesh I shall see God,
>
> 27: whom I shall see on my side, and my eyes shall behold, and not another. My heart faints within me!

The reference to the fleshly nature of human eyes is also mentioned in Job's allusion to the nature of Yahweh's visuality in Job 10:4: "Hast thou eyes of flesh? Dost thou see as man sees?"

There is certainly indication that Job wants to hear from God (Job 31:35), and where seeing/hearing are paired as in Job 13:1: "Lo, my eye has seen all this, my ear has heard and understood it." But in the latter case, he is referring to information he is hearing from his so-called friends. What is significant is how often we do not find seeing/hearing paired in similar statements, but rather just other synonyms for "seeing," as in Job 23:9: "On the left hand I seek him, but I cannot behold him; I turn to the right hand, but I cannot see him."

Furthermore, it appears that hearing God's voice does not provide understanding, as in Job 37:5: "God thunders wondrously with his voice; he does great things which we cannot comprehend." Likewise, Job 26:4: "Lo, these are but the outskirts of his ways; and how small a whisper do we hear of him! But the thunder of his power who can understand?" All of this might be an expression of awe, but it could also express the idea that hearing only provides incomplete understanding, which is fulfilled only later, judging by the exclamation of Job 42:5.

In fact, it is remarkable how often more extended statements about existence itself are linked only to seeing (see Terrien). For example, in Job 7:7–8, Job seems to equate existence with seeing and with being seen: "Remember that my life is a breath; my eye will never again see good. The eye of him who sees me will behold me no more; while thy eyes are upon me, I shall be gone."

Likewise, Bildad's speech in Job 8:18 indicates that being seen is the mark of existence: "If he is destroyed from his place, then it will deny him, saying, 'I have never seen you.'" Zophar makes a similar statement in Job 20:7–9 (cf. Eliphaz in Job 4:15–16):

> 7: he will perish for ever like his own dung; those who have seen him will say, "Where is he?"
>
> 8: He will fly away like a dream, and not be found; he will be chased away like a vision of the night.

> 9: The eye which saw him will see him no more, nor will his place
> any more behold him.

Danger of losing one's life is associated with not seeing in Job 22:10–11: "Therefore snares are round about you, and sudden terror overwhelms you; your light is darkened, so that you cannot see, and a flood of water covers you."

Otherwise, even when hearing and seeing are discussed in a passage, hearing seems to take second place to seeing. Job 28:20–28 illustrates one such case:

> 20: Whence then comes wisdom? And where is the place of
> understanding?
>
> 21: It is hid from the eyes of all living, and concealed from the birds
> of the air.
>
> 22: Abaddon and Death say, "We have heard a rumor of it with our
> ears."
>
> 23: God understands the way to it, and he knows its place.
>
> 24: For he looks to the ends of the earth, and sees everything under
> the heavens.
>
> 25: When he gave to the wind its weight, and meted out the waters
> by measure;
>
> 26: when he made a decree for the rain, and a way for the lightning
> of the thunder;
>
> 27: then he saw it and declared it; he established it, and searched it
> out.
>
> 28: And he said to man, "Behold, the fear of the Lord, that is
> wisdom; and to depart from evil is understanding."

The passage emphasizes the search for "the place" of wisdom, and this search primarily involves vision. Hearing can only provide "rumors" about its location (v. 22). Likewise, creation itself foregrounds vision in establishing existence ("he saw it" in v. 27).

And even if we go to the epilogue of the entire book, we are told that, after seeing Yahweh, "Job lived a hundred and forty years, and saw his sons, and his sons' sons, four generations. And Job died, an old man, and full of days" (Job 42:5). So even if the epilogue were an additional component of Job, it continues the theme of "seeing." In particular, seeing his descendants, not just God, indicates that he had lived a fulfilled life.

Many scholars have already observed that Job reflects a theodicy that is different from that of Deuteronomy. In Deut 28, illness is the inevitable result of the violation of the covenant, and health is the inevitable reward for keeping the covenant. Job provides an alternative moral universe, in which people are not sick because of any transgression. The book of Job, after all, begins with the premise that Job was upright and blameless. Note also that words similar to those found in Deut 28:35 are used to describe Job's affliction in Job 2:7.[2] However, another difference between Job and at least parts of DtrH might be in the manner in which they value vision and hearing. Unlike the case of Job, DtrH repeatedly indicates that vision is not necessary to perceive God, and hearing is sufficient. In Job, hearing is not sufficient and, at the very least, must be complemented or completed by vision.

Conclusion

"Sensory criticism" is not only possible, but also necessary to gain a better appreciation of how biblical authors conceptualize and treat human embodiment. Biblical authors do recognize what we regard as "senses" (seeing, hearing, smell, taste, touch) that are, in great part, tools for obtaining information. However, we have learned that ancient cultures also saw certain features of human existence (e.g., sexual desire) as belonging to the same class of phenomena as our five senses.

If "criticism" is a term that signals that a particular feature of the biblical corpus merits attention (e.g., the text in textual criticism, rhetoric in rhetorical criticism), then the place of the senses and the body should receive parity by the term "sensory criticism." Sensory criticism has a discrete subject and an approach that is no less worthy of attention than rhetoric, text, or redaction, which are also different features of textual "bodies." And it is also feasible to see sensory criticism as part of a larger inquiry we may call "corporeal criticism" and which encompasses the whole experience of embodiment.

More important, my preliminary exploration indicates that the senses are not all equal in value, and sometimes there is antipathy toward particular senses in certain contexts. Even if DtrH is not a unified composition, we can find a sustained sonic theology. Even if Job is not a unified composition, we can find that 42:5 is consistent with many other statements throughout its earlier chapters about the value of seeing. I have demonstrated that such differential valuations of the senses are intertwined with larger social, literary, political, and theological agendas.

The entire discussions about the value of hearing and seeing in both DtrH and Job may be considered part of a larger struggle with epistemological questions that continue today, namely, what are the best instruments available to human beings to perceive the world and the divine? In DtrH, we see a continuing effort to identify how the audience can know that they have received a communication from God (see Deut 18:21). These

---

2. My thanks to Jeremy Schipper for this insight and other comments, and to Sarah Melcher for her comments.

questions had personal and national implications that were intertwined with legitimizing the proper channels of authority.

With regard to how sensory criticism contributes to disability studies, one must begin by noting that some of what are classified as disabilities in our society are related to the senses (e.g., hearing, seeing). However, it seems clear that the type of information that is valued also affects how disability is conceptualized. Ahijah, the unsighted prophet, for example, was fully capable of receiving all the information he needed through hearing. In such a context, he might not have been regarded as disabled. Biblical materials tell us that even ancient societies would understand that there were alternative means to accomplish the same goals (e.g., to receive information). There were ways to compensate for the lack of sight.

On the other hand, we can also see how even a biblical corpus identified as relatively unified has varying and contradictory valuations of the senses. The biblical authors valued senses depending on their own goals, politics, and theological presuppositions. Such variegated and contradictory attitudes among biblical authors should dissuade us from taking any particular view of the senses in biblical authors as "normative" today.

Sensory criticism can render us more sensitive to how the gathering and processing of information has been a continuing theme in the differential treatment of human beings that underlies all notions of disability, whether in the medical or social models. With the increase in the use of cyberinformation, human nature itself may be reconceived and new configurations in the valuation of senses may result (Baillie and Casey; Baldi). Therefore, current debates about the role of cyberinformation in shaping human nature can be regarded as a continuation of discussions about the role of the senses in evaluating information that were first recorded in the ancient Near East.

4

"Be Men, O Philistines!" (1 Samuel 4:9)

ICONOGRAPHIC REPRESENTATIONS AND REFLECTIONS ON FEMALE GENDER
AS DISABILITY IN THE ANCIENT WORLD

Carole R. Fontaine

> . . . an analysis of these women's texts affirms that the disabled body,
> like the female body, is a socially constructed symbol of powerlessness
> and deviation, created by social organizations and imbued with mean-
> ing by cultural ideologies. . . . In telling . . . their most intimate stories,
> they "authored" themselves, their narratives richly illustrating how their
> "deleted" and "crooked" bodies function as cultural metaphors . . . (Phil-
> lips 1993:397)

It is important to begin this essay by making clear that I am a handicapped
female elite. Because medical care is available to elites, I am able to work.
Because I work, I have status and some might say, "a purpose." But the reality is that I am not living a normally "abled" life and that inevitably colors
my reflections on the interpretations of everything—including the Bible.

Disability plus female gender presents a potent "double whammy"
of cultural constructions. Being a "handicapped" female in a masculinist
setting involves double "cultural performances," ones that simultaneously
force the deviant subject to submit to twin requirements: first erasing the
female body and then the disabled body. Struggling for the elusive "reasonable accommodation" requires me to be less (or, more!) than female,
since that term involves passivity, silence, compliance. Likewise, because
I am profoundly *more* disabled by the inaccessibility of professional settings, I become more disabled in the public domain than in my private
one, and become more noticeable as such. A person who resists her own
disappearance becomes viewed as cantankerous, carping, idiosyncratic,
self-absorbed, always requiring and asking for more. A female who must
continually serve as her own advocate is easily characterized as a "bitch";

a female who refuses to die obediently when issued a death sentence by those in white coats is but a few steps from being "witch."

Reading current works on the social construction of the body is very telling: it is, by and large, *not* those in the culturally preferred bodies—healthy males of a certain class—who are discussing the fluidity or cultural "making" of the body. Rather, the theories are proposed by those who have been "de-classified" as Perfect Body, those who will never be able to move into the preferred category (Grosz 1994; Butler 1990; Kampen 1996; Parpola and Whiting 2002; Rautman 2000). For whatever reason, critics writing on these topics have vested interests in de-inscribing "classical" male perfection as the ideal human form. When such personal or professional interests are at stake, it is only sensible to offer a reality check to the theories with a little data.

While I quite agree with the quote by Phillips opening this essay, I have some hesitation in applying the insights wholesale to the ancient Near East and the world of the biblical text. Is there anything in the ancient world that can shed light on the proposed identity of "female as disabled" and "disabled female" as the ultimate disability? Elsewhere, I have offered some studies on how the disabled and chronically ill are used as literary props for the *real* action in many biblical stories (Fontaine 1996). Now I turn to art history to offer a few snippets of data that support the contention that in ancient patriarchal societies, the low-status disabled female sits at the very bottom of the ladder of cultural preference. This doubly devalued woman has been so successfully erased from the archaeological and iconographic record that she can only be recovered by intimation—establishing her status by the views and representations of the male world that abhors her.

Gender and Disability in Ancient Near Eastern Art

As studies on the representation of the body proceed, we find much attention being given to our earliest documented cultures—Egypt, Mesopotamia, Anatolia, whose traditions often had pronounced impact on the iconography of the kingdoms of Judah and Israel and later communities of synagogue and church. While we have not always looked at material culture for its "symbolic" meanings, or even acknowledged fully the places where excavations shed doubt on biblical narratives, this is no longer considered acceptable practice by most. I use the comparative method here because one of the target cultures, Egypt, has been so obliging as to encode its ideologies of gender, nationality/ethnicity, and supposed abilities into the conventions of its art (Whitney Davis 1989). If biblical writers were so free in their compositions that they could pick up a text wholesale from Egypt with only a few modifications (the NK Instruction of Amenenope finds its way into Prov 22–24), then it is likely that they were likewise influenced in artistic conventions from time to time, especially ones reproduced on scarabs, although as with "borrowed" texts, quite able to give new and altered meanings to the items borrowed as necessary.

The Art of Smiting and Feminization of the Enemy in Egypt

Unlike Mesopotamia, where we must seek indications of gender in presence or lack of beards, counting the number of horns on the headdress for a status index, the Egyptian canon of art made such identifications much simpler: males were painted in dark brown colors, representing their exposure to the public outside world; females were painted with yellow ochre, reflecting their domestic world where sunburn was a less frequent occurrence. That the colors are clearly gender-coded and carry gendered meanings for the creator and viewer is clear from the treatment of queen burials in NK tombs: a queen, as wife of the god (Pharaoh) and mother of the god (Pharaoh), could not be imaged in the same limited iconic vocabulary normally applied to regular women. NK Queens are "gendered" male in their appearances in mythological scenes in their tomb paintings by being painted dark brown. A wall painting from Theban Tomb of Kynebu of Queen Ahmose Nefertari (EA 37994 in the British Museum) provides an excellent example of a "blackened queen" shown deified (Twentieth Dynasty, ca. 1130). Ann M. Roth speculates that this gender-bending switch takes place as queens are identified with Osiris in the process of rebirth, symbolically possible because he had no phallus, according to myth (Roth 2000). The point: they are transfemale, female-to-male redeemers who freely delete male military elements from tomb iconography to be replaced with more nurturing divine elements of the customary mythological narrative of life in the Underworld (McCarthy 2005).

When surveying the pictographic elements of the hieroglyphic language, we can see that some of the stereotypic meanings of the "coloring" of the genders are reflected there as well. Gardiner's classic *Egyptian Grammar* records fifty-five signs of male body "in action" in its index to the sign list in Section A (of course!), "Man and his Occupations" (Gardiner 1957). Section B, "Woman and Her Occupations," has all of seven signs, five of which include reference to motherhood or fertility (pregnant woman, child exiting woman's body; squatting woman, child nursing; child sitting on lap). It is easy to imagine that the presence of a female disabled with respect to her fertility might leave her as a functional "non-person"—the visual language cannot even express her being.

There are, of course, other telling "gender conventions" in Egyptian art. Male figures, even in the charming family tomb scenes that seem to gesture toward real family affections, are placed in different positions which effectively express not just status but preference for male gender. Males are on the left; females and children are on the right. Men are invariably shown in a position of "half" movement, one foot placed in front of the other as though they are striding out into eternity in the fullness of their bodily integrity. Sometimes, the male in the composition is even shown twice (!) to emphasize his importance in the family unit or the eyes of the world ("multiply constituted," as one would say in corporeal studies). Women are often portrayed with one arm around the husband's back, holding onto the far side of his torso for support. Most disturbing is the placement of the woman's feet: precisely together, indicating a stationary position within the family and society—at least for the purposes of tomb art. As one of my students commented during a museum visit to Old Kingdom free-standing and bas-relief family sculptures, "She's certainly going nowhere fast compared to him!" Indeed.

It is when we add a third category of representations—that of foreigners or enemies (often the same thing)—that we are able to better triangulate the relationship of female gender as a primary and basic disability outweighing all others. By the time of the predynastic period, iconographic standards were already set for the presentation of Pharaoh's enemies. These canons of art are clearly visible in the so-called ritual "palettes": the Hunter's Palette, the Battlefield Palette, the Narmer Palette, and so on. These are especially important pieces of visual ideology, as they are examples of official, "state" art and, as such, seek to inscribe the reality of the new form of leadership onto the viewers' and users' consciousness. While it is not possible to date these entirely accurately (Naqada I or II periods) or to tell their exact use in a particular ritual, both the time period and the function seem clear enough (Koehler 2002; O'Connor 2004a, 2004b). Such palettes of stone, plain and in much smaller sizes, were used privately to grind, mix, and apply eye makeup, which was worn by both men and women. It is assumed that the large ritual tablets covered in iconography were used in temple or military ceremonies to "open the eyes" of the statues of the gods—certainly an advantage if one would like the god's participation in the current smiting of foreigners.

While earlier art tended to focus on the representation of processions of offerings and activities having to do with the hunt, the production of food, or the domestication of animals, these later official palettes make an interesting and disturbing move: the foreign enemy replaces the animal in the scenes of slaughter. Later, most caught or wounded animals disappear in favor of foreigners treated the same way. The Oxford Palette may mark the transition here: it shows an upright jackal figure, piping to animals all around, but its association with the ideology of the predynastic period remains unclear. While it may have been important for early leaders to show their worthiness for that position by their ability to lead successful hunts, to instigate and control food production, later rulers of the "unified" land favor a different job description of the elite male: he smites people, thereby providing the "food" of the empire—subjugated populations, slaves, tribute, favorable treaties, and so on.

The focus on the "foreignness" of the one being smote may be a sop to the real violence that undergirds any positive-sounding "unification" program (if that is indeed the historical referent of these symbolic scenes). While cities and enemies being subjugated in the Narmer Palette have been widely identified with a variety of foreign groups, the real message *may* be one of internal relief: although the king had to smite locally to make himself an empire, he now turns his attention to those outside of his newly crafted realm. The vision of the foreigner in mid-smiting, then, became both a statement of national security and a refocusing of the might of the state in its willingness to smite, all the while providing a subtle warning to any who found themselves unhappy with this state of affairs (Goldwasser 1992). To say "no" to the power of Pharaoh rendered one "foreign" and an enemy to be crushed—so it had been, and so it would be, proclaims this art.

It is not simply that foreigners replace cattle in early times of state formation in Egypt; other artistic signals are being sent in the new "Pharaoh Smites Foreigner" icon. The foreigners are placed to the right of Pharaoh in the "female" position and often kneeling before him as he grabs a hair forelock to pull back the neck for easier beheading. Foreign fighters are shown in attitudes of flight, legs at full gallop, although in these vignettes they never succeed in escape. Unlike Pharaoh in all his battle regalia, the enemies are usually shown clad only in loin clothes, penis sheaths, or entirely naked, emphasizing their lack of status vis-à-vis the Egyptians. Other dead prisoners are shown with no genitalia at all but peculiar sausage-like items on their heads, possibly the severed penis, representing perhaps a reference to the full feminization of the slain enemy (Davies and Friedman 1998). In other cases beyond the scenes on palettes, foreigners are portrayed as female: they are painted in yellow ochre colors, have full flowing hair as appropriate to their nationality (we can never see Pharaoh's hair under his battle headdress), and are shown with a flaccid penis or none at all.

One should not assume that this early predynastic canonical tradition of manhood, femaleness, and foreignness is unfamiliar in ancient Canaan: in fact, numerous ties have been established between the southern Levant and Egypt in the predynastic periods and beyond. The hieroglyphic *serekh* (standing for Narmer's palace façade) as well as Narmer's name sign ("raging catfish") have been found inscribed on artifacts from Canaan at places like Nahal Tillah, indicating a robust trade network between the two regions (Levy et al. 1995; van den Brink and Levy 2002; Miroschedji 2002; Stanley 2002).

The canonical treatment of the "Other" as female, whether in overt moves such as using the female color to portray them, or in more subtle ways such as treatment of hair, position of legs, and genitalia, becomes standardized within Egyptian art. The glyph of the captive foreigner, kneeling with arms drawn back and pinned behind the back, becomes a

Fig. 1. Wooden Execration Figure, end of the MK, Louvre E27204; drawing by author.

common background cartouche for the writing of names of foreign nations, or particular groups a Pharaoh may have conquered. This convention may be found from earliest times right up into the Ptolemaic Period (examples abound in the Louvre and British Museum). Another group of artifacts which can help elucidate the relationship between "captivity/limitation" and "femaleness"—a prime concern of our Philistines in 1 Samuel—is a group of execration figures from the late Middle Kingdom, now in the Louvre (E16492–E16501, terra-cotta figurines; E27204, painted wood, see below).

These models of human enemies were used in execration rituals, a form of sympathetic ritual magic, which allowed the actors to name the figure for a certain enemy and, by destroying the figure, obliterate the powers of the enemy to do harm. While all of the figures in this group are clearly men (they have no breasts), they have been thoroughly feminized, which reflects the desires of the ritual actors. The figures in terra-cotta have been given huge incised pubic triangles, a familiar form of gendering the female figurine in ancient Levantine and Mesopotamian sculpture, but have no penis. The painted wood figure shows an even more ominous form of gendering: standing in the female position, arms pulled back, face alive with horror, this enemy has an ominous absence where his penis should be—perhaps representing its having been hacked off, inferred from the exceptionally rough condition of the wood where his legs meet the torso.

The desire to make one's enemy into a female, suitable for destruction or enslavement, becomes the hallmark of such "military" art, and this is the folk idea behind the outcry of the Philistines as they invoke the ideology of gender. Maleness is a symbolic construction, representing potency, activity, agency, courage, movement, and, by inference, choice. Female-ness is characterized as the binary opposite, and, for the male worldview, to be female is to be handicapped in all essential ways.

The Case for Feminization in the Bible: The Philistines

התחזקו והיו לאנשים פלשתים פן תעבדו לעברים כאשר עבדו לכם
והייתם לאנשים ונלחמתם:

> Be strong, and be men, O Philistines, lest you become slaves to the Hebrews just as they became slaves for you. Be men, and fight! (1 Sam 4:9)

We come now to our fearful Philistines and other examples of the horror of gender-bending in the Hebrew Bible. Their concerns are highlighted in the verses prior to 1 Sam 4:9:

> When the ark of the covenant of the LORD came into the camp, all Israel gave a mighty shout, so that the earth resounded. When the Philistines heard the noise of the shouting, they said, "What does this great shout-ing in the camp of the Hebrews mean?" When they learned that the ark of the LORD had come to the camp, the Philistines were afraid; for they said, "Gods have come into the camp." They also said, "Woe to us! For nothing like this has happened before. Woe to us! Who can deliver us from the power of these mighty gods? These are the gods who struck the Egyptians with every sort of plague in the wilderness. Take courage, and be men, O Philistines, in order not to become slaves to the Hebrews as they have been to you; be men and fight." So the Philistines fought; Israel was defeated, and they fled, everyone to his home. There was a very great slaughter, for there fell of Israel thirty thousand foot soldiers. (1 Sam 4:5–9 NRSV)

We may extract key points from the scene: the Philistines hear and fear; as foreigners, they do not quite understand what is going on in terms of the divine reality but they know the story "on the street"; they believe that "being a woman" leads to enslavement (and to other forms of humiliation, no doubt); *and even in the presence of the mighty Ark of the Covenant, their self-admonition is effective.* Dread of being female outweighs dread of the Ark that smote Pharaoh and his men, and the former serves as an effective counter to the latter condition. That we find these literary tropes inscribed in texts having to do with military contexts makes perfect sense: in the all-male world of soldiering and conquest, the tendency rigidly to stereotype the other absent gender, as well as one's own, is a bonding mechanism that also works to motivate the flagging combatant—*don't* behave like a woman! Of course, the Hebrew Bible presents us with a few crafty women who *are* dangerous to men in battle, especially foreigners (Deborah and Ya'el, the unnamed woman at Thebez in 2 Sam 11:21, Judith), a trope which also has a payoff in humiliation of the one who fell by the hand of a woman.

The fears of the Philistines of what it would mean to be turned into women are further elucidated in an Akkadian translation of a Hittite text concerning the siege of Urshu:

> The king waxed wroth and his face was grim: "They constantly bring me evil tidings; may the Weather-god carry you away in a flood! . . . Why have you not given battle? You stand on chariots of water, you are almost turned to water yourself . . . You had only to kneel before him and you would have killed him or at least frightened him. But as it is, you have behaved like a woman." (Gurney 1981:180–81)

As Cynthia R. Chapman has pointed out, in the ancient Near East the only place where the commonplace domain of "soldier" overlaps with the domain of "woman" is in elements of weakness, fear, inactivity, and inability to handle weapons usefully (2004:13). The Urshu text confirms this in its rehearsal of unsuitable soldiering: failure to give battle (inactivity), chariots of water (inability to use weapons), turning into water (fear), and failure to challenge the enemy one-on-one (cowardice). References to ritual curses that change the enemy or treaty-breakers into women is proof enough of the desire to feminize the enemy combatant and can be found verbally in Assyrian, Anatolian, and Aramaic curses and treaty texts among others (documented by Chapman and others), and visually in the Egyptian positioning of the captured enemy as female within a visual field. What is interesting in the story of the Philistines and the siege of Urshu is that it is *one's own soldiers* who are warned of feminization, rather than placing that curse upon the enemy.

Of course, the Bible also applies such imagery to foreign enemies. In Isa 19:16, we learn what YHWH has planned for the men of Egypt: under a spirit of confusion, they will become like women (יהיה מצרים כנשים) and stagger like vomiting drunkards, a nice reversal of Pharaoh's smiting of foreigners. In the tirade against Nineveh in Nah 3:13—feminized as the worst sort of female, a sorcerous prostitute—the writer slanders the defenders of the city with the stereotype *"your people (troops) are women in your midst,"* leading to the opening of the city's gate (a sort of vagina?) and ultimate vulnerability for the inhabitants. The imprecation that all Babylon's warriors in her midst should "become women" in Jer 50:37 functions as a verbal ritual of gender switching, here carried out by YHWH, just as a masculinized Ishtar is invoked to break bows and to turn enemies into women in texts from Mesopotamia (Chapman 2004: 50–57). Jeremiah 51:30 tells us that Babylon's warriors have turned into women (היו לנשים), and it is not a pretty sight for the successful waging of war. "The warriors of Babylon have given up fighting, they remain in their strongholds; their strength has failed, they have become women; her buildings are set on fire, her bars are broken." The key action motifs are giving up, hiding, weakness—all forms of feminization that lead to destruction and increased vulnerability for the population.

The message (and hope) is clear: men can be disabled as warriors simply by regendering them.

In Search of the Handicapped Female

If being in a female body is a handicap from the perspective of male military ideology and iconography (no wonder Queen Hatshepsut kept cross-dressing with false beards!), what must be the situation for the *disabled* female in such a matrix of cultural stereotypes continually reinforcing the message of preference for what is male (strong, powerful, effective)? Again, we are hampered by lack of direct representation; we must draw our inferences from male stereotyping and concerns reflected in medical texts. We must begin therefore by asking if there are any *positive* images of a feminized male body in art historical sources.

The most famous example in Egyptian art may be the portrayals of the heretic king Akhenaten, of the Amarna Period in the New Kingdom. The feminization there *may* represent genuine articulation of illness and disability. Scholars debate whether the elongated face, thick lips, the narrow shoulders, almost female-like breasts, pendulous belly, broad hips, fat thighs, and matchstick legs always shown in representations of Akhenaten are a snide comment by workshop artists who were by no means happy with the new trend in more naturalistic representations of royals and elites. If so, the king was remarkably benign in allowing these clear deviations from the pharaonic ideal to stand as official works, and, eventually, the peculiar form of Akhenaten was applied to other royals and even ordinary citizens, although in a far less exaggerated way. Other views include the notion that we have a real artistic revolution in representation on our hands, or that the peculiar shape of the head of Akhenaten and his family may be a symbolic reflection of the cosmic egg. Perhaps heads were bound in childhood to produce the peculiar egg-shaped skull, much as body-sculpting continues to take place in indigenous cultures around the world (Arnold 1996:19)

Another theory favors the view that Akhenaten was in fact handicapped and that the portrayals of him reflect his actual appearance. For whatever reason, the heretic king may have allowed this to be represented to his subjects. By producing children and happily portraying them, the image of Akhenaten acquits itself from any notion of disability in the realm of fertility, however unusual the king might look. The so-called expressionist or even surrealist tendency in the art of the Amarna period carries over into subject matter illustrated: Akhenaten and his family are shown in intimate family scenes, embracing each other under the life-giving rays of the solar disk and basking in the rule of this king who referred to himself in inscriptions as "the mother who gives birth to everything" (Shaw 2000:281–82). Could it be that the king appropriated the *female* iconography to himself by *choice*? A heretic, indeed!

With regard to other portrayals of the disabled, the evidence is rather sparse if one excludes the altering bodies of the aged or the crumpling bodies of slaves under the weight of heavy loads, both of which experience a certain lack of ability but are not precisely handicapped as we would think of the term. The great exception to this is the presence of representations of dwarves in Egyptian art and the subsequent correlation of skeletal tomb evidence that show that dwarfism was indeed present in the societies of ancient Egypt (Dasen 1993). We see a blind harper in the Saqqara tomb of Paaetenemheb, dated to about 1212 B.C.E. (Achtemeier 1996:715). Queen Tiye, the wife of Amenophis III, comes in for the most representations of a woman of advanced years, yet because of her role as wife and mother of kings and her own powerful personal presence, she is imaged as anything but dried up and weak, a "reading" of her character well borne out by her political activities in the Amarna letters (Fontaine 2002:62–63).

The woman handicapped from birth by defects or congenital conditions, injured by an accident in the daily round of grueling domestic duties, the one with chronic illness, or deliberately mutilated in a permanent way—for these persons (who must surely have existed, at least briefly even if they did not live to old age), there is only the silent gap with no word or image to even gesture toward the existence of a less than perfect female body in the Egyptian corpus surveyed (canonical art from predynastic to Ptolemean).

In the area of infertility, because of its immense impact on the entire construction of femaleness, we find hints of what the lives of such women must have been like. If a woman's most powerful positive aspect was her ability to give birth, then any condition or situation that prevented that was grave indeed for the woman, her family, and her community. Medical/magical texts are notorious for their focus on male and female fertility, and it is here, perhaps, as well as in omen texts, that we glean some trace of the women for whom we are looking. The Kahun Gynecological Papyrus, and the Ebers Medical Papyrus (esp. paragraphs 783–839) give us a look at the obsession with predicting, validating, and successfully fulfilling female fertility (Nunn 1996). Indeed, in the literature of Sumer and the Hebrew Bible, mass or personal infertility was an indication of divine wrath or disarray (Gen 29:31; 30:1–2; Innana-Ishtar's Descent to the Underworld), so it is no surprise to find such conditions and their diagnosis and treatment given considerable attention in related texts.

Given the absence of the handicapped woman in official, public iconography, it is something of a surprise to find her given such narrative space in the texts of the Hebrew and Christian Bibles, at least with respect to her infertile infirmity. Perhaps it is ancient Israel's adoption of a "slave subjectivity" to understand its conception in Egypt, a theoretically shameful instance of classic reversal of expected claims of exalted origins, that gives the biblical text its moment of pity for the barren woman. It may be that the Bible's penchant for the "success of the unsuccessful" or second-born motif that breeds this openness to the portrayal and redemption of the infertile—an ultimate handicap in a cultural performance as woman. While it is true that such women characters are used to demonstrate the astonishing power of God or his surrogates when they announce or cause an extraordinary birth or to highlight the extraordinary healing powers of the Messiah, nevertheless, *they are there*, bearing witness to the exigencies of changeable bodies in a world of subsistence agriculture and medical naïveté. Fertility is the arena in which women fight their battle against death and social meaninglessness, call upon their deities as redeemers and helpers, and realize the fullness of the limited biological roles assigned to them (Miller 1994:237–39).

Yet there is trouble here for someone whose fertility does *not* reassert itself after divine intervention, or whose issue of blood does *not* go away. Other than providing images of weakness and exclusion (2 Sam 5:6–8, "The blind and the lame shall not come into the house"; Prov 26:7, "The legs of a disabled person hang limp; so does a proverb in the mouth of a fool," with the NRSV's gender-neutral translation), the handicapped women of the Bible most often represent the trope of healing, *not* disability. Indeed, we must look at childless widows or rape victims not forced into marriage with their rapists to see what happens to a woman whose fertility never found full expression: she is apt to be placed in harems without much protest on the part of her husband, sent back to her family's home in infertile disgrace and suspicion of some awful sin after the death of her son-less husband, or simply narratively erased (Sarah, Dinah, the Tamars, Michal, Ruth and Orpah). One way or another, she dwells desolate, even if she is wife or daughter to a king.

Beyond this, there is no extended consideration of the state of health and life conditions of the accident victim, the chronically ill, or the disabled. Farming accidents, domestic accidents, disease, and war were realities that could inflict massive damage onto bodies, and most healing consisted of home care performed by women. What might be expected for a one-armed woman who could not engage in the twenty-some steps involved in turning flax into yarn, or find a husband willing to marry her, given her disability? To what even more menial and marginal work would such a one be assigned by her family or village? Toward what hope could she press? What does the Bible have to say, if anything, to the woman who does not get well when it can barely acknowledge her existence?

A Modest Conclusion

Bodies do not exist apart from their physical environments, nor do minds exist apart from the body. For this reason, even though one's defining interest might be in the intellectual realm of theology, considerations of corporeal and socio-environmental factors must continue to be an ongoing part of our investigations of the past. Although she is largely absent from text or image, the handicapped female, representing the far end of the continuum of power and preference, is important to us precisely for the questions her absence raises. She was and is a survivor, forced to write her own story and to craft her own image in self-defense against erasure. There is wisdom, power, courage, agency, and movement in her life as there is in any warrior's, and she obtains her meaning without having to kill or dehumanize any Other. Her situation continues to be dreadful even in the modern world, but increasingly visible—which can only be good for us all.

I end with a recent study by the United Nations on the economic, social, and cultural rights of disabled persons, especially women and children, whose human rights are coming into social consciousness for increasing positive legislation and defense:

> While women the world over are striving for equality with men, women with disabilities struggle to be recognized first as persons and then as being female. There is a tendency for care-givers, whether at home or in institutions, to treat disabled persons as objects without feelings or the right to decide on matters concerning them. This is particularly the case with those who are extensively disabled and fully dependent on others for daily activities. In the case of women, the gender bias in society imposes a subordinate status on them, and increases the likelihood that disabled women will have their individuality and rights ignored. (http://www.unescap.org/esid/psis/disability/decade/publications/wwd1.asp)

5

Masculinity and Disability in the Bible

Thomas Hentrich

1. Gender and Disability

1.1. Introduction

The objective of this essay is to address disability issues in the Bible from a gender-related perspective. In modern disability studies, gender issues play an important part, as a disability tends first to overshadow and then to highlight traditional gender roles: a disabled person is often seen as a disabled person and only secondarily as a man or a woman. Helen Meekosha states that disabled people are often considered "without gender" (3), and, in order to compensate for their lack of gender identity, disabled men and women would be encouraged to participate in gender-typical activities (8) and would therefore inadvertently strengthen traditional stereotypes (10).

1.2. Masculinity in the Bible

When discussing gender issues in the Bible, feminist theology has made great progress highlighting a woman's perspective, since this view of the biblical narratives is generally neglected or ignored. After all, the majority of biblical stories are about men and their achievements. Why should masculinity in the Bible then be an issue in the first place? Various scholars have nevertheless researched the role of men in the Bible and paid specific

A preliminary version of this article was presented at the Annual Meeting of the Society of Biblical Literature in Philadelphia in November 2005. The author wishes to thank the attending members for their input and constructive comments on this topic.

attention to their relationship with God as well as the anthropomorphic image of God.

Stephen D. Moore reflects in *God's Gym* on the statement in Gen 1:26: "Let us make humankind in our image, according to our likeness." Despite the claim of God's unimaginability, references "to certain synecdochically charged body parts do abound—Yahweh's face, eyes, mouth, ears, arms, hands, and feet are frequently mentioned . . ." (86). Furthermore, since Adam was made in God's likeness, he too is described in ancient Jewish sources as being gigantic with a perfect physique, reaching from heaven to earth. Yet with all this perfection, the Bible mostly refers only to his face (89–90). Based on early rabbinic literature, Moore concludes that the corporeal God, just like Adam, was androgynous and at creation possessed two faces, one male and one female. It therefore follows that both male and female components are equally and complementarily present in God's embodiment (91).

Mark S. Smith discusses gender issues in relation to the development of biblical monotheism in the ancient Near East with reference to the quite sexual nature of the deities in the Ugaritic pantheon (86–93). He disagrees with Moore's notion of androgyny in YHWH's image and with Howard Eilberg-Schwartz's equally daring concept of "homoeroticism" (Mark S. Smith: 248 n. 50), which is based on the assumption that "these men [Moses and the patriarchs] love, in ways that are imagined as erotically and sensually, a male deity" (Eilberg-Schwartz 1994:3), a consequence of imagining Israelite religion and its predominantly male representatives as God's wife. While recognizing the value of "corporeal god" theories for a psychoanalytical discussion, Smith concludes:

> Biblical monotheism is expressed through anthropomorphism, through gendered language, yet it relativizes anthropomorphism, perhaps even subordinates it to the divine one known only by the name of Yahweh. However, this view of anthropomorphism and divine sexuality in the Bible may have resulted at least in part from a de facto omission of older, more sexually explicit descriptions of the divine. (Mark S. Smith: 93)

In my opinion, this omission mainly affected the female side of God's image, since divine sexuality and fertility was associated in a large part with goddesses in the ancient Near East (see Hentrich 1986 for details).

Finally, David J. A. Clines examines David's role as a man in the Bible and compares it with today's standards. The assumption is that many of the interpretations of the biblical texts are influenced by modern perceptions of a given situation, such as the role of men in society. Just as men today are thought to be successful, aggressive, sexual, self-reliant, and above all anything but female (1995:213–14), David is portrayed in much the same way. First Samuel 16:18 identifies various characteristics of David: "skillful in playing" (ידע נגן), "a mighty man of valour" (גבור חיל), "a man of war" (איש מלחמה), "intelligent in speech" (נבון דבר), and "a beautiful person"

(איש תאר). Clines attributes to him the following traits: the fighting male, the persuasive male, the beautiful male, the bonding male, the woman-less and the musical male (217–30). He then asks the question whether David does not indeed stand for a new, regenerated masculinity in the Bible, a so-called new man who through his actions breaks out of the tra-ditional male role, especially considering his ambiguous relationship with Jonathan. After considering the episodes in which David appears to be vulnerable and showing signs of weakness (the Absalom revolt in 2 Sam 15:13–23; Batsheba's dying child in 2 Sam 12:15–23), Clines comes to the devastating conclusion that

> There is no "new man" here in the David story. There is a fully fledged traditional male, who for the most part recapitulates everything scripted for him by his culture, but now and then conspicuously fails—so con-spicuously that any non-feminized reader knows immediately that it is a failure that is not to be excused or imitated, but is a sorry example that serves only to reinforce the value of the traditional norms. (233)

In all, there does not seem to be too much room for experiments in the role of men in the Old Testament. For the most part, men not only represent the patriarchal society of Ancient Israel, but as such also deter-mine the predominating male image of the "God of the fathers."[1]

1.3. Gender and Disability in the Bible

Disability studies has demonstrated that disability narratives tend to be in "gendered terms, with both the content and styles reflecting the way in which gender-expectations are modulated by disability status" (Meekosha: 10). The same applies to biblical stories: Most stories of disabled people do involve men and the perspective is predominantly male, but the reason why they are in the story is less because they are disabled *men*, but because they are *disabled* men and how this may affect the relationship to God. The central issue is: Does a disability affect the human interaction with God? This becomes clear when we look at the role of priests in ancient Israel.

Two aspects need to be considered separately when it comes to mas-culinity and disability in the Bible: first, masculinity as an indication of ancient Israel's patriarchal society including the dominant male images of YHWH. At the same time, in an article about the perceived male image of God and His representatives on earth, it is impossible to ignore the reverse issue of the lack of female representations of God in the Bible. I briefly ad-dress this issue without getting too sidetracked on this intensely debated topic.

Second, there is the general aspect of illness and disability in the Bible. In the ancient Near East, disabilities were approached with some ambigu-

---

1. For further reading on masculinity concepts, see also Berger et al. and Timothy C. Edwards.

ity. As much as there was an obligation for charity toward disabled people, those same people were also considered as carriers of the gods' wrath for an unnamed sin in the past. In the Old Testament, the multitude of gods and demons responsible for a disability was reduced to just YHWH, but the situation for disabled or otherwise afflicted people was compounded by the impact of the purity laws on any illness or injury. They essentially turned them into outsiders and second-class citizens, at least where temple worship is concerned (Braddock and Parish: 14–15).

When the Bible addresses disability issues, it does so mostly with a male disabled person: the priests in Lev 21, David's nephew Meribaal in 2 Samuel, or the "lame and blind" on top of Jerusalem's wall to defend the city in 2 Sam 5:8.

In early Christianity, the situation has changed slightly, but disabled men are still the norm, and the notion of sin and healing still appears to be present during Jesus' healing practices (Braddock and Parish: 17), even though Jesus will dismantle this causality. The difference is that these healings challenge the traditional views of purity. Jesus approaches and heals disabled and sick people despite their perceived impurity and especially during Sabbath (Luke 5:12–26; 6:6–11; 8:40–56; 13:10–17; Acts 3:1–10). Only when these purity restrictions are being challenged can an independent view of disabled women and men be developed.

After a brief overview of the basic terminology concerning men in the Old Testament, I then undertake a theological examination of God's perceived masculinity that I believe is the underlying cause for the lack of female representation among disabled people at least until the New Testament, when some of the traditional conventions were questioned. Second, I survey some of the available data concerning disabled people in biblical stories with special attention to a "minor" detail in the purity laws that specifically addresses the male species.

2. God's "Masculinity" as a Model for "His" Representation

2.1. Definition of Masculinity in the Bible

2.1.1. Basic Terminology

In the Old Testament, various meanings of the word "man" appear 2,615 times. These are the most important meanings:

- אדם (e.g., Gen 1:26–27; 6:1), meaning man or mankind in the sense of human being and as a general term for the human race. The first man Adam represents here *pars pro toto* of all humanity. Out of 552 occurrences in the Hebrew Bible, 529 refer to the general meaning of "human" either in singular or plural form as "man" or "men" and 13 more describe the figure of Adam in Gen 1 (BLB 1996–2002a).
- איש (1,639 occurrences): the true meaning of "male" as opposed to

female (1,212 occurrences; e.g., Gen 4:1; 1 Sam 1:11); it is also used to designate the word husband (69 times; e.g., Ruth 1:11; Gen 3:6; 29:32). Other designations indicate "man as opposed to God" (Job 9:32; 12:10) or a "virile man" (1 Sam 2:33) (BLB 1996–2002f).

•   The ambiguous גבור (e.g., Gen 10:9; 2 Sam 17:10), meaning "strong man" or "hero" (158 occurrences): Contrary to its original meaning though, the alleged hero in the Hebrew Bible is often described as somewhat "unheroic," almost too human (BLB 1996–2002e). The reason is that the power and might of the גבור does not lie within the hero himself, but is rooted entirely in YHWH who lets the hero partake in it. Richard Hooker describes this relationship as follows:

> The gibbor is not really a "hero" in our sense of the word; the gibbor gains heroism not from inherent power and autonomy, but from obeying god. Any power or capability the gibbor has, comes from Yahweh; in the Book of Judges, the Hebrew phrase most often used to describe how the gibborim become powerful is: "and Yahweh breathed his spirit into him." (2)

One example of such an anti-hero who also relates to the topic of disability is Moses himself. When called upon by YHWH to guide the Israelites out of Egypt, he refers to his stuttering and slow speech as reasons why he would not be qualified for the job of hero (Exod 4:10). Nevertheless, YHWH insists that he rely on God's power to succeed in his task.

•   סריס: Another controversial male figure with a "disability" in the Hebrew Bible is that of the eunuch (42 occurrences, 17 of them as eunuch). The word derives from סרס (to castrate) and designates men who were to oversee the care of women in the royal household (Esth 2:3, 14, 15; 4:5), hence the סרס. Eunuchs also functioned as government officials (e.g., 1 Sam 8:15; 1 Kgs 22:9; 2 Kgs 9:32) (BLB 1996–2002b).

2.1.2. Examples of Masculine Able-Bodied Features

Throughout the Old Testament, the editors of the various books stress the importance of able-bodied functions of mainly male characters, the reasons for which have been outlined above. Adam's presumably astronomical proportions of his perfect, divine body have already been mentioned. Ironically, Moses, who portrayed himself at first as physically inadequate to perform YHWH's demands, is considered in best physical condition at his death: "Moses was a hundred and twenty years old when he died, yet his eyes were not weak nor his strength gone" (Deut 34:7 NIV). In case of warfare, all of Israel, meaning all able-bodied men, was called upon to serve, as was the case in Saul's war against the Ammonites (1 Sam 11:1–11). The only exemptions are known for economical (building a new house, recently married, etc.) or psychological (faint-heartedness or fearfulness) reasons (Deut 20:5–9).

Again, the average and therefore normative Israelite in the eyes of the Old Testament editors was an able-bodied male, who was the head of the family and could sufficiently contribute to Israelite society. This would also apply to Israelite cultic life as will be discussed further below.

2.2. The Analogy of God and "Man"

As Thomas Aquinas's *Summa theologica* argued, all human beings are imperfect beings in the eyes of the perfect God; every imagination of God must therefore be incomplete. Consequently, we can speak about God only in an imperfect way or in an analogy (1:13:2). This also applies to "His" sexual connotations: Every attempt to identify God with one of the two sexes is by definition insufficient, since God transcends all human imagination and that includes also sexual ones (Ruether: 88; Schmidt: 121). In theory, this would lead to a divine "transcendence of sexuality."

Why only in theory? The fact is, despite the presumed transcendence of sexuality, practically all gender-related connotation is expressed in masculine or paternal metaphors. The Old Testament refers to YHWH as judge, king, warrior, and so on, and in the New Testament, Jesus calls God "father" or αββα (Hamerton-Kelly 1981:97–98; Hanson: 317; for a more detailed discussion of God's anthropomorphisms, see Hamerton-Kelly 1979; Gerstenberger: 1–12; Moore: 82–86). Nowadays, this nominal transcendence of human sexuality is used as a reason for no longer questioning the imagination of the divine "Father" figure. If God is transcending sexuality anyway, why not just keep the traditional image of God? As Edmond Jacob puts it, there would be no real need to change the image:

> C'est pourquoi parler de Dieu comme du Père qui est aux cieux reste le langage le plus adéquat pour exprimer la souveraineté et l'amour de celui qui par son altérité confère à l'homme son identité filiale. Invoquer à côté de ce Père la «Mère qui est sur la terre» ne ferait que troubler cette relation en la transformant en une autodéification. (230)

On the contrary, because God transcends human sexuality, it should be legitimate to speak of God not only in male imagery, but also in feminine figures. This would truly express his general transcendence of sexuality and not only his "masculinity" (Mulack: 17). Yet since the image of any god is a product of the society it comes from, and since ancient Israel was definitely a patriarchal society, therefore not only is God portrayed in masculine terms, but also "His" representatives are male: priests, kings, and family fathers, and so on. As Paul Hanson pointed out:

> The dominance of the male metaphor . . . is the product not of a society which could freely choose the gender of its primary metaphors, but of a society driven to choose male metaphors by virtue of patriarchal structures predicated upon sexual inequality. (317)

The problem begins when some of YHWH's representatives are physically less than perfect. This stands diametrically opposed to the Israelites' imagination of YHWH as the perfect (male) human. Any disabled woman probably also had an added handicap to deal with: the purity prescriptions in Lev 12 and 15 concerning menstruation and childbirth. Women would already spend a large part of their adult life in a state of impurity, and an added disability may have been deemed irrelevant by the editors to be mentioned in the Old Testament. The only exceptions are cases of infertility when YHWH heals Samuel's mother, Hannah (1 Sam 1:11–2:10), and Abraham's wife Sarah (Gen 21:1–2) to ensure the survival of the (male) family line.

3. A Survey of Masculinity and Disability in Biblical Texts

As stated above, the normative Israelite citizen was an able-bodied male person. Nevertheless, there are several stories about disabled people in the Old Testament, each with its own purpose. The first two examples refer to the person of David as the main protagonist, whom we have learned stands for the "ideal man" in ancient Israel. In the first story, the disabled person is a potential threat to his position as king and highest priest in union and therefore has to be a male person. But we also learn about David's unique friendship with Jonathan that is a highly debated issue among scholars (Clines 1995:243–44). The second story revolves around the capture of Jerusalem and some disabled Jebusite soldiers that appear to be mocking David's presumably able-bodied male army. Last are the prescriptions concerning priests with physical disabilities, an obvious "male-only" domain.

3.1. 2 Samuel

The Second Book of Samuel contains two separate accounts about the "lame" who are somewhat involved in David's consolidation of his throne: first is the story of Jonathan's son, commonly identified as Meribaal or Mephiboshet, depending on the preferred tradition,[2] whom David saves from the fate of the rest of Saul's descendants (4:4; 9:1–13; 16:1–4; 19:18b–19, 25–31; 21:7–9a). A second story mentions the "lame and the blind" who are supposed to prevent David's army from conquering the Jebusite capital, Jerusalem (5:6–8).

3.1.1. Meribaal and Mephiboshet (2 Sam 4:4 et al.)

Jonathan, son of Saul, had a son whose feet were lame (נכה)

He was five years old when the news about Saul and Jonathan came from

---

2. For the discussion about the authenticity of "Meribaal" or "Mephiboshet," see Veijola 1978:338 n. 1; Schorch.

Jezreel. So his nurse picked him up and fled, but in her panic to flee, he fell and was crippled (יפסח).

His name was Meribaal.

Chapter 4 describes the demise of the house of Saul that is to be replaced by the house of David. Of course only the male members are important here: Saul's son Ishboshet is killed, and a disabled descendant appears seemingly out of nowhere. It appears that this verse was inserted here to indicate that Meribaal is no serious threat to the throne due to his disability. It is not clear whether this disqualification would be based on his physical inabilities or on purity laws that may prevent a future king and highest cult officer in Israel at the time to hold office. Therefore, most scholars connect this episode with chapter 9 (Ackroyd: 50–51; Stoebe: 150; Grønbæk: 244). Only Andersen (67) and Veijola (1978:345) place the story after Ishboshet's death.

Another issue in this story surrounds the exact identity of Meribaal. In some translations he is referred to as Mephiboshet. The reason for this confusion is that Saul also had a son with the same name, Meribaal/Mephiboshet. Which part of the story relates to which person? Are we dealing with two personalities here, and does the text always refer to the same person but use different names due to different traditions?

I believe the most likely possibility is that there were probably indeed two different personalities, one called Meribaal, Jonathan's son, the other one Mephiboshet, Saul's son. Due to the similarity of their names and probably other political or religious reasons, both personalities may have merged at one point in the tradition. Only the first and last episodes of the story (2 Sam 4 and 21) refer to the "historic" figures of "Meribaal" as Jonathan's son and "Mephiboshet" as the son of Saul.

Going back to the introductory text, 2 Sam 4:4, we see that already at this stage, the text is showing signs of the integration of Meribaal/Mephiboshet's two identities. The text begins with Jonathan's son, who became lame through an act of נכה, an "injury with intention to kill" (v. 4:4a), and v. 4:4c identifies him as Meribaal. Although the major versions (MT, LXX, Targum) read "Mephiboshet" in 4:4c, in my opinion, Meribaal represents the original reading (in bold) and forms the base for its recital in 2 Chronicles, minus the information of the condition of lameness that the Chronicler deemed unnecessary. I think that v. 4:4b does not refer to Jonathan's son, but already gives an indication of Saul's son Mephiboshet. Not only did they have similar names as Andersen stipulates it, but they both may also have been lame. Mephiboshet's injury likely resulted from the accident that is being described in v. 4, rendering him פסח in the sense of "becoming lame as consequence of a dislocation following a fall" and not נכה (in *italics*). Questions remain about the historical accuracy of this episode; this event would have had to take place about twenty years earlier to match the ages of Mephiboshet with Meribaal, but according to Veijola this is not impossible (343–44). In the eyes of the redactor, it lets David appear generous and reliable, pointing simultaneously toward chapter 9 and back in history to the oath between David and Jonathan.[3]

3.1.2. The "Lame and the Blind" (2 Sam 5:6–8)

⁶ Then the king and his men went to Jerusalem against the Jebusites, the inhabitants of the territory, who said to David, "You will not enter here;

even the blind and the lame could turn you away"

(meaning, "David cannot enter here").

⁷ However, David took the stronghold of Zion:

that is the city of David.

⁸ That day David said, "Whoever would conquer the Jebusites must take possession of the water supply . . ."

David hates the lame and the blind; therefore it is said,

"The blind and the lame shall not come into the house."

This passage is generally considered as an etiological justification of the nonadmittance of disabled people into the temple. In Saul Olyan's opinion, it is difficult to discern whether the set phrase "the blind and the lame shall not come into the house" addresses priests only (based on Lev 21:17–26) or the ordinary worshiper in general (based on Deut 23:2). At the least it might indicate a yet to be determined time period when the exclusion of disabled people from temple worship was generally accepted (1998:226–27). This general attitude toward disabled people was then woven into the story of David's conquest of Jerusalem to give the subsequent Levitical laws Davidic, and therefore unquestionable, authority.

The underlying reason for the exclusion of disabled people was their perceived impurity (Ackroyd: 56–57). The "lame and blind" (and we will presume here that these were indeed mainly [male] injured soldiers that were called upon) are placed in an exposed position to defend Jerusalem from David and his army. Jan Heller considers them Jebusite cultic personnel because of the attached word פסח (to limp) and argues that as such they were regarded as taboo by Jebusite standards (254). Disabled people in a temple function may not have been so uncommon. According to Johannes Renger, in ancient Mesopotamia people afflicted with a disease or disability would often end up working at the temple, because their immediate family could no longer take care of them (123–24). Gilbert Brunet stresses the presumed "magic" protection the lame and blind might have exerted on David's soldiers by building a "moral wall" on top of the actual

---

3. For a more detailed analysis, see Hentrich 2005.

city walls. If the soldiers had removed them by force they would have risked becoming lame and blind themselves (71).

Considering that from an Israelite standpoint, certain disabled people may have been considered impure[4] outsiders due to their physical "incompleteness," I am proposing an interpretation that explains this situation quite simply: Even though blindness could have been considered a curse by YHWH for disobedience (Deut 28:29), the soldiers likely did not fear becoming blind or lame when touching them in order to remove them from the wall. Considering the "lame and blind" indeed being some sort of Jebusite temple personnel as Heller stipulates, the Israelite soldiers may have applied the purity prescriptions concerning priests to them. What they may then have feared was a possible notion of impurity attached to their physical disability. The Jebusite leaders could have even exploited this fear by placing the "lame and blind" purposely at that position. The physical removal of supposedly impure people would then automatically render the soldiers impure, should they attempt such a seemingly easy task (Hentrich 2003:26–27).

The final redactor of 2 Samuel is justifying the actual practice of non-admittance to the temple through an authorization by David himself, which would then make it irreversible. Even though nothing is said about their presumed impurity, this episode would indicate that David himself ordered their expulsion from the temple because of their opposition to him during the capture of Jerusalem.

3.2. Leviticus 21:17–23

[17] Tell Aaron,

"No man

from your descendants throughout their generations

who has a physical flaw is to approach to present the food of his God.

[18] *Certainly,*

no man who has a physical flaw is to approach: a blind man, or one who is lame, or one with a slit nose, or a limb too long,

[19] **or a man who has had a broken leg or arm,**

[20] **or a hunchback, or a dwarf, or one with a spot in his eye, or a festering eruption, or a feverish rash, or a crushed testicle** (מרוח אשך)**.**

---

4. For a discussion about the origins of impurity, see Neusner: 9–11; Wright; Milgrom: 953–57.

²¹ No man from the descendants of Aaron the priest who has a physical flaw may step forward to present the Lord's gifts;

he has a physical flaw, so he must not step forward to present the food of his God.

²² *He may eat both the most holy and the holy food of his God,*

²³ *but*

he must not go into the veil-canopy or step forward to the altar because he has a physical flaw.

So he must not profane my holy places, for I am the Lord who sanctifies them."

This is probably the most important text regarding the issue of masculinity and disability in the Bible, since temple priests were considered the closest persons representing God's "perfect" incarnation on Earth. In what follows I briefly summarize the findings that have been documented in more detail elsewhere (Hentrich 2003:9–20) and elaborate on a specific body part that is mentioned in the above list.

Concerning the integrity of this passage, I have previously established a three-part redactional history of this text based on the three repetitions of the demand that no person with a blemish or מום is to enter the temple. The prescriptions start with an appeal to the general public not to admit disabled persons to the temple. I consider this passage (in bold) the underlying base tradition of this episode, containing simply a list of twelve blemishes and their consequence (vv. 18–20, 23). The only blemish that somewhat falls out of line is the ominous "crushed testicle" that may have been inserted at a later stage to match the twelve animal blemishes in Lev 22.

The next layer (in *italics*) restates the first basic prescription (vv. 17, 18a, 21b–23a) and extends its function to include the presentation of food. At this point, the law enters the domain of a temple priest, namely the presentation of the sacrifices to YHWH. However, even though a disabled priest may not present the sacrifice, he is nevertheless allowed to eat from it. Purity issues now play a major role, as a disabled priest would likely "contaminate" the sacrifice that is to be presented to YHWH. Yet once that is done, for the simple consumption of the sacrifice a disability seems irrelevant to YHWH.

The third layer (vv. 17a, 21, 23b, in normal print) first provides another repetition of the previous food provisions, but also connects the law to Aaron, the ancestor of all priests. The vocabulary is definitely more monotheistic, from "food of *his* God" to "the Lord's gift," indicating a later stage in the edition. But most important, this editor expands the priestly restrictions now to the actual presence at the temple. The reason for that is again the fear of profanation of the entire temple area by a presumed impurity that might be attached to a physical blemish. In this editor's mind, it would be directly opposed to the wishes of YHWH, who requires perfect physical condition in order to sanctify the temple (Hentrich 2003:17). Saul Olyan makes a case that despite this apparent discrimination against disabled priests, Lev 21 also establishes a two-tier hierarchy of blemished and unblemished priests who, due to the different restrictions and permissions in the temple, nevertheless remain superior to regular worshipers:

> By allowing him to retain certain other privileges, the text asserts indirectly that the blemished priest remains the superior of the whole nonpriest. (2000: 112)

3.2.1. The Issue of the "Crushed Testicle" (מרוח אשך) (Lev 21:20)

As mentioned above, the "crushed testicle" appears out of place in the entire list of twelve blemishes. This is underlined by the fact that this is the only occurrence of the expression מרוח אשך in the entire Old Testament (BLB 1996–2002d). The only other passage that refers to a genital defect as a reason for non-entry into the "house of the Lord" is Deut 23:1. The only difference here is that this redactor uses the expression פצוע־דכה, likely to be Deuteronomistic: "He whose testicles are crushed or whose male member is cut off shall not enter the assembly of the LORD" (RSV). It is understood that this passage (Deut 23:1) refers to the institution of eunuchs not being able to enter the temple (BLB 1996–2002c).

Having injured genitalia seems irrelevant to the functions of a priest and only makes sense when placed into a context with the following chapter (Lev 22) about blemishes of sacrificial animals. I want to explore another indirect connection, as remote it may appear. Genesis 17:10 and Lev 12:3 require all males to be circumcised at a very young age. This requirement is considered part of the initial covenant between Abraham and YHWH and is understood as a law directly given by YHWH. Therefore, it is conceivable that any deviation from this law may be seen as a violation against God's will. Ironically, a circumcision is practically the only physical "defect" that is not viewed as a blemish and is actually desired in Israelite men, much to the contrary of the Greek and Roman contemporary environment (Olyan 2000:114).

But considering the rather crude medical circumstances of how circumcisions were performed in the ancient Near East (fig. 1), it becomes clear that there may have been a fairly high rate in "unsuccessful tries" or "accidents." Since the Old Testament places a very high value on the genetic succession of priests from the house of Aaron, it also seems clear that a priest with "injured genitalia" may not be qualified enough to perform his duties properly and that such a state could not be forgiven in the eyes of YHWH (Olyan 2000:108). Even though testicles and foreskin are indeed not the same organ, they are nevertheless closely enough related. I am suggesting that the "crushed testicle" in Lev 21:20 may be interpreted as

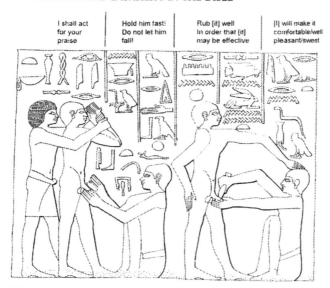

| I shall act for your praise | Hold him fast! Do not let him fall! | Rub [it] well in order that [it] may be effective | [I] will make it comfortable/well pleasant/sweet |

Fig. 1. Circumcision scene from the tomb of Ankh-ma-hor, 6th Dynasty, Saqqara (after Nunn: 170).

an "imperfect circumcision." The expression מרוח אשך could have found its way into the text as a replacement for this rather embarrassing condition and at the same time inconspicuously makes the connection with the following chapter (22) on sacrificial animals.

What do these three Old Testament texts (Lev 21; 2 Sam 5; and the Meribaal episode in 2 Sam 4–21) tell us about disabled men in ancient Israel? Due to the patriarchal nature of the Israelite society, they were predominant in positions of leadership, such as kings and especially priests who were genetically traced back to Aaron. Yet different positions may have had a different way of dealing with a disability of one of their members. There were quite severe restrictions concerning their cultic functionality. According to Lev 21, physically disabled priests were not allowed to serve at the altar for fear of polluting the "House of YHWH" with their perceived impurity. On a profane level, though, these restrictions may not have been so rigid. Meribaal was reinstated as landowner, even though he was physically unable to work the land that was returned to him as owner, but in Ziba and his family was given an aide who was in fact the administrator and eventually became part owner himself. I believe that Saul's son Mephiboshet was not actually disabled and his persona was only used as a literary ploy.

3.3. Mark 2:2–12 (par. Luke 5:17–26; Matt 9:1–8)

> [2] So many gathered that there was no longer any room, not even by the door, and he preached the word to them.

[3] Some people came bringing to him a paralytic, carried by four of them.

[4] When they were not able to bring him in because of the crowd, they removed the roof above Jesus. Then, after tearing it out, they lowered the stretcher the paralytic was lying on.

[5] When Jesus saw their faith, he said to the paralytic, "Son, your sins are forgiven."

[6] Now some of the experts in the law were sitting there, turning these things over in their minds:

[7] "Why does this man speak this way? He is blaspheming! Who can forgive sins but God alone?"

[8] Now immediately, when Jesus realized in his spirit that they were contemplating such thoughts, he said to them, "Why are you thinking such things in your hearts?

[9] Which is easier, to say to the paralytic, 'Your sins are forgiven,' or to say, 'Stand up, take your stretcher, and walk'?

[10] But so that you may know that the Son of Man has authority on earth to forgive sins,"—he said to the paralytic—

[11] "I tell you, stand up, take your stretcher, and go home."

[12] And immediately the man stood up, took his stretcher, and went out in front of them all. They were all amazed and glorified God, saying, "We have never seen anything like this!"

I now only briefly address one episode from the New Testament that is commonly placed at the center of the discussion about the relationship between sin and disability.[5] In this story Jesus confronts the traditional belief that a disability, or any other illness for that matter, is a consequence of a previous sin against God, and therefore only YHWH would have the authority to remove the blemish and heal the afflicted person. Kerry Wynn's analysis of this passage shows how Jesus deconstructs this cause-and-effect belief and instead replaces it with a new kind of relationship between forgiveness and healing under the direct authority of God represented by the "Son of Man" (or The Man as other translations have it).[6] Effectively turning the traditional belief on its head, the Markan Jesus does not see the relationship between sin and disability as one of cause and effect. Rather it sees a categorical relationship between forgiveness and healing. Both acts are "acts of God." The division between forgiveness and healing and sin and disability is further evidenced in the fact that the forgiveness does not result in healing. Jesus' forgiveness is an act of compassion that is given in

---

5. For a detailed comment on this episode and its parallels, see Mann: 221–25; Beare: 220–24.

6. For a discussion of the term "Son of Man" in Mark, see Mann: 225–28.

light of faith and results in a holistic restoration of the individual. Physical healing is a sign giving evidence of this greater restoration and the in-breaking of the kingdom of God. The faith of the man with paralysis is the basis of his forgiveness but is insignificant for his cure (Wynn 1999:8).

The practice of forgiveness established here forms a genuine "Christian" approach that is rooted neither in Judaic nor pagan practices (Beare: 224), which is why the present scribes describe it as blasphemy. A common human could have never had such an authority.

4. Conclusion

In the Old Testament, the image of an able-bodied person was very much oriented on YHWH's image of a "perfect" body. Anyone falling outside these rigorous categories may have been considered an outsider. Nevertheless, not all disabilities were treated alike: a blind person probably had a different status than a lame person, and, especially in cultic life, a disability likely weighed heavier than in normal life. An indication are the purity laws for priests and that Meribaal was still able to inherit land.

In the New Testament, the gender-related status of disabled people started to change. For obvious reasons, Jesus is still referred to as the "Son of God" and likely follows here the traditional masculine God imagery set out in the Hebrew Bible. But, with Jesus' revolutionary and holistic approach to purity laws, disability, illness, and sin, he also gives a chance to disabled and ill women who otherwise would be lost in oblivion to be recognized and healed. The focus is no longer on disability of men (as "imperfect" representatives of God) and their potential exclusion from society, but on forgiveness and healing and therefore inclusion of disabled persons of both genders. Examples hereof are the stories of Jairus's daughter (Mark 5:21–43; Matt 9:18–26; Luke 8:40–56) or the healing of Peter's mother-in-law (Mark 1:29–34; Matt 8:14–15).

PART TWO
BIBLICAL TEXTS AND DISABILITY STUDIES

6

The Normate Hermeneutic and Interpretations of Disability within the Yahwistic Narratives

Kerry H. Wynn

The most widely held perspective within disabilities studies today is that disability is a social and cultural construction embedded within society rather than a medical condition imbedded within the individual. Simi Linton writes:

> Across the world and throughout history various terminologies and meanings are ascribed to the types of human variations known in contemporary Westernized countries as disabilities. Over the past century the term *disabled* and others, such as *handicapped* and the less inclusive term *crippled*, have emerged as collective nouns that convey the idea that there is something that links this disparate group of people. The terms have been used to arrange people in ways that are socially and economically convenient to the society. (9)

This statement reveals several problems that arise when the "social model" of disability is brought to bear on the study of the Pentateuch. Since the social construction of disability varies "across the world and throughout history" there is likely to be multiple layers of social constructions of disability that have an impact on the development and interpretation of scripture. Biblical understandings vary from the Yahwistic view in Exod 4:11 that maintains that disability is part of God's intended creation to the Priestly perspective that disability is primordial chaos breaking into God's created order (Lev 21:17–23; Wynn 2000). This study will focus on the contemporary interpretation of the Yahwistic narratives rather than on the legal Priestly materials in their historical context. Exodus 4:11 is viewed as the author's theological perspective on disability:

Then the Lord said to him, "Who gives speech to mortals? Who makes them mute or deaf, seeing or blind? Is it not I, the Lord?" (NRSV)

The Normate Hermeneutic

Contemporary interpretation of disability within the narratives attributed to the Yahwist shows that a "normate hermeneutic" dominates modern biblical thought. The term "normate" was coined by Rosemarie Garland Thomson and refers to the socially constructed ideal image "through which people can represent themselves as definitive human beings." Those who approximate this "constructed identity . . . can step into a position of authority and wield the power it grants them" (1997:8). In traditional American culture the normate is an able-bodied white Protestant male heterosexual. The further one moves from the normate image, the more powerless and marginalized one becomes. This has clearly been the experience of disabled people.

The "normate hermeneutic" is the means by which scripture is interpreted so that it complies with and reinforces the socially constructed norms. This hermeneutic imposes a society's interpretation of disability on the text without due consideration to the text itself. The normate hermeneutic has been applied by Bible translators and commentators throughout the centuries and continues to be imposed today.

Thomson describes how the "normate" norm affects disability:

> As the norm becomes neutral in an environment created to accommodate it, disability becomes intense, extravagant, and problematic. Disability is the unorthodox made flesh, refusing to be normalized, neutralized, or homogenized. . . . Shaped by history, defined by particularity, and at odds with its environment, disability confounds any notion of a generalizable, stable physical subject. (24)

For Thomson, however, the value of the otherness of the "extraordinary body" serves as "proof that the myriad structures and practices of material, daily life enforce the cultural standard of a universal subject with a narrow range of corporeal variation" (24). Her goal is to "render physical difference as distinction, uncoupled with modernity's devaluation of the atypical" (137). Her aim is

> to critique the politics of appearance that governs our interpretation of physical difference, to suggest that disability requires accommodation rather than compensation, and to shift our conception of disability from pathology to identity. (137)

The following discussion will examine the impact of the normate hermeneutic on the understanding of disability in the Yahwistic narratives. I will show that the normate bias is not limited to traditional white male scholars but is infused into contemporary liberatory hermeneutics such as feminist interpretations. I will also provide an interpretation of these narratives from a disability perspective consistent with the biblical text and the aims identified by Thomson.

The Blindness of Isaac

Genesis 27:1–45, the story of Isaac's blessing, provides the classical example of a biblical character disabled by the normate hermeneutic. Bill Moyers's PBS series *Genesis* (1996) showed how it is possible to have an intelligent and engaging discussion about sacred texts within the public forum. Yet the series illustrates how accepted the normate hermeneutic is within American society. Marianne Meye Thompson reflected this hermeneutic when she described Isaac:

> In some ways, he's just a transition figure. But who is he on his own? He's blind. Rebekah has the word from God, but we don't know whether Isaac has ever been told how it will turn out. (259)

A similar disabling hermeneutic is found in Susan Niditch's book *Underdogs and Tricksters*. Isaac's visual impairment is the result of the natural aging process. He serves as a reminder that anyone who lives long enough will inevitably become disabled. Niditch, however, asserts that old age parallels blindness in Gen 27:1 and death in Gen 27:2 (83). The implication is that blindness and death are to be seen as the same experience. Sharon V. Betcher asserts that "one of the most subtle and persistent theological encodings of disability is that which views us as 'close to death'" (344).

This image of powerlessness and dependency is a hermeneutic that has been shared with femininity. Thomson says: "Femininity and disability are inextricably entangled in patriarchal culture, as Aristotle's equation of women as disabled men illustrates" (1997:27). Susan Wendell concludes:

> [F]eminist ethics needs the insights of people with disabilities, that people with disabilities need feminist ethics, that some people involved in disability ethics and politics are already practicing feminist ethics, and that more feminist ethicists should be practicing disability ethics. (10)

Yet Thomson warns, "Even feminists today invoke negative images of disability to describe the oppression of women" (1997:19). We have already seen this in Thompson and Niditch. Leon R. Kass advances this normate view metaphorically when he says:

> Rebekah figures out a way through a very bad situation in a male-dominated world. Sometimes harsh confrontation is not the most loving way. I would even argue that Rebekah gives Isaac a gift in this deception, in that she enables him to see. He's been blind a long time—not just dim of sight, but blind to the question of his own sons and what it is only his place to transmit. Thanks to this deception, he now behaves in the last scene like a true patriarch. (Moyers: 253)

The metaphor interprets blindness as a state of weakness and ignorance. The literary device only works because such is the broader social view of those who are blind. Thus the woman oppressed by a patriarchal society is able to achieve liberation by gaining domination over the disabled, and therefore powerless and incapable, patriarch. This domination is for his own good, and, indeed, he should be grateful. Naomi Rosenblatt asserts that this shift in roles is possible "now that Isaac is infirm and blind" (Moyers: 260). Kass says "Rebekah is in the place of Abraham" and because of her, God's plan, "this fragile way, barely begun, survives in this generation, despite the weakness and blindness of her husband" (256). Thus Kass felt free to erase the disabled patriarch by altering "the God of Abraham, the God of Isaac, and the God of Jacob" into "the God of Abraham, the God of Rebekah, and the God of Jacob" (256). In this way the disturbing disabled person is removed from the public view. He is moved from "close to death" to dead. This modern normate interpretation is in direct conflict with the actual content of the biblical text.

The normate perspective can also be seen at play in Niditch's identification of parallelism between blindness, old age, and death in our biblical passage. It must be kept in mind that we are dealing with narrative in this passage and not Hebrew poetry. While age is identified as the cause of Isaac's blindness as well as the cause of his awareness of his impending death, blindness and death are separate issues in these verses. Indeed, Isaac's declaration to Esau, "I am old," reflects the ancient Hurrian legal formula for a deathbed will found in the Nuzi texts (Westermann: 437). The characteristics of the legal genre are more applicable to the text than that of a poetic genre. There is no basis for associating blindness in this passage with either death or powerlessness.

Isaac retains the power of the patriarch, and this can most clearly be seen in the nature of the patriarchal blessing that is the center of the account in Gen 27. Walter Brueggemann drives home the power of Isaac's blessing when he explains:

> This family in Genesis is preoccupied with blessing, as though it matters more than things visible. As it is here sought and given, the blessing combines all of the *primitive power* of a spoken word (which has a life of its own) with the *high theological claim* of special vocation for its addressee . . . Blessing is understood as a world-transforming act which cannot be denied by modern rationality. For the son as for the father, indeed for the entire family, the matter of the blessing is as dangerous as it is compelling. (1982:227–28)

Gerhard von Rad acknowledges the power of the word which Isaac maintains but fails to escape the dominant normate bias. When a very lucid and skeptical Isaac, who knows his family well, questions who Jacob really is in Gen 27:18–24, von Rad concludes, "Isaac's questions show pathetically how the blind man cannot at first master a feeling of uncertainty" (277). When Isaac pronounces a blessing on Esau in Gen 27:39–40 "he no longer has the same powers" because of "the irrevocability of the blessing once it has been given" (278–79). Here von Rad exhibits a normate bias against age and blindness that is not inherent to the text. It is because of Isaac's power and not his weakness that the word cannot be revoked. To revoke the word would be to question the power of the one who spoke that word. As the Lord's word "shall not return to me empty" (Isa 55:11), neither will the patriarch's word return to him empty. Isaac's inability to revoke the blessing does not lessen his patriarchal power any more than the monarchical power of Darius (Dan 6:6–18) or Ahasuerus (Esth 1:19 and 8:8) is reduced by their inability to revoke their own decrees when they are deceived. To revoke his word is to treat him as powerless. Indeed, the powerful word of cursing that Rebekah is willing to take upon herself in Gen 27:13 would come as the word of the patriarch as well. Jacob will not move to receive the word of blessing until he is protected against the word of cursing (von Rad: 277). Claus Westermann clarifies the locus of power in relation to the person and to the word:

> [I]t is vitality that is passed on by the one who is departing from life; in this process no distinction is made between the corporal and the spiritual and so both action and word are required. Because the blessing is concerned with vitality as a whole, the blessing cannot return or be subsequently altered. (436)

The dysfunctional nature of Isaac's family predates his visual impairment. Isaac's disability is the context for the deception that follows and not the cause. His personal weaknesses and those of his family are well established prior to his loss of vision. Even a metaphorical use of visual impairment in relation to this narrative implies some degree of just punishment that is not warranted by the text.

Isaac's decision to bestow the blessing on Esau at this time is not the result of his disability but his uncertainty about the hour of his death (27:2). Indeed, we see no loss of social authority or power on the part of Isaac as a result of his disability. Isaac retains both his social status as head of the clan and his theological import as the heir of the promise regardless of his loss of vision. While his family takes advantage of his disability to further their own ends, there is no judgment or ridicule associated with his disability. It is not seen as a divine judgment but part of the natural course of life.

Rebekah does not become the empowered matriarch by dominating Isaac because he is the disabled patriarch. If Isaac is powerless due to his blindness, there is no power to be gained in dominating him. Isaac, however, is powerful. He maintains all the power of the patriarch. Here Niditch provides us with a model for understanding the empowerment of Rebekah through the folk hero known as "the trickster." This narrative presents Jacob as the trickster with Rebekah in the role of "a veritable co-conspirator" (100). The trickster is one who "brings about change in a situation via trickery" but they "never gain full control of the situation around them and often escape difficulties in a less than noble way" (xi).

Niditch maintains that the central issue of a trickster story is that of status, but it is the trickster who is without status, who gains status, and who ultimately loses status (99–100). It is the status of Jacob and Esau that is at stake. The status of Isaac as patriarch and his power to grant the blessing are never brought into question in light of his age or his blindness. It is because Isaac has the status and authority that Rebekah must become a "co-trickster" and in the end loses the company of her beloved son because she is powerless to protect him save by sending him away.

While Isaac is no longer able to see he remains a keen observer. He has learned to accommodate his disability by relying on his ability to reason as well as his other senses. He examines Jacob with questions (27:18–20) while relying on his sense of touch (27:21), of hearing (27:22), and, according to von Rad (277), of smell (27:26–27). This in no way implies that his other senses are enhanced. What it does show is a keen mind that has learned to adapt to the life situation of his impairment. Isaac attempts to use skills that he has developed which Jacob with all his vision fails to use upon his wedding night (Gen 29:23–25). Isaac is a capable patriarch who requires those around him to provide the accommodations that enable him to fulfill his role in society. That Rebekah and Jacob disable Isaac through dishonesty in accommodations does not reflect on the ability of Isaac but upon Rebekah and Jacob.

When the text of Gen 27 is freed from the normate hermeneutic and examined in light of what it actually says and in light of the historical context of its writing, a totally different picture of the patriarch appears. We must reject the traditional Isaac as a "powerless dependent" for Isaac, the "powerful patriarch" with all the sexist implications that come with his patriarchal role.

The Disabling of Jacob

The second Yahwistic narrative that I consider is the account of Jacob wrestling at the Jabbok in Gen 32:22–32, an encounter of which Walter Brueggemann writes:

> Meeting this God did not lead, as we are wont to imagine, to reconciliation, forgiveness, healing. It resulted in a crippling. The *new name* cannot be separated from the *new crippling*, for the crippling is the substance of the name. So Jacob's rendezvous in the night is ambivalent. He has penetrated the mystery of God like none before him. . . . And he has prevailed. But his prevailing is a defeat as well as a victory. There is a dangerous, costly mystery in drawing too near and claiming too much. (1982:271)

The account of Jacob's impairing experience at the Jabbok provides a classical case in which the normate hermeneutic of the tragic hero or, to use Brueggemann's phrase, "a cripple with a blessing," has been regularly applied. Naomi Rosenblatt provides a good description of our tragic hero:

> Even when Jacob prevails over the angel, he walks away limping. Unlike the famous painting of St. George slaying the dragon, where the handsome young knight emerges victorious and unscathed, Jacob limps away. This is my favorite part of the story. In life, there's no such thing as absolute victory. Even though Jacob has been chosen, he will be a bit of a cripple for the rest of his life. (Moyers: 264)

Rosenblatt sees Jacob as a hero because "Jacob prevails over the angel" and because "Jacob has been chosen." Yet he is a tragic hero because "he walks away limping" and "he will be a bit of a cripple for the rest of his life." We, like Jacob, are all tragic heroes because "there's no such thing as absolute victory."

Moyers abandons "cripple" terminology for "a permanent wound" (264). Such terminology implies a lack of healing. When disability is tragedy, the only remedy is liberation from the impairment itself. "Healing," here meaning the erasure of the physical impairment, is the only resolution for the tragic disability. For the tragic hero, the solution is to be found in changing the individual to conform to the normate expectations of an ablest society. When the "wound" becomes "permanent," the tragedy cannot be escaped.

Echoing Moyers, John Kselman states that Jacob "comes away wounded, limping." Kselman immediately turns this into a metaphor that "reminds us that encounters with God are very serious experiences, and we come away wounded—but believing" (Moyers: 280). Brueggemann reflects a similar metaphoric interpretation of disability:

> If one extrapolates from the personal woundedness to the sense of community, it means that the community—whether Israel or the Christian Church—is never going to be the beautiful people. They're always going to be weird and odd misfits. . . . What is now being rediscovered, as the Church is being disestablished in the West, is that we are having to face up to our weirdness and the sense of being a misfit in the world. I suppose we always chafe against it, but it seems to me it's a given in the nature of this community of faith. (Moyers: 305)

This treatment of impairment as metaphor affirms marginalization by assuming disabled people are rightfully perceived as "weird and odd misfits" who are "never going to be the beautiful people." Disability, or "woundedness," is synonymous with powerlessness, ugliness, weirdness, and oddness. All are metaphors of loss for the Western church. While Brueggemann believes this loss is a positive event in the life of the church, he maintains a negative view of disability reflecting "modernity's devaluation of the atypical" (Thomson 1997:137).

The prior quote from Rosenblatt claimed "Jacob prevailed over the angel" (Moyers: 264). Westermann disavows any identification of Jacob's opponent with either God or an angel. "It was neither Yahweh nor the God of his father who attacked Jacob at the ford, but the river demon who

wanted to stop him from crossing" (521). Westermann is not only uncomfortable with any implication that God would be afraid of the dawn's light
but that God would disable Jacob.

> A hostile demon, an evil spirit, attacks someone so as to cause harm. This
> can happen in a variety of ways. In the New Testament it is predomi-
> nantly the evil spirit that causes illness; here it is the demon of the night
> or the river. (516)

Westermann cannot imagine that the Yahwist would portray God
attacking "like a thief in the night." Furthermore, he cannot see the biblical author portraying God as the source of disability—a normate bias not
shared by the Yahwist in Exod 4:11. Contrary to Westermann, evil spirits
have very few roles in causing illness or disability in the New Testament.
Regardless, Brueggemann is correct when he asserts that attempts to identify the man with "a demon or a Canaanite numen" ultimately do "not
help us to interpret the present form" (1982:266–67).

Von Rad, like Westermann, had identified Gen 32:25 as a later addition, but for opposite reasons to those of Westermann. The removal of this
phrase leaves the touch of the assailant but it does not describe the dislocation of his hip. The purpose of this addition for von Rad is to mask the
"monstrous conception . . . that Jacob nearly defeated the heavenly being"
(321). This addition makes the following verse absurd, in his opinion, "for
the request to Jacob to be released is now poorly motivated, since Jacob is
after all, crippled" (321). And with this, Westermann would agree:

> There is no reason for the attacker's request to let him go . . . if he has
> already injured his opponent severely. This has long been noted and
> there has been a variety of attempts to explain it. (517)

This "variety of attempts" has involved limiting or removing Jacob's
impairment. The normate hermeneutic assumes that Jacob cannot win
once he is disabled for it imposes the disempowerment of the normate bias
without examining the evidence found in the history of warfare. There are
many accounts of soldiers who have continued to fight when wounded
only to learn the severity of their wounds after the battle was over. Disabled people have often proven their capabilities in areas where normate
social constructions have held them incapable. Such interpretations com-
promise sound biblical interpretation in favor of normate misconceptions
of the nature of disability. The determination of Jacob to achieve his goal,
to receive the blessing, and his being strong enough and capable enough
to accomplish this, even with a newly acquired disability, is overlooked by
a normate hermeneutic.

Brueggemann, on the other hand, does allow that the "hidden One has
the power to injure Jacob" yet "he does not finally defeat him" (1982:267).
However, he also asserted that Jacob's impairment is a "mark left on his
very manhood and future" (270). There is no better example of the nor-

mate emasculation of disabled men as noted in the previous discussion of Isaac. There the disabled male was demeaned to enhance the feminine. Here, both the female and the disabled body are mutually demeaned. Thomson observes:

> Many parallels exist between the social meanings attributed to female bodies and those assigned to disabled bodies. Both the female and the disabled body are cast as deviant and inferior; both are excluded from full participation in public as well as economic life; both are defined in opposition to a norm that is assumed to possess natural physical superiority. Indeed, the discursive equation of femaleness with disability is common, sometimes to denigrate women and sometimes to defend them. (1997:19)

Brueggemann's emasculation of Jacob reflects a social construction of disability as effeminate, a perspective that is not original to the text.

The second issue Rosenblatt raises by her comment is that of the permanence of Jacob's impairment. Rosenblatt says that "he will be a bit of a cripple for the rest of his life," and Moyers agrees "that the struggle with the angel led to a permanent wound" (270). Westermann, however, maintains that "there is not indication that he was permanently lamed" (520). Yet he correctly sees that the disability is meant as a reminder when he says Jacob "limped past Penuel and the limp reminded him of the mortal danger that he had narrowly escaped." Such a reminder would not be necessary the day after the event while within sight of Penuel. The reminder would be needed when time had faded the memory and distance had obscured the vision of Penuel. If the disability was temporary, it would hardly be worth noting. One would assume that the hip was not the only sore joint in Jacob's body the day after such a strenuous workout. We will see that the disability truly served as a reminder, but not a reminder of the danger of Penuel. Any attempt to make the disability temporary is an attempt to deny Jacob's disability and to reestablish his normate status.

Jacob's opponent requested release from the disabled patriarch who would not let him go without a blessing. Genesis 32:27–29 returns us to the power of the spoken word in its most intense form, the power of the name. The change of the name Jacob, which contained the essence of his character as a trickster (Gen 27:36), is now to be changed to a name that should, by the power of the word, transform Jacob's character. The passage explains the meaning of the new name, Israel, as evidence that he has "striven with God and with men and has prevailed." Jacob, however, will show that his old character is not so easily given up by immediately trying to trick his disabling benefactor into revealing his own name so that Jacob can gain power over him as well. Westermann establishes the significance of this new name when he writes:

> The change of Jacob's name presupposes the establishment of Israel. This means that only when Jacob, as the father of the 12 sons who gave rise to

the 12 tribes, had become the forefather of the people comprising these 12 tribes, was he given the title "Israel." The addition regards Jacob as a representative of Israel; the title sees in him the people of Israel. (518)

Not only would the name represent the people or nation of Israel, but the land of Israel as well. The meaning of the name as a blessing is not to be found in its etymology but in this representation. The conferral of the name bears the patriarchal blessing as it was reiterated to Abram when his name was changed to Abraham in Gen 17. The name was the conferral of the patriarchal covenant on Jacob for Israel would be the people, the nation, the land, and the blessing conferred on Abraham.

How does Jacob's disability relate to this blessing-in-a-name? First, we must note that the disability was neither the cause nor the result of the blessing/name. The disabling touch occurs before the request for a blessing and the references to the disability in Gen 32:25 and 31 create an *inclusio* around the blessing/naming account. The disability is related to the blessing by association rather than by cause or effect. This association with the blessing transforms the disability into the sign of the covenant for Jacob, as circumcision is the sign of the covenant for Abraham in Gen 17. Just as the "sons of Israel" would participate in circumcision as a sign of the covenant given to Abraham, so with the inclusion of the dietary practice set forth in Gen 32:32 they would participate in Jacob's disability as a sign of the covenant.

Once it is recognized that Jacob's disability is a sign of the covenant, one must be cautious in drawing a conclusion that this meeting "did not lead . . . to reconciliation, forgiveness, healing" but that it "resulted in crippling" (Brueggemann 1982:270). The widely held view that Jacob leaves Penuel "broken" or "wounded" becomes questionable as well. We hear no more of Jacob's disability throughout the remainder of his life. It did not alter his lifestyle. He maintained his patriarchal status and continues his patriarchal duties unaltered by his disability. The difference with Isaac's disability is that while Isaac's blindness did not hinder his authority as the patriarch, Jacob's disability is the sign and vindication of his authority. Jacob is not a tragic hero or "cripple with a blessing" (Brueggemann: 271). As with Abraham, he is a patriarch with a sign of his covenantal encounter with his God. The normate hermeneutic reverses the process advocated by Thomson by shifting the perception of disability from identity to pathology instead of from pathology to identity (1997:19).

Thus Gen 32:22–32 can be understood free from the normate hermeneutic. While alone at night on the banks of the Jabbok, Jacob was confronted by a theophanic figure. Jacob and the "man" struggled throughout the night and when the "man" realized that the fight was coming to a draw, he touched Jacob's thigh and dislocated his hip, causing a permanent disability. Jacob would not be diverted from his course by such a disability. Jacob used other strengths to compensate his loss and successfully continued his fight. The "man" requested to be released when he saw that Jacob's disability would not deter him from achieving his goal. Jacob would not release him until he had obtained his objective—a blessing. In response, Jacob's opponent granted Jacob a new name, which acknowledged that he had prevailed in the struggle even after being disabled. The disability was Jacob's sign of the covenant. The blessing was not a result of the disability, nor was the disability a result of the blessing. It is something he took away as a lifelong reminder of what happened there—lifelong for Jacob but, for all of Israel, a sign for all time.

Conclusion

This study has shown how the contemporary normate bias that views disability as dehumanizing continues to shape and mold the interpretation of the Yahwistic narratives. This bias is not only found among lay readers but among biblical scholars ranging from traditional white male scholars to feminist interpreters as well. The normate bias misconstrues the disability theology of the Yahwist, who understands disability to be a part of God's created order. This order can be realized through natural processes or through divine intervention. Disability is not a reason for loss of status and indeed can be a mark of status.

A full understanding of disability within the Pentateuch will have to take into consideration the P and D legal materials. Whether or not the authors use "collective nouns that convey the idea that there is something that links this disparate group of people" (Linton: 9) and whether or not this constitutes a "cultic model" that parallels the contemporary "medical model" of disability will need to be addressed. One thing is clear from this study. Any attempt to understand the meaning of disability within the Pentateuch will need to be viewed on its own merits devoid of the modern normate hermeneutic.

7

Disabling Israelite Leadership
2 SAMUEL 6:23 AND OTHER IMAGES OF DISABILITY IN THE DEUTERONOMISTIC HISTORY

Jeremy Schipper

[T]extual embodiment provides a concrete visible form to an otherwise abstract idea. To give an abstraction a literal body allows an ideology to simulate a foothold in the material world that it would otherwise fail to procure.

—David T. Mitchell,
"Narrative Prosthesis and the Materiality of Metaphor"

The epigram for this essay comes from David T. Mitchell's discussion of disability in Sophocles' *Oedipus the King*. Among other things, he observes that literary images of disability tend not to concentrate on the lived experience of disability. Rather, these images serve as metaphors that extrapolate the so-called meaning(s) of the disability into "cosmological significance. . . . Blindness may represent the incapacity of humanity to see into the future; lameness can designate the crippling effects of social ideologies; . . . amputation can provide evidence of an unchecked medical industry; and so on" (2000:25). Mitchell also suggests that Sophocles' ancient story can function as a paradigm for literary approaches to disability because bodies with disabilities allow writers to establish a connection between abstract ideologies and concrete experiences (27). Informed by Mitchell's observations, this essay will examine uses of disability in another ancient text, the Hebrew Bible's so-called Deuteronomistic History (Deuteronomy–2 Kings). Specifically, I examine the use of images of disability during key transitions in Israelite leadership.

As Mitchell suggests regarding *Oedipus the King*, images of disability rarely help to narrate or develop how a biblical character experiences his or her disability in everyday life. Rather, they provide the text with a means of ideological commentary on the state of national leadership. I begin by examining Michal's childlessness (2 Sam 6:23) in relation to David's solidification of power. After providing evidence that infertility was recognized as a disability in antiquity and that the text presents Michal as infertile, I consider the relationship between her condition and other images of disability that appear during David's solidification of power in the opening chapters of 2 Samuel. Together these images help to reinforce an ideological justification for the transfer in leadership from Saul's house to David.

Yet, in the end, no model of leadership, even the Davidic dynasty, can live up to the standard set by Mosaic leadership. Although the historian draws on sources composed before the end of the Davidic dynasty, he or she first edited his or her work after its end and stresses retrospectively the point that one should judge all models of Israelite leadership by their (in)fidelity to Mosaic authority as expressed in his interpretation of the law, preserved primarily in Deuteronomy. This form of the Deuteronomistic History (which includes all the texts treated in this essay) employs specific images of disability to help communicate this abstract point. The book of Deuteronomy concludes by presenting Moses as a having a hyper non-disabled body even at his life's end. I conclude by showing how this depiction contrasts with the images of disability that continually mark the decline of subsequent modes of leadership throughout the Deuteronomistic History.

I. Interpretative Difficulties in 2 Samuel 6:23

Second Samuel 6:20–23 contains Michal's final major appearance in the Deuteronomistic History. In these verses, Michal confronts her husband, David. She criticizes him for "uncovering himself" before his servants' maids as he brought the ark to Jerusalem (v. 20). David responds by saying that he danced before YHWH, who chose him in place of Michal's father, Saul, and all Saul's household and that his maids will honor him (vv. 21–22). David has the final word in this argument. The text does not record any response by Michal. Rather, this episode ends with an odd verse that has provided scholars with an interpretative crux. Verse 23 reads, "Now Michal the daughter of Saul did not have a child until the day of her death."[1] Since at least the Talmud, interpreters have puzzled over the significance of this story's final statement and its ambiguous connection to the preceding verses. Yet understanding Michal as infertile and infertility as a disability helps to uncover an important, but often overlooked, aspect of 2 Sam 6:23.

---

1. All biblical translations are my own.

II. Infertility as a Disability in Antiquity

Biblical, comparative ancient Near Eastern, and early rabbinic material all contain examples of infertility treated as a disability or illness. As a blessing for Israel's obedience, Moses promises a lack of both male and female barrenness (עָקָר וַעֲקָרָה לֹא־יִהְיֶה בְךָ) alongside a removal of every "sickness" (חֹלִי) and any "malignant disease of Egypt" (מַדְוֵי מִצְרַיִם) in Deut 7:14–15 (cf. Exod 23:25b–26a). That Gen 20:17 uses the word "heal" (רפא) to describe the divine removal of infertility further strengthens this association since the Hebrew Bible often uses רפא to describe the healing of sickness and disease (Avalos 1995a:332; cf. Exod 15:26; Lev 13:18; Deut 28:27; Ps 103:3; and so on). As in Mesopotamian texts concerning illnesses, a number of biblical texts present infertility as under the direct control of a divine "sender/controller" (Avalos 1995a:332; cf. 128–221; Gen 16:2; 20:18; 25:21; 30:1–2; Judg 13:2–3; 1 Sam 1:5). Exodus 4:11 depicts a handful of disabilities such as lameness, blindness, and muteness in a similar fashion.

Also, one sees infertility connected with other disabilities in comparative ancient Near Eastern literature. In the Sumerian myth "Enki and Ninmah" (circa third millennium B.C.E.), the god Enki and the goddess Ninmah enter into a contest while drinking beer. Ninmah creates several types of humans for which Enki must assign a function within society. A number of Ninmah's creations have disabilities, but Enki assigns each of them a particular, and at times prominent, social function. For example, Enki allotted the blind person to "the musical art, and seated it (as) chief-[musician] in a place of honor, before the king." One should note that along with humans who are either blind or lame in both feet, Ninmah creates "a woman who could not give birth" (COS 1.159:518; cf. Benito: 20–76; Kramer and Maier: 31–37).

One finds a further connection between infertility and both physical and cognitive disabilities in early rabbinic literature. While discussing Sarah's pregnancy with Isaac following a long period of infertility (Gen 21:1–7), Gen. Rab. 53:8 notes, "But when the matriarch Sarah was remembered [gave birth], many other barren women were remembered with her; many deaf gained their hearing; many blind had their eyes opened, many insane became sane" (H. Freedman: 1:218–19). Given these representative examples from biblical, comparative ancient Near Eastern, and early rabbinic literature, it appears that writers in antiquity could categorize infertility with other illnesses or impairments, such as deafness, lameness, or blindness.

III. Michal's Infertility

Good evidence exists that v. 23 presents Michal as infertile, even if the cause of the infertility remains a matter of speculation. Second Samuel 21:8 does refer to "the five sons of Michal" (so MT). Yet, following the scholarly consensus, I would read this phrase as "the five sons of Merab" (so LXX). The same verse also reports that the five sons were born to Adriel, who is Merab's husband, not Michal's husband (1 Sam 18:19). Thus, the context suggests that the mother is Merab rather than Michal (McCarter 1984:439; Walters: 290–96; cf. *b. Sanh.* 19b).

Some scholars argue that Michal's childlessness does not have a biological cause, but results from a forced sexual abstinence (Henry Smith: 297; McCarter 1984:187, 188). They suggest that David ended sexual relations with Michal, as he did with his ten concubines in 2 Sam 20:3b (Exum: 32). Nevertheless, 6:23 does not mention David ending relations with Michal explicitly, as he does with the ten concubines in 20:3b. Furthermore, regardless of when or how David's and Michal's sexual relationship ended, Michal loved David early on in their relationship (1 Sam 18:20) and they shared a bed at one point (1 Sam 19:13). Considering David's great procreative success with all his wives except Michal (2 Sam 3:2–5; 5:13–15; 11:5; 12:24), the text seems to suggest Michal's infertility, especially since the Hebrew Bible often understands the woman as the cause of infertility. That Michal does not have any children with her other husband, Paltiel (1 Sam 25:44), even though he appears to love her deeply (2 Sam 3:16), further supports this conclusion.

Scholarly attempts to understand the literary significance of her infertility usually involve speculation on its cause. Often, interpreters suggest that YHWH causes Michal's infertility as YHWH had in the cases of Sarai (Gen 16:2), the unnamed women of Abimelech's house (Gen 20:18), Rachel (Gen 30:2), and Hannah (1 Sam 1:5). In Michal's case, the proposed reasons for the (alleged) divine action have ranged from a punishment for her pride (Calvin: 279–94), her rejection of YHWH (Hertzberg: 281), or even her idolatry (Lillian Klein: 37–46). Yet, whereas the text notes explicitly God's involvement in the cases of divinely caused infertility mentioned above, it does not do so in Michal's case. In the end, the text does not provide enough evidence to speculate on the cause of Michal's infertility. Scholarly concern over whether her condition results from a divine action or a human one may reflect a tendency to approach images of disability from a "medical model" standpoint. This approach focuses on "diagnosing" the cause of her condition as a phenomenon isolated in an individual body, rather than understanding it as an example of an ideologically charged literary motif (disability) open to critical reflection.

Moving beyond speculation on the cause of her infertility, one may examine the contribution it makes to the political rhetoric surrounding David's rise to power. To be sure, some scholars explore the practical implications of her childlessness. Her infertility eliminates the possibility of another Saulide heir and separates David's bloodline from Saul's line (McCarter 1984:188). In this sense, 2 Sam 6:23 contributes to the further solidification of David's power and the demise of Saul's house. Yet the contribution of this verse to this transfer of royal power does not end with the practical fact that Saul will not have an heir. In the midst of David's increasing power, this verse also depicts a Saulide who opposes David as having a disability when it presents Michal as infertile.

Disability scholars have examined how images of disability often become metaphors for social downfall in literature from throughout the world. For example, David T. Mitchell and Sharon L. Snyder observe, "[Disability] serves as a metaphorical signifier of social and individual collapse. Physical and cognitive anomalies promise to lend a 'tangible' body to textual abstractions" (2000:47–48). Along these lines, one should note how Michal's infertility helps to "lend a tangible body" to the abstract theme of the Saulide collapse in the face of David's rise to power by interpreting it in light of other images of disability in the early part of 2 Samuel.

IV. Michal and 2 Samuel's Ideological Use of Disability

The case of Jonathan's son Mephibosheth, who becomes "lame in both his feet" (2 Sam 9:13; cf. 4:4; 9:3; 19:27), arguably provides the most recognized image of disability in 2 Samuel. Yet, if one studies 2 Samuel closely, an unusually frequent number of disability images appear in its opening chapters, such as the lame and the blind in 5:6–8 or those with a skin disease and unusual bodily discharge in 3:29. Images of disability in 2 Samuel do not appear as isolated or random occurrences. Rather, they participate in a larger rhetoric program that supports the solidification of David's power and the demise of Saul's house (Schipper 2005a:422–34; 2006:88–98). Second Samuel 6:23 contributes to this rhetorical use of disability in the opening chapters of 2 Samuel.

In 2 Sam 3:27, David's general Joab assassinates Abner, the general of Saul's son Ishbosheth. While this murder proves politically convenient for David, the king needs to distance himself from Joab's actions since 3:37 hints that some people suspect David's involvement in the murder (cf. *Sanh.* 20a). Thus when David first hears of the murder, he claims his innocence immediately and distances himself from Joab by cursing Joab's household.

> I and my kingdom are innocent before YHWH forever regarding the blood of Abner son of Ner. May it fall on the head of Joab and all the house of his father. One who has an unusual genital secretion (זב) or a skin disease (מצרע) or is supported by a spindle (פלך)² or falls by the sword or wants food will never be lacking (אל־יכרת) from the house of Joab. (3:28b–29)

One should take note of the fact that, among other things, David's

---

2. Scholars dispute the exact meaning of פלך. It may also mean "crutch," which would fit in with the images of disability earlier in the verse (McCarter 1984:118; but see also Holloway: 370–73; Layton: 81–86).

curse on Joab's house involves perpetual disabilities. As David continues to solidify his power over the next several chapters, the text characterizes parties from whom he needs to distance himself or who present an obstacle for him with images of disability. In ch. 4, the text portrays Saul's son Ishbosheth's hands as "enfeebled" (v. 1)[3] and Saul's grandson Mephibosheth's feet as "crippled" (v. 4). This same chapter narrates Ishbosheth's assassination (v. 7) and reminds the reader of Saul's and Jonathan's deaths (v. 4a). By the end of ch. 4, Mephibosheth represents the only surviving Saulide heir (cf. 9:1). Since his disability may have socially disqualified him from assuming the throne, a son born to Michal provides the only hope for a continued Saulide dynasty.

In chs. 5–6, David establishes the capital of his new kingdom in Jerusalem. In these chapters, images of disability mark those parties that oppose David's entry into Jerusalem. As in both Sumerian and early rabbinic literature, the story of his entry connects infertility with disabilities such as lameness and blindness. When David first captures Jerusalem in 5:6–8, images of disability saturate this short episode as the primary characterizations of David's opposition. The words for "blind" (עורים) and "lame" (פסחים) each appear three times in vv. 6–8. In fact, v. 8a uses these words to describe those people whom David "hates." This method of characterization follows a pattern that has grown subtly during David's rise to power. Thus, it seems fitting that after David brings the ark into Jerusalem, the text would portray Michal, the last person to oppose David's establishment of his kingdom (6:20) and one who "despises" David (6:16), as having a disability.

Chapter 6 sets the announcement of her infertility in the context of the struggle for power between David and Saul's household. In his response to Michal's criticism of his dance, David claims that YHWH chose him as king over her father Saul and all Saul's household (v. 21). While noting that Michal did not have any children, v. 23 also emphasizes that Michal is "the daughter of Saul." In fact, ch. 6 never refers to Michal as David's wife. Rather, it stresses her connection to Saul by referring to her as "the daughter of Saul" repeatedly (vv. 16, 20, 23). It reinforces her connection to the party that has served as David's major opposition over the last several chapters. Verse 23 provides the concluding remark on the long battle between David and the Saulides, first introduced in 2 Sam 3:1. Indeed, the very next verse begins a new phase in David's rule when it states, "Now David dwelled in his house. YHWH gave him rest from all his enemies who surrounded him" (7:1). When David returns to the matter of Saul's house in ch. 9, only the "lame" Mephibosheth remains (9:3, 13). In other

---

3. To be sure, the phrase "his hands were enfeebled" (וירפו ידיו) used in 4:1 does not describe a physical condition, but appears as an idiomatic expression for a lack of courage on Ishbosheth's part.

words, the note that Michal remains childless provides closure to David's rise to power in at least two ways. First, it eliminates the possibility of a future Saulide heir who could challenge David for the throne. Second, as the text had done with others who appear politically dangerous to David over the last several chapters, v. 23 dismisses the last of the opposition to David's rise to power through disability imagery when it hints at Michal's infertility. When one considers her infertility in relation to other images of disability in 2 Samuel, it foregrounds how images of disability underwrite the ideologically charged narration of the royal transition from Saul's house to David.

V. Disability and Other Leadership Transitions in the Deuteronomistic History

The power struggle between Saul's house and David provides the Deuteronomistic History with its longest narration of a transfer in national leadership. As seen above, images of disability supply an important means of articulating this transfer. Yet the Deuteronomistic History does not limit this narrative technique to this one case. Rather, moving beyond the so-called David Story, one should note that images of disability often surface at other key points of transition in national leadership within the Deuteronomistic History.

I begin with the death of Moses, Israel's first major leader. Deuteronomy 34:5–6 narrate his death and burial. Verse 7 follows this scene up by noting that "Moses was 120 years when he died. His eyesight had not dimmed (לֹא־כָהֲתָה עֵינוֹ) and his vigor had not fled" (but see Deut 31:2). This description sums up Moses' life as one lived under divine favor. One finds a parallel in the inscription of Adad-guppi, when the mother of Nabonidus declares that the godhead Sin blessed her so that she lived to 104. She claims "my eyesight was good, my hearing excellent, my hands and feet were sound, my words well chosen, food and drink agreed with me, and my mind happy" (ANET, 561c). Likewise, Si'-gabbar's inscription claims that as a priest of Sahr in Nerab he lived a long life because of his righteousness and could see his descendants with his own eyes until the day of his death (ANET, 661d; cf. Tawil: 60–63). These parallels suggest that the physical description of Moses at the time of his death signals that he lived under divine favor. Indeed, vv. 10–12 conclude the book of Deuteronomy with the claim that no other prophet has arisen in Israel who can compare to Moses. Moses sets the standard for all future leaders in Israel. Although Joshua takes the mantle from Moses (v. 8), he inherits some but not all of Moses' spirit (Num 27:20; cf. 11:17; Coats: 37). He leads Israel according to the Mosaic interpretation of YHWH's command rather than speaking to YHWH "face to face" as Moses did (Deut 34:10; cf. Exod 33:11; Olson: 168–70). Indeed, no other leader will live up to this standard. As the Deuteronomistic History unfolds, the connection between disabilities,

particularly "dimmed" eyesight, and Israelite leadership underscores this
point at various other transitions in leadership.

Following the conquest and settlement of Canaan, a series of judges
provide charismatic leadership for the tribes of Israel. Yet this system of
leadership begins to break down by the time the reader reaches the story
of Samson in Judg 13–16. Samson hardly fits the mold of a traditional Israelite judge. Unlike other judges, he does not lead Israel into battle, but
fights the Philistines alone as more of a personal vendetta (Judg 15:11–12).
In 16:21a, the Philistines capture Samson and forcibly remove his eyesight:
"The Philistines seized him and gouged out his eyes (וינקרו את־עיניו)." Unlike Moses, Samson dies without his eyesight.[4] Following his death, the
last chapters of Judges do not focus on any further judges, but foreground
the issue of a possible change in leadership systems through the repeated
phrases "everyone did what was right in their own eyes (בעיניו)" (17:6;
21:25) and "there was no king in Israel" (17:6; 18:1; 19:1; 21:25). Although
the first phrase represents a common idiom employed throughout the Hebrew Bible, here the use of the metaphor suggests that kingship as a new
form of leadership might "see properly" for the people.

Nonetheless, in regards to the eyesight of Israelite leaders, 1 Samuel
picks up right where Judges left off. The books of Samuel open with Eli
judging Israel (1 Sam 4:18). Yet Eli cannot control his corrupt sons (2:22–
25), and YHWH revokes the divine promise of a perpetual priesthood for
Eli's house (2:30–36). First, an unnamed man of God announces this divine
judgment to Eli (2:30–36), and then Samuel receives word that this judgment is about to take place and announces it to Eli (3:11–18). In between
these two announcements, 3:2b–3a informs the reader that "[Eli's] eyes
began to dim (ועיניו החלו כהות [MT qere]) and he was not able to see, but
the lamp (נר) of God had not yet gone out." The root for "to dim" (כהה)
appears in both Deut 34:7 and 1 Sam 3:2. Yet the story of Moses ends by
noting that his eyesight never dimmed, whereas the notice that Eli's eyes
have indeed dimmed comes right in midst of announcements of Eli's end.
In fact, the Masoretes point the word in 3:2 according to the qittēl noun
pattern, which they often employ to indicate a disability. This pointing
connects Eli's condition to other images of disability, such as muteness,
deafness, lameness, or blindness (cf. Exod 4:11; Lev 21:18–20; 2 Sam 5:6–8;
9:13; and so on). As with Samson, the loss of sight accompanies the continued breakdown in leadership.

---

4. The Philistines blinding Samson provides an ironic twist to his fate.
His first reported contact with the Philistines comes when, against his parents'
wishes, he demands that they get an unnamed Philistine woman as a bride for
him since he claims in 14:3 that "she is beautiful in my eyes" (היא ישרה בעיני). This
action triggers a series of events that results in the Philistines gouging out his
eyes in 16:21.

At the same time, as with Samson, the issue of kingship emerges once again in the wake of Eli's demise. Immediately after the notice about Eli's dimming eyesight, the next verse introduces the image of a "lamp" (נִיר) into the Deuteronomistic History. As the History progresses, it will repeatedly associate the image of the lamp with the divine promise of fidelity to the Davidic dynasty (2 Sam 21:7; 22:29; 1 Kgs 11:36; 15:4; 2 Kgs 8:19; cf. Polzin: 49–54).

In 1 Sam 8:4–5, the issue of kingship surfaces less subtly when the elders of Israel demand that Samuel appoint a king for them. Following the capture of the ark by the Philistines (4:1–7:2) and that Samuel's sons, like Eli's sons before them, fall into corruption (8:3), the elders call for a new form of Israelite leadership. Eventually, Samuel proclaims Saul as the first king over Israel (10:20–24). As with Eli before him, YHWH makes a divine promise to Saul (12:14–15, 25). At first, Saul seems to turn things around for Israel. Like the judges of old, he leads Israel into battle and successfully defeats their oppressors (11:1–14). In fact, he halts a loss of eyesight in Israel with his first military campaign when he defeats Nahash the Ammonite. Nahash began the process of "gouging out" (נִקּוֹר; cf. Judg 16:21) the right eye of everyone in Jabesh-gilead in order to "place a reproach on all Israel" (10:27 [4QSam^a]; 11:2). Initially, Saul's leadership halts this loss of eyesight and seems to break the link between impaired eyesight and the demise of Israelite leadership.

By ch. 13, however, Samuel declares that Saul's kingdom will not continue (vv. 13–14). From 1 Sam 13–2 Sam 9, Saul's household slowly crumbles, and more images of disability slowly pile up. The text never mentions an impairment of eyesight during the long transfer of leadership from Saul's house to David. Nonetheless, as seen above, a handful of other images of disability mark the demise of his house. While this association may begin as early as Saul's own cognitive breakdown in 1 Sam 16:14–23, it culminates with his daughter Michal's infertility (2 Sam 6:23) and his grandson Mephibosheth, who, as the text notes repeatedly, is "lame in both his feet" (9:13; cf. 4:4; 9:3; 19:27). As yet another form of Israelite leadership passes away, the images of disability continue to build around these moments of transition.

After David takes control of Jerusalem, his dynasty retains power until the very end of the monarchical period nearly five hundred years later. Nevertheless, even David's body does not live up to the extraordinary non-disabled standard set by the elderly Moses at the end of Deuteronomy. Unlike Moses whose vigor never leaves him even in old age, when David dies at an old age, he cannot keep himself warm even with the aid of blankets (1 Kgs 1:1). Likewise, other Davidic rulers end their lives with chronic disabilities (1 Kgs 15:23; 2 Kgs 15:5). In contrast to Moses, Adad-guppi, or Si'-gabbar, kings in the Davidic house do not share the same sign of divine favor by living to an old age while remaining physically unimpaired. Although images of disability and old age seem to overlap in these cases, one should note that deciding what counts as disability and what counts as old-age imagery may reflect an able-bodied interpretative bias. As several disability scholars note, the process of aging exposes the socially constructed aspects of disability. How abruptly or at what point in life one becomes impaired often influences whether or not society labels the impairment as a disability as opposed to a "natural" by-product of aging. Some members of the disability rights movement refer to people who identify themselves as nondisabled as "TABS" or "temporarily able-bodied" in order to foreground this point (Thomson 1997:13–14, 141 n. 14).

To be sure, of all the modes of national leadership, David's dynasty comes the closest to producing a leader like Moses. At first, the Deuteronomistic History seems to portray the northern king Jeroboam as a Mosaic figure who nearly replaces the Davidic dynasty (1 Kgs 11:31–32). It connects him with Egypt (11:40) and narrates how he freed his people from forced servitude (12:1–20). Yet in 13:2–3 an unnamed man of God condemns an altar built by Jeroboam, claiming that David's descendant king Josiah will desecrate it (cf. 2 Kgs 15:27–29). In v. 4, Jeroboam raises his hand and orders the man of God's arrest, but the king's hand withers (ותיבש ידו). Although his hand heals, the incident signals his dynasty's downfall. The chapter concludes by noting that Jeroboam did not learn from this incident, and thus his dynasty was destroyed (vv. 33–34; cf. 2 Kgs 17:21–23). On the other hand, the aforementioned Josiah appears even more like Moses. In fact, 2 Kgs 23:25 describes him with language that seems very much like the description of Moses in Deut 34:10 (cf. Deut 6:5). Yet, like Joshua, Josiah leads the people according to the Mosaic interpretation of YHWH's law rather than through direct revelation. Furthermore, unlike Moses (Exod 32:9–14), Josiah's actions cannot turn back YHWH's "fierce anger" from against the nation (2 Kgs 23:26–27; cf. 21:10–15), due to the corruption of Manasseh.

In the end, even David's monarchy goes the way of other post-Mosaic modes of leadership. Zedekiah is the last Davidic king to rule in Jerusalem. When the Babylonians invade, he flees the city. The Babylonians capture him, kill his sons, and blind (עור) him (2 Kgs 25:7). Throughout the Deuteronomistic History, no one, not even a Davidic ruler, can live up to the standard of leadership set by Moses back in Deuteronomy. The literary use of disability provides the Deuteronomistic History with one means of illustrating this point.

VI. Conclusion

I began this essay by studying one verse (2 Sam 6:23) and moved on to connect this verse to the use of other images of disability in 2 Samuel. Then, I suggested that these images in 2 Samuel participate in a larger rhetorical technique that runs throughout the Deuteronomistic History's reflection on national leadership. Its images of disability lend support to Deut 34's presentation of Moses as an unparalleled leader in the nation's history. Certainly, I have not exhausted the images of disability that appear in the Deuteronomistic History. One could also study the Philistine tumors (1 Sam 5:12), the blindness of Ahijah the prophet (1 Kgs 14:4), or the skin disease of Naaman the Aramean (2 Kgs 5) to name just a few examples. Furthermore, one could focus on certain traditions in the Deuteronomistic History that seem to devalue eyesight and prioritize audition (see Avalos's essay in this volume). Nonetheless, I have limited my study to images of disability that relate to an abstract reflection on national leadership. Rather than attempting an exhaustive catalog of images of disability in the Deuteronomistic History, I have explored how the narrative employs disability as one means of embodying an ideologically charged commentary on the state of Israelite leadership.

As Mitchell observes in regards to Sophocles' work, the images of disability treated in this essay provide little insight into the experience of disability in the biblical world. The narrative passes over the lived experience of disability in favor of the metaphorization of disability as a tool for social commentary. For the most part, the narrative shows little interest in developing the implications of certain characters' disabilities once it has noted the fact that they have a disability. Rather, it appears more interested in using images of disability to help provide a "tangible body," to borrow Mitchell's and Snyder's words, for an abstract ideology regarding national leadership based on a limited and a highly stereotyped range of "meanings" for disability.

8

With Whom Do the Disabled Associate?

Metaphorical Interplay in the Latter Prophets

Sarah J. Melcher

An important principle of metaphor theory is to discern the meaning of metaphors within their entire context, including their literary context. This essay builds on my previous work (Melcher 2004) by examining more fully the literary context of metaphors of impairment in prophetic passages. By studying the interaction of metaphors of impairment with other prophetic metaphors, the essay will begin to flesh out how metaphors of disability help articulate the prophets' conception of ideal divine/human relations. Thus this study will begin to map out how these metaphors communicate the prophets' theological conception of divine sovereignty.

This essay explores three general areas: the role of metaphors of impairment within a prophetic emphasis on healing; prophetic metaphors of impairment and the depiction of moral deficiency; and prophetic resources for a disability liberation ethic. These three general areas of investigation were chosen because a survey of prophetic passages dealing with impairment suggests these as three primary foci within the prophetic books.

The reader will note, undoubtedly, a preference for the term "impairment" over the term "disability" in this essay. The term "disability" tends to evoke past social judgments about "any lack of ability—fiscal, physical, legal, and so on" (Lennard J. Davis 1995:xiii). As Lennard J. Davis states, "'Disability,' on the other hand, survives from a usage that links any impairments—not pigeonholed as physical limitation—together without creating a discourse of disability" (xiii). Thus, the term "impairment" is preferred here, but with the acknowledgment that it, too, is a term that has been used by an ableist society to designate something that departs from an "ideal" construct. As Davis points out, however, all such terms are "hopelessly embroiled in the politics of disability" (xiii). To me, the term "impairment" seems less socially loaded, but it is certainly not a neutral term.

This article broadens the understanding of impairment used in a previous article (Melcher 2004), defining impairment here to include injury, congenital impairment, chronic illness, cognitive impairment, and, in one instance, death.[1] Rosemarie Garland Thomson acknowledges how broadly (and somewhat artificially) disability is defined in our cultural milieu:

> Disability is an overarching and in some ways artificial category that encompasses congenital and acquired physical differences, mental illness and retardation, chronic and acute illnesses, fatal and progressive diseases, temporary and permanent injuries, and a wide range of bodily characteristics considered disfiguring, such as scars, birthmarks, unusual proportions, or obesity. (Thomson 1997:13)

Nevertheless, this broader definition better reflects a consistent view of disability among the Latter Prophets in their articulation of metaphors of impairment. These books view the issue of disability in a broad way.

In addition, methodological considerations have been broadened to include more of the literary context when analyzing metaphors of impairment. When the previous article was summarized at the Society of Biblical Literature's Annual Meeting in 2004, Bruce C. Birch suggested that a broader examination of the literary context would provide a different perspective on these metaphors. Thus, this essay attempts to incorporate his suggestion.

Of course, this study shares some of the weaknesses common to many survey articles. Because of the immensity of the prophetic corpus, the article can only explore some of the pertinent passages and suggest only a few of the significant themes that arise in prophetic passages about physical and cognitive impairment. A survey article may overlook some of the differences that exist among prophetic texts that were composed in various historical periods and social contexts. Nevertheless, preliminary surveys are valuable for outlining important areas for future consideration and are a necessary first step in such a nascent enterprise as the study of disability in biblical texts.

Several disability studies theorists advise researchers to investigate figures of disability within a broad context. Davis argues that disability is part of a "historically constructed discourse, an ideology of thinking about the body under certain historical circumstances. Disability is not an object—a woman with a cane—but a social process that intimately involves everyone who has a body and lives in the world of the senses" (Lennard J.

---

1. See the discussion of Ezek 37:1–14, p. 120.

Davis 1995:2). Since disability is a historically constructed discourse, it is important to see how it fits into a system. "In the task of rethinking and theorizing disability, one of the first steps is to understand the relationship between a physical impairment and the political, social, and even spatial environment that places that impairment in a matrix of meanings and significations" (Davis: 3). Thomson, too, stresses the importance of examining how disability relates to social processes and discourses—noting the consequence of exploring how the disabled figure relates to that of the "normate," Thomson's term for the socially constructed "normal" individual (1997:8–9).

Looking at how metaphors of impairment interrelate with other metaphors within prophetic passages is one way to flesh out the broader discourse within which metaphors of impairment function. Examining metaphors of impairment with the broader literary context in mind can help us to see how disability fits into a conceptual system as well as to discern how the prophets saw the phenomenon of impairment within their social milieu.

1. Metaphor Theory and Methodology

The methodology employed in this article has been influenced in an informal way by the work of George Lakoff and Mark Johnson (Lakoff and Johnson 1980; 1999), especially as it has been applied to Second Isaiah in *Mixing Metaphors: God as Mother and Father in Deutero-Isaiah* by Sarah J. Dille. In both *Metaphors We Live By* and *Philosophy of the Flesh*, Lakoff and Johnson argue that a single conceptual or structural metaphor can give rise to multiple linguistic metaphorical expressions. They contend that an individual's conceptual system is metaphorically structured and defined. In fact, Lakoff and Johnson suggest that "metaphors as linguistic expressions are possible precisely because there are metaphors in a person's conceptual system" (1980:6). Even though multiple linguistic metaphors arise from a single concept, they may not be consistent with one another—consistency meaning that "a single clearly delineated metaphor" may satisfactorily account for all of the linguistic metaphors under consideration. Nevertheless, though inconsistent, they may still share a certain coherence—that is, they may share an overlap of entailments, "those concepts that logically follow from a metaphor or a metaphoric statement" (Dille: 10; cf. Lakoff and Johnson 1980:95–96). These entailments can form a network of associations surrounding a central metaphorical concept. These various linguistic metaphors flesh out the primary conceptual metaphor, often in a creative fashion. Thus, there can be a network of innovative subordinate metaphors that relate to this more central concept (Dille: 8–20).

Another important contribution from Lakoff and Johnson is the idea that multiple metaphors can interact. As mentioned above, linguistic metaphors that explore the same subject or concept are likely to be inconsistent, but it is possible that they share an overlap or coherence of entailments. However, coherent metaphors may highlight or emphasize different aspects of the subject or concept. Dille suggests a very useful way to think about metaphors in prophetic poetry: "By the interweaving of metaphors, *the text creates coherences* not previously evident" (Dille: 15). Lakoff and Johnson's theory about the interaction of metaphors—through an overlap of entailments—suggests a way to explore how metaphors about impairment interact with other metaphors in a prophetic passage.

Also helpful theoretically is Paul Ricoeur's idea of a "root metaphor," which will aid in exploring how metaphors of impairment may relate to a more central "root metaphor" in prophetic passages (64; see also Melcher 2004:3–4). In Ricoeur's explanation, root metaphors "are capable of both engendering and organizing a network" of metaphors (64). This means that subordinate metaphors can be brought into association within the network connected with and surrounding the root metaphor. Root metaphors have a strong generative capacity to spawn innovative metaphors that add richness to the primary relationship (Melcher 2004:3–4). When the idea of "root metaphor" is used here, it is with the understanding that there may be multiple root metaphors in the prophets (see Dille: 3).

2. The Role of Metaphors of Impairment within a Prophetic Emphasis on Healing

An attention to literary context quickly reveals a prevalent assumption of the prophetic books that illustrates the conceptual universe into which metaphors of physical and cognitive impairment fit. For the prophets, YHWH wields punishment, imposes discipline, or bestows blessing with the goal of shaping the behavior of God's people. The ultimate aim of such shaping by YHWH is the restoration of the divine/human relationship.

In fact, YHWH is frequently depicted as one who restores a people, so that "God as restorer" could be considered a "root metaphor" in Ricoeur's sense (64; see also Melcher 2004:3–4). "God as restorer" functions as a root metaphor or major conceptual metaphor in many prophetic passages, while the metaphor of "God as healer" can be seen as a subordinate metaphor that adds richness to a network of metaphors that convey God's restorative power. The passages that speak of YHWH's restorative actions most often use some form of the root שׁוב (in Qal or Hiphil), although the Hiphil of חלם is used in one instance to communicate that God will restore the health of someone (Isa 38:16). In Jer 30:17, the phrase אעלה ארכה, "I will restore health," is employed, and a similar phrase occurs in Jer 8:22 and 33:6 (cf. Isa 58:8). The prophets frequently use the metaphor of "YHWH heals" (with root רפא) to convey God's restorative work. This restorative effort often focuses on Israel, but not exclusively so.

In many passages, there is interplay between metaphors of punishment and healing, an interaction found in Isa 19:22.

> YHWH will strike Egypt, striking and healing; they will return to YHWH, and he will hear their entreaties and heal them.[2]

Isaiah 57:14–21 reflects this interplay of punishment and restoration—striking and healing—that are a part of YHWH's efforts to redirect human behavior. Except for the unrepentant wicked in vv. 20–21, YHWH's goal is restoration for God's people (Goldingay: 324; Michael L. Brown: 199). That restoration is depicted in terms of healing, as well as of providing comfort and peace. Jeremiah 3:6–4:4 speaks of God's disciplinary work with Israel, but also relates God's mercy, generosity, healing, and salvation (3:12, 19, 22, 23).

A brief section of the longer pericope, Jer 30:1–24, also serves as an example of the frequent interplay of punishment and healing as the larger passage moves toward restoration.

> [14] All your lovers have forgotten you; they do not care for you; for I have struck you the blow of an enemy, the punishment of a cruel one, because your guilt is great, because your sins are so numerous. [15] Why do you cry out over your brokenness? Your pain is incurable. Because your guilt is great, because your sins are so numerous, I have done these things to you. [16] Therefore all who devour you shall be devoured, and all your foes, every one of them, shall go into captivity; those who plunder you shall be plundered, and all who prey on you I will make a prey. [17] For I will restore health[3] to you, and your wounds I will heal, says YHWH, because they have called you an outcast: "It is Zion; no one cares for her!"

As noted for other passages, when Jer 30:1–24 moves toward restoration, it employs metaphors of divine healing. Earlier, the passage depicts God as saying that pain had been inflicted through divine intention and that this pain was incurable. Hosea 6:1–3 refers explicitly to YHWH's ability to punitively strike out or to heal (see v. 1, especially). Numerous prophetic passages repeat this pattern of punishment then restoration for God's people, with "healing" as a primary metaphor of restoration: Jer 33:1–13; Hos 6:4–7:10; 11:1–12:1; and so on.

In contrast to the examples above, metaphors of healing can be used to convey an irredeemable situation—to represent an incurable condition, as in Jer 30:15. Similarly, when Jer 51:1–19 tells of YHWH's irreversible judgment against Babylon, it employs metaphors of healing to refer to that nation's incurable wounds: "We tried to heal Babylon, but she could not be healed" (v. 9aα). Babylon was not amenable to divine redirection. In

---

2. All translations are my own.
3. More literally, "bring up new flesh" upon the wound.

another example, Hos 5:1–15 speaks of attempts at healing to emphasize YHWH's irreversible judgment against Israel: "When Ephraim saw his sickness, and Judah his wound, then Ephraim went to Assyria, and sent to the great king. But he is not able to cure you or heal your wound" (v. 13). Hosea 7:1 employs metaphors of healing to convey the incurability of Israel's unrighteousness. (See also Jer 15:18; 17:14; 46:11; Nah 3:19; cf. Isa 3:7.)

These passages emphasize that God can restore and renew Israel, with figures of physical and cognitive impairment or illness serving to illustrate God's power to wound or heal. See Hos 14:4–9, where restoration is conceived as God's healing power.

However, Isa 6:1–13 takes a decidedly different tack, where YHWH inflicts physical impairments on Judah, so that its people may not be healed: "Make the heart of this people dull, and stop their ears, and shut their eyes, so that they may not look with their eyes, and listen with their ears, and comprehend with their heart, and turn and be healed" (v. 10). YHWH causes many kinds of impairment—both cognitive and physical—for Judah so that the people are incapable of understanding and unable to pursue their own healing. On the other hand, Isa 52:13–53:12 suggests that one person's affliction may be redemptive or healing for others: "But he was wounded for our transgressions, crushed for our iniquities; upon him was the punishment of our wholeness, and by his stripes we are healed" (53:5)

Of course, the preeminent example of physical impairment and healing is Ezek 37:1–14, although the root רפא does not appear. Perhaps this common root for healing is absent because the passage depicts a miracle beyond normal healing. Nevertheless, the passage presents the extraordinary capacity of YHWH's power to restore. The dry bones represent the very limits of death—death long established. YHWH's restorative power far exceeds even death's tenacious grasp. Death—the ultimate physical and cognitive impairment—is reversed by YHWH, who has sovereignty even over death. Thus, the passage—through an extended metaphor—demonstrates that YHWH can restore Israel the nation to good health in its land (vv. 12–14), in spite of its apparently incurable situation (v. 11).

In several instances, the physically and cognitively impaired appear in prophetic passages as the example of God's restorative power, although metaphors of healing are absent. In Jer 31:1–27, YHWH indicates the divine intention to rebuild Israel and return the exiles to the land. As the passage envisions restoration, it pictures how the extraordinarily complete return of the exiles will look. The character of YHWH speaks of the physically impaired persons who will be returning.

> [8] See, I am going to bring them from the land of the north, and gather them from the remotest parts of the earth, among them the blind and the lame, the pregnant one and the woman in labor, together; a great company, they shall return here. [9] With weeping they shall come, and with consolations I will lead them back, I will let them walk by brooks of water,

in a straight path in which they shall not stumble, for I have become a
father to Israel, and Ephraim is my firstborn.

Here, the metaphorical figures of "the blind (עור) and the lame (פסח)" serve
as vehicles to convey divine restorative power. The return from exile shall
be so inclusive and YHWH's protection shall be so effective that even those
who are physically weakened will make the trip to Israel. The physically
impaired, in this instance, include pregnant women and those who are in
labor, who are linked through the commonality of their physical vulnerability. These metaphors are connected through God's ability to make safe
their passage to Judah. YHWH explains the nature of the divine concern
for the vulnerable: "for I have become a father to Israel . . ." God becomes
Israel's parent, which entails a concern for all God's children, especially
the most vulnerable. The relationship between God and the people has
been fully restored.

Notably, the subsection of Jer 31:7–9 reverses previous motifs of YHWH's
punishment of Judah. God had predicted stumbling blocks that would
make "this people" stumble in Jer 6:21–22 and an invasion from the north,
ironically the same direction from which the impaired will return in Jer
31:7–9. Jeremiah 18:15 implies that immorality makes the people stumble,
while they receive safe passage in Jer 31 (cf. 25:32 and 50:41; Lundbom:
420).

Jack R. Lundbom argues that "the lame and the blind" are healed of
their impairments in Jer 31:7–9, but the passage is ambiguous (424). Lundbom's solution would certainly fit our previous observations about the
place of healing in God's restoration, but the healing of the disabled is not
clear here. Yet the disabled have become YHWH's firstborn, precious among
God's children (Brueggemann 1998:284)—constituting a reversal of their
disadvantaged position.

Similarly, Zeph 3:14–20 depicts the return of physically impaired persons as an illustration of YHWH's restorative power, but does not indicate
their healing. Before the lame one (הצלעה; literally, "she who limps") is
saved and the outcast (הנדחה; literally, "she that is outcast;" Sweeney:
206–7) is gathered, the judgments against the people of Judah have been
lifted. Of course, it is noteworthy that the lame person is paired with the
outcast (v. 19). Perhaps this indicates some sort of social equivalence. Nevertheless, both characters are gathered in, and both experience renewal
(יהריש; v. 17).

Of concern to this study is the depiction of the "limping one" as the
recipient of shame and reproach. Verse 18 indicates that the people of
Judah, including the disabled, had been rebuked because of the disaster
the nation has experienced: "Those who suffered from the appointed time
I removed from you; they were a burden upon her, a reproach" (חרפה). The
following verse portrays a transformation in the disabled person's reputation: "I will deal with all your oppressors at that time, and I will deliver

the lame and gather the outcast, and I will change their shame (בשתם) into praise and renown in all the earth." Thus, God's restoration can include an elevation in status or reputation. Nevertheless, the passage implies that the physically impaired person, the "limping one," could be the recipient of social reproach and, like the metaphorical partner, "the outcast," could experience social ostracism. The explicit point of commonality is the shame that both parties share.

Several commentators propose that the metaphors in v. 19 evoke the root metaphor of YHWH as shepherd and Israel/Judah as the flock of sheep. As Adele Berlin argues, "The image is of a shepherd rescuing his sheep from predators and keeping them from straying. The shepherd image is commonly used for kings in the ancient near east, and this metaphor continues the picture of God as king in v. 15" (Berlin: 147; see Vlaarding-erbroeck: 218).

In contrast to Jer 31:1–27 is Isa 29:15–24, which clearly associates YHWH's restoration with the healing of the deaf (החרשים) and the blind (עורים).[4] The passage begins with a warning (הוי) to Judah's leaders, who attempt to hide their schemes in deep places (v. 15). Verse 16 reminds the arrogant that YHWH's creative power is vast. The assumption that their schemes are not known is perverse. Like Assyria, they have overthrown the relationship between the potter and the clay, the creator and the created (cf. 10:15; Miscall: 77). Though Judah's leaders fail to understand God's sovereignty, they will soon see God's restorative power in action (Childs: 219). The passage then moves to nature's restoration, when Lebanon is transformed into a fruitful field and later into a forest (v. 17). Next, the healing of the deaf and the blind—illustrative of YHWH's extraordinary restoration—comes about at the same time as nature's renewal: "On that day, the deaf will hear the words of a scroll and out of gloom and darkness, the eyes of the blind will see" (v. 18). The disabled are healed so that they can appropriate YHWH's word. Their new ability to hear and see God's word can be compared with the restoration depicted in verse 24, "And those who err in spirit will come to understanding, and those who grumble will accept instruction." God's restorative aim is to make God's people more capable of understanding God's purposes. Indeed, they shall come to a more enlightened vision of God—treating God as holy and awe-inspiring.

Along with the disabled, the afflicted (ענוים) and the neediest of people (ואביוני אדם) will also experience greater joy and will rejoice in the Holy One. The entire passage is about reversal. The arrogant leaders will be brought low. The disabled, the oppressed, and those in desperate need will experience a reversal of fortunes. The disabled will be healed, the op-

---

4. Sweeney and Childs argue that the passage begins with verse 15 because of the repetition of the woe particle. This resembles the pattern in 29:1 and 30:1. The passage then begins and ends with a polemic against Judah's leaders (Sweeney: 377; Childs: 219).

pressed will experience joy, and the neediest of people will praise God. All of these groups represent people in vulnerable circumstances and those who are devalued by the leadership in power. YHWH will reorder an oppressive society so that the marginalized will experience restoration and justice. Those of humble social status will be raised up, while the arrogant oppressor will be brought low. God's restorative power will correct the disparities.

Of course, a very positive aspect of the passage is the contrast of the deaf, blind, afflicted, and the neediest with the arrogant, the tyrant, the scoffer, and the unjust. The recipients of God's restorative power are those who are in humble positions socially, while those who abuse their power will be eliminated (v. 20).

There are additional passages that use healing as a metaphor illustrating YHWH's restorative powers (for example, Mic 4:6–14 and Isa 35:1–10), but the scope of this article does not permit exploration of all relevant passages. However, having illustrated the central place of metaphors of healing, this study now explores other ways of using metaphors of physical and cognitive impairment in prophetic texts. Metaphors of impairment are often used to indicate moral deficiency. On the other hand, some passages suggest that helping a disabled person is a righteous act. See, for example, Zech 11:4–17, which indicates that the righteous leader will aid the physically or cognitively impaired. Ezekiel 34:4 reflects a similar point of view (Michael L. Brown: 199–200). Isaiah 58:1–14 argues that if a person feeds the hungry, houses the poor, and clothes the naked (v. 7), then the one helping will be rapidly healed (v. 8) and develop strong bones (v. 11)!

3. Prophetic Metaphors of Impairment and the Depiction of Moral Deficiency

As noted above, metaphors of physical and cognitive impairment sometimes serve as figures of moral deficiency.[5] Isaiah 1:2–20 portrays chronic illness as God's punishment for sin. The metaphor of chronic and pervasive illness in this passage serves to associate sin with illness, and, on the other hand, to use illness to describe the devastation of the land after siege. Leading into the metaphors of illness with a woe saying, the passage depicts the people of Judah as sinful in the extreme: "Ah, sinful nation, people laden with iniquity, offspring who do evil, children who act corruptly, who have forsaken YHWH, who have despised the Holy One of Israel, who are absolutely estranged!" (v. 4). Judah suffers as the result of God's beatings, yet such punitive measures have not caused Judah to change its course (v. 5). God's punishment is full; all of Judah is affected

---

5. The Targum understands several prophetic metaphors of impairment as symbolic of sin and exile: for example, Isa 1:6; 35:6; 42:19; Mic 4:6–8; and Zeph 3:19. See Evans: 80–82 and Houtman.

by YHWH's beatings: "The whole head is sick, and the whole heart faint!" (v. 5b). Verse 6 elaborates on the full extent of Judah's wounds: "From the sole of the foot even to the head, there is no soundness in it, but bruises and sores and bleeding wounds; they have not been drained, or bound up, or softened with oil."

In this passage, the metaphors of physical impairment serve to illustrate YHWH's attempts to prod the people of Judah into turning again to YHWH. But, in spite of repeated bludgeoning by YHWH, Judah appears willing to accept its badly wounded state without modifying its actions. Thus, the prophetic passage portrays God's beatings as a means to motivate the people of Judah to return to proper relationship with God.

This is not the only instance in the prophetic books in which YHWH inflicts physical impairment to punish the nation and/or to motivate the people to return to a proper pious interaction with YHWH. Isaiah 10:5–19 uses metaphors of impairment to illustrate how YHWH will punish the arrogant nation of Assyria. A few verses are particularly relevant:

> Therefore the Sovereign, YHWH of hosts, will send wasting sickness among his stout warriors, and under his glory a burning will be kindled, like the burning of fire. The light of Israel will become a fire, and his Holy One a flame; and it will burn and devour his thorns and briers in one day. The glory of his forest and his fruitful land YHWH will destroy, both soul and body, and it will be like when an invalid wastes away. The remnant of the trees of his forest will be so few that a child can write them down. (vv. 16–19)

To destroy Assyria's army, YHWH afflicts hefty warriors with a wasting disease. YHWH and the nation of Israel will destroy the forests and agricultural land like a fire. The passage moves easily from images of nature to human images, where the reference to "soul and body" (מנפש ועד־בשׂר) applies to the forest and the fruitful land. The destruction of these natural resources will be like the invalid who wastes away. The punishment of arrogant Assyria, inflicted by YHWH, will be like the chronically ill person, who grows weaker and smaller until death.

In this example, YHWH inflicts a disease that will cause a reversal. For the arrogant, YHWH will turn the stout warrior into one who wastes away. YHWH causes a deadly physical impairment to punish a nation for their arrogance. A nation and its resources will die away, and the plight of an invalid is the image that brings this home.

Ezekiel 12:1–16 uses images of physical impairment to describe moral deficiency, particularly in vv. 2 and 3:

> Mortal, you are living in the midst of a rebellious house, who have eyes to see but do not see, who have ears to hear but do not hear; for they are a rebellious house. Therefore, mortal, prepare for yourself an exile's baggage, and go into exile by day before their eyes; you shall go like an exile from your place to another place before their eyes. Perhaps they will see, though they are a rebellious house.

This pericope presents non-functioning eyes and ears as symbols for the inability to hear and understand God's word. Verse 2 emphasizes Judah's deliberate disobedience to God's will. The phrase "rebellious house" (בית־המרי)—employed three times in this passage—conveys throughout Ezekiel the prophet's appraisal of Judah as relentlessly disobedient from the time of the exodus from Egypt until now (Tuell: 251). Thus disability in this passage represents Judah's recalcitrance—its persistent moral failure. The one who does not see and the one who does not hear are equated with the rebellious house. As Moshe Greenberg observes, it is Judah's willfulness that is at issue—their *refusal* to see (Greenberg 1983:208–9).

The following verse commands the prophet to pack up "an exile's baggage" (כלי גולה) and, ironically, to go into exile "before their eyes." The passage states explicitly YHWH's hope that the people of Judah will see (יראו) this time, implicitly hoping for their repentance. Yet there is no guarantee that their eyes will choose to see, that is, understand. The prophet is exhorted to make the people see; the phrase "before their eyes" is repeated seven times throughout the passage (Greenberg: 209). Thus, obedience is depicted as eyes that see, in contrast to disobedience, which is symbolized as eyes that do not see and ears that do not hear.

At the time of the "great day of YHWH," Zeph 1:14–18 pictures YHWH's punishment of the people in terms of disability: "I will bring such distress upon people that they shall walk like the blind; because they have sinned against YHWH, their blood shall be poured out like dust, and their guts like dung" (v. 17). To express the extent of YHWH's punishment, the passage turns to the familiar figure of the blind person, whose walk is affected by his or her impairment. The punishment will be dire as "the whole earth shall be consumed; for a full, indeed, terrible end he will make of all the inhabitants of the earth" (see v. 18).

Ironically, in Zech 11:15–17, YHWH punishes the people by sending a "worthless shepherd" to lead them, then the divine strikes the shepherd with various physical impairments. YHWH "raises up" a shepherd

> who does not attend to the perishing, nor seek the scattered, nor heal the maimed (והנשברת), nor nourish the healthy, but devours the flesh of the fat ones, tearing off even their hoofs. Oh, my worthless shepherd, who abandons the flock! May the sword strike his arm and his right eye! Let his arm be completely withered, his right eye utterly blinded! (vv. 16–17)

The divine in Zechariah can raise up a shepherd who will neglect the needs of God's human flock in order to punish them, but can also inflict multiple physical wounds—wounds that cause permanent disability—upon the leader who fulfills the divine intention to punish the flock. Physical impairment is one of YHWH's tools for enacting the divine purpose—for inflicting punishment upon God's people.

Zechariah 14:1–21 mentions YHWH's punishment of the nations that wage war against Jerusalem: "This shall be the plague with which YHWH

will strike all the peoples that wage war against Jerusalem: their flesh shall
rot while they are still on their feet; their eyes shall decay in their sock-
ets, and their tongues shall rot in their mouths" (v. 12). In this context, the
striking of bellicose nations with disease is an illustration of what YHWH
will do to keep Jerusalem safe from destruction, so that its inhabitants can
live there securely (v. 11). Yet it shows YHWH's willingness to inflict a debilitating disease upon those peoples who are aggressive toward Jerusalem.
Thus, YHWH will use disease as a defense of Jerusalem, as well as a punishment against those who fall short morally.

Malachi 1:6–2:9, although it speaks of disabled animals, may shed
light on prophetic attitudes toward disabled persons. The passage rebukes
the priesthood for not treating YHWH with proper honor. YHWH accuses the
priests of offering polluted food upon the altar: "'When you offer blind
(עור) animals to sacrifice, is that not wrong? And when you offer those that
are lame (פסח) or sick (חלה), is that not wrong? Try presenting that to your
governor; will he be pleased with you or show you favor?' says YHWH of
hosts" (1:8). The same principle is repeated in vv. 13 and 14:

> "'What a weariness this is,' you say, and you sniff at me," says YHWH of
> hosts. "You bring what has been taken by violence (גזול) or is lame (הפסח)
> or sick (החלה), and this you bring as your offering! Shall I accept that from
> your hand?" says YHWH. "Cursed be the cheat who has a male in the flock
> and vows to give it, and yet sacrifices to the Lord what is ruined; for I am
> a great king," says the YHWH of hosts, "and my name is revered among
> the nations."

In this passage, ironically, the priesthood is admonished by YHWH for
offering animals that have been polluted because of their physical imperfections. This matter is ironic because elsewhere it is the priesthood who is
charged with observing certain restrictions about appropriate animals for
sacrifice (see Lev 22:17–33; cf. Deut 15:19–23, which may mitigate the requirements somewhat). Leviticus 22:20 makes it clear what the standards
were for sacrificial animals: "You shall not offer anything that has a defect
(מום), for it will not be acceptable on your behalf." The Leviticus passage
lists several different examples of physical impairment, which disallow the
animal as an offering upon the altar. The admonition is very serious in the
eyes of Malachi, for the individual who violates it will be cursed by YHWH
(וארור; 1:14).

The same principle applies to persons from priestly families who have
a physical imperfection, according to Lev 21:16–24. The major premise is
summarized by verse 21: "No descendant of Aaron the priest who has a
defect shall come near to offer the LORD's offerings by fire; since he has a
defect (מום), he shall not come near to offer the food of his God." This passage, like Lev 22:17–33, lists some examples of unacceptable imperfections.
The issue is likely centered in the holiness of YHWH's altar, because it is

potentially dangerous for impure persons to come into contact with pure items. Nevertheless, the two passages from Leviticus establish a relative devaluation of human beings and animals that have a physical imperfection. The passages from Malachi, Leviticus, and Deuteronomy imply that those with a physical imperfection are not worthy to approach YHWH (see Melcher 1998).

Most scholars place Malachi in the time frame of the fifth century B.C.E., and the interests of the book fit an era when the priesthood was prominent. It seems probable that a similar priestly requirement lies behind Mal 1:6–2:9. Malachi 1:11 makes the ideal clear: " 'For from the rising of the sun to its setting my name is great among the nations, and in every place incense is offered to my name, and a pure offering (ומנחה טהורה); for my name is great among the nations,' says YHWH of hosts." To properly acknowledge YHWH's great name, an offering must be pure (without imperfection).

There are other passages which depict YHWH's punishment for moral failure in terms of disability, such as Isa 56:9–12; 59:1–21; and Mic 7:10–17. The scope of this article does not permit examination of every passage. Yet this is an indication that the topic of physical and cognitive impairment deserves more complete study.

4. Prophetic Resources for a Disability Liberation Ethic

While this article has explored several examples of problematic passages in fleshing out how metaphors of disability fit into YHWH's plan for divine/human relations according to the prophets, this closing section explores a passage that could serve as a resource for a prophetic liberation ethic of disability: Isa 45:1–19. The passages discussed above are problematic for those who are impaired in our current day, for they craft a relationship between disability and moral lack, they emphasize the necessity of healing and YHWH's power to remove all impairment, and they suggest a social devaluing of persons with disabilities. All of these motifs could be challenged by a liberation ethic that is rooted in the current real experience of persons with impairments. Although this essay makes it clear that a more thorough reading of the prophets from a disability liberation perspective is needed, that is beyond the scope of this essay. Nevertheless, a brief look at Isa 45:1–19 suggests that the prophetic corpus could provide the resources for constructing a disability liberation ethic. Verses 9–12 stress YHWH's sovereignty as revealed in divine creative acts.

> Woe to one who quarrels with his Maker—a pot among earthen pots! Does the clay say to the potter, "What are you making?" or "Your work has no hands"? Woe to one who says to a father, "What are you begetting?" or to a woman, "What are you bearing?" Thus says YHWH, the Holy One of Israel and its Maker: Will they ask me things to come about my children, or instruct me about the work of my hands? It was I who made

the earth and created humankind upon it. My own hands stretched out
the heavens, and I commanded all their host. (45:9–12)[6]

Like many prophetic passages, Isa 45:9–12 presents YHWH's creative history as support for God's free exercise of divine sovereignty. God's creative
power is the primary theme of the larger discourse, 44:24–45:25. In this
smaller section, YHWH offers a defense to the nations for the choice of Cyrus
as God's anointed (see v. 1; Childs: 354). YHWH indicates that the divine
purpose will employ whatever instrument (or whomever among God's
children) serves the divine will, despite the objections of the nations.

God's sovereign freedom over human beings (God's children, vv.
11–12), which is rooted in God's creative power, has broader implications. YHWH's question could very well apply to persons with a physical
impairment. God asks whether any person has the right to question God's
purpose—whether in creating human beings or selecting them for special tasks. Verses 9–12 suggest that the work of God's hands is valuable in
its own right and that people are not qualified to question God's creative
work.

The passage suggests that all persons are created through the will of
God, in ways that reflect God's sovereign choice. In addition, these verses
argue that God continues to work with creation, bringing God's purpose
to fruition through unexpected means. For persons with a physical or cognitive impairment, the passage suggests that the divine purpose can be
fulfilled through a great variety of people, from all walks of life.

Several other prophetic passages support the idea that YHWH has deliberately shaped human beings from the womb. In several verses from
the book of Isaiah, the metaphor of YHWH as potter is evoked (see Isa 27:11;
29:16; 43:1, 7, 21; 44:2, 21; and 49:5; cf. Jer 1:5). These passages support
the idea of YHWH's sovereign power of creation—that YHWH deliberately
shaped human beings in the manner of YHWH's choice. According to these
verses, YHWH has a purpose in forming human beings in various ways. The
implication is that God chooses the shape of every person so that every
type of person should be valued, as she or he is. In addition, passages that
stress YHWH's creative acts also underline God's sovereign purpose.

5. Conclusion

I have explored three major themes within the prophetic corpus that have
clear implications for the study of metaphors of impairment in that context. We have learned that metaphors of impairment play a prominent
role in passages that predict God's restoration of the covenant people.
While God as restorer is the primary conceptual metaphor, an important
subordinate metaphor is that of God as healer. Of course, not all passages of God as restorer refer explicitly to the healing of the disabled, but

---

6. This translation has been strongly influenced by Childs (346).

healing does occupy a significant place in passages with metaphors of impairment.

I also illustrated that there is often a relationship between impairment and moral deficiency. While the use is metaphorical, it suggests an underlying social association of disability and moral laxity.

Finally, I briefly explored how a particular prophetic passage might serve as a basis for the development of a biblically based liberation ethic for the disabled. This section hints at the possibilities of constructing such an ethic.

This study also makes evident how important it is that more extensive studies of impairment in the prophetic books be undertaken. Further studies that are more sensitive to varying historical and social contexts among the prophetic books will likely yield more insight about how the construction of disability in ancient Israel is related to its social context.

9

"Living among the Tombs"

Society, Mental Illness, and Self-Destruction in Mark 5:1–20

Holly Joan Toensing

> Mental illness, despite the many recent advances in scientific understand-
> ing and medical treatment, retains about it the musty and unpleasant aura
> of the asylum—and no one, from bioethicists to the mentally ill them-
> selves, cares to visit that place if it can be avoided. (Janet R. Nelson: 190)

In a recent presentation developed for Christian-education classes during
Lent, I express some of the theological and ecclesial dilemmas I have en-
countered since my brother's suicide in 1986 when he was thirty-one years
old. The degree to which Christians have continued to stigmatize, or even
to outright condemn suicides, reverberated into my life and, over the years,
created a spiritual riptide so powerful that to survive I just stopped talking
about it and I just stopped going to church. Only within the last few years
have I come to realize that I had been "standing guard" at my brother's
tomb for nearly twenty years, in part to protect my brother from God's
supposed rejection. There is a sense in which the demoniac story of Mark 5
tells my story of keeping this vigil; harassed by Christianity's demons, I
am the demoniac living among the tombs, shrieking in perpetual mourn-
ing, unwilling to give my brother into hands so bent on delivering him to
hell. Again. For prior to his death, my brother was already living a hell so
intensely real that death seemed his only relief. Pieced together from what
I have been told about my brother's last few years and, occasionally, from
what I directly experienced of him during that time, I discern in the story
of the demoniac my brother's story of struggle with mental illness, which
was most likely (although undiagnosed) paranoid schizophrenia. Critical
reflection on the text of Mark 5 provides a means to "visit that place" so
often avoided, as the epigraph by Janet R. Nelson notes.

The story of the demoniac in Mark 5:1–20 shows both the hope in and
limitations of disability studies—as applied to theological understand-

ing—when it is read as a story of severe mental illness. On the one hand, the demoniac is a man, suffering like so many men and women today, with a stigmatized ailment. On the other hand, miraculous cures may not be available for those living with such mental illnesses today, and a community's long-term, consistent, and compassionate care is vital for confronting our greatest fears about our lives and ourselves.

Mark 5:1–20—Context and Summary

The story of the Gerasene demoniac appears in Mark's Gospel after a long teaching section with parables (3:19b–4:34) and may relieve narrative tension with its bizarre, yet entertaining, details (Tolbert: 166). More specifically, the story occurs immediately after Jesus calmed the waters and winds of a storm on the Sea of Galilee, which he and his disciples were crossing (4:35–41). Having just witnessed Jesus' ability to control natural phenomena, the disciples were left a bit shaky-legged, wondering as others in the Gospel already had, "Who then is this?" (4:41).

The crossing "to the other side" (εἰς τὸ πέραν) (4:35; 5:1) is important because it is the first time in the Gospel that Jesus takes his ministry into predominantly Gentile territory, considered ritually unclean, also signaled by the presence of pigs (5:11–13) because Jews were not allowed to eat, let alone keep, them. The narrative emphasizes this point explicitly by describing Jesus' first encounter in the foreign territory as a man with "an unclean spirit" (πνεύματι ἀκαθάρτῳ), typically referred to simply as the Gerasene demoniac (5:2). Traditional scholarly interpretations of the story focus on the first-century religious conflicts between Jews and Gentiles, claiming that Jesus' exorcism suggests a cleansing of the land of pagan idols and readying it for further mission (Jasper: 68–69; Wefald: 14–15).

In a Gospel that clips along with apocalyptic urgency, the story of this demon possession captures readers' attention because of its length; at twenty verses, the Gerasene demoniac story is the longest healing story in Mark's Gospel. Its relative length invites a sort of settling into its story-world. The plot has three overlapping foci, each of which I elaborate on in the essay and relate to severe mental illness: it describes first the demoniac's situation or experience; second, the surrounding community's usual response to the demoniac; and then, last, Jesus' exorcism of the demon from the man.

From the vantage point of where he had been living among the tombs near the mountains, the demoniac saw Jesus arriving and went to meet him. The demoniac had been living in the tombs for some time, engaging in self-destructive behavior and howling day and night (5:2, 5). Apparently with some success early on, the surrounding community had often restrained the man, but was no longer able to do so because he had grown so strong that he was able to break the chains that bound him (5:3–4). However, Jesus proved stronger than the demon, demanding that it come out of the man and permitting it to enter into a herd of pigs instead, which promptly rushed to destruction over a cliff and into the sea (5:8–13). Jesus' actions made the community afraid, and they begged him to leave (5:15–17). When the man who had once been possessed by the demon wanted to leave with Jesus, too, Jesus refused and instead commanded him to go home and tell everyone about what had happened to him (5:18–20).

Methodology—Disability Studies Approach and Mental Illness

Some scholars may object to interpreting Mark's story of the demoniac in terms of mental illness today because modern, Western notions of self that ground contemporary psychology contrast so greatly with what has been argued as the concept of self for the ancient first-century Mediterranean personality (Strecker: 120). Certainly, examining the first-century Mediterranean context of the story of the demoniac elicits useful insights that expand and can transform one's understanding of the text. However, the demand to see the text only through this lens at the exclusion or denigration of other perspectives threatens the idea that biblical texts are living traditions that are challenged and renewed by lived experience of ongoing generations of Christians.

Given the fact that throughout most of Western history people believed that behaviors associated with what we call mental illness today were caused literally by demon possession, the demoniac story of Mark 5 and others like it certainly contributed to the stigmatization and ill treatment of the mentally ill. Mentally ill persons were perceived as weak-willed or flawed in some way to have given the demon—even Satan himself—a foothold in their lives, even welcoming it. Moreover, what was associated with the demonic or Satan was often perceived to be violent and so the mentally ill were feared, segregated, restrained, and even executed. Although other etiological theories of mental illness have come to dominate since the eighteenth century, the theory of a spiritual cause still persists, as does the stigmatization of the mentally ill. Interpreting the demoniac story of Mark 5 using the lens of disability studies gives readers an opportunity not only to understand how such texts may contribute to this stigmatization, but also to explore the textual resources for changing those perceptions or for thinking differently about the theory of a spiritual cause for mental illness.

Two models within disability studies are useful for interpreting the story of the demoniac of Mark 5. The medical model understands disability as a loss of function or ability of a particular body part (McCloughry and Morris 2002; Mitchell and Snyder 1997). The disability itself lies within the body of the individual and is a medical or biological condition. The goal is to correct, cure, or restore that loss of function/ability in order to bring the affected area back into "normal" range. In contrast, the minority or social group model argues that the problem of disability does not reside

within a particular body part of the individual, but in the way society creates physical and attitudinal barriers that limit a person's ability within
society (Eiesland 1994 and 1998). Society not only stigmatizes disabled
bodies as flawed, inferior, dangerous, and dependent, but also erects social
and physical barriers to marginalize, segregate, devalue, and discriminate
against people with disabilities.[1]

Both models in disability studies have offered more fully integrated
and hopeful lives to many people with mental illness who in decades past
would have been institutionalized. Examining mental illness as a biochem-
ical brain disease, the medical model encouraged the development of new
drug therapies to restore proper brain chemical balance. Indeed, deinstitutionalization of mentally ill patients became a reality in part because of
these medications. Similarly, the minority group model has done much
to confront society's prejudices. It fueled the disability rights movement
of the 1960s and '70s that supported the deinstitutionalization of the disabled by emphasizing the principle of autonomy, that is, the right of the
person to be self-determining and to exercise individual freedom through
independent living and equal access. With the new residential programs,
new medications, new therapies, and new systems of providing care that
have emerged, 50 to 80 percent of mentally ill individuals may improve
and recover (Neugeboren: 338).

However, both the medical model and the minority group model have
limitations that certain mental illnesses bring to the fore. Some mental illnesses are resistant to pharmacological therapies and therefore challenge
the medical model approach that mental illness is "just a chemical imbal-
ance" that can be "fixed" with the proper medicine. Similarly, those with
mental illnesses that significantly diminish decision-making capabilities,
making them "feel like they cannot trust their own thought processes and
feelings" (Black: 164), challenge the minority group model that emphasizes
rationality as the necessary and sufficient condition for autonomous moral
action taken by an independent agent (Janet R. Nelson: 186). Rational self-
determination may remain elusive or greatly compromised in certain cases
of mental illness. Jay Neugeboren pointedly reminds us that "these same
statistics [that between 50–80 percent of individuals with mental illness
improve or recover with treatment] . . . are telling us that twenty or thirty
or forty or fifty men and women out of every hundred afflicted with serious mental illness do *not* improve or recover" (338). These experiences
invite closer attention, and the demoniac story of Mark 5 offers a way to
understand their complexities.

---

    1. For a description of how stigmatization emerges and functions within so-
ciety, see Erving Goffman's book *Stigma*.

Demon Possession and Severe Mental Illness— Similarity of Experience

When Jesus arrived in the Gentile territory of the Gerasenes,[2] a man with an "unclean spirit" (πνεύματι ἀκαθάρτῳ) immediately met him (5:2). This spirit presumably had entered into the man from the outside because Jesus commanded the demon to "come out" (ἔξελθε) of him (5:8), and when it does, it "entered into" (εἰσῆλθον) a herd of pigs nearby (5:13). By the second century C.E., virtually everyone in the Mediterranean world believed that good and evil spirits/demons lived in a realm immediately above the earth and that they would harass people or enter into and take possession of them (Dodds: 38; Frieden: 44–46; Koester: 141). Certain possessions were viewed more positively, if the possessed person could be shown to work miracles, speak in the language of angels, foretell the future, and read people's minds (Collins: 47; Dodds: 55). Earlier in Mark's Gospel, Jesus' healings had prompted some to wonder if he had become possessed. This is expressed in the Gospel as an accusation that Jesus "had gone out of his mind" (ἐξέστη) (3:21). The Jewish leaders are depicted as characterizing Jesus' actions less ambiguously as the work of an evil spirit associated with Satan (3:22). Readers of the Gospel know, however, that the Holy Spirit—not an evil spirit—descended upon Jesus at his baptism when God verbally affirmed Jesus as his son (1:10).

Because the self-proclaimed name of the demon, "Legion" (λεγιὼν) (5:9), designated a military command of Roman soldiers, some scholars explored the first-century Mediterranean experience of the Roman military as suggestive of what may have caused demon possession. Developing Frantz Fanon's contemporary theory of the "Manicheism" of colonization, these interpretations highlight the degree to which Roman techniques for military conquests and colonization terrorized populations. In the experience of villagers in Palestine, they argue, the Roman legions "would more than once have attacked their villages unmercifully, burning their houses, slaughtering or enslaving the people, [and] plundering their goods" (Horsley: 140). The population could do little but comply or find indirect ways to protest, for example by expressing the hopelessness and madness of their existence through the experience of demon possession. Thus, demon possession was a sanctioned way to act and speak out against one's oppressed situation, a strategy then vicariously participated in by the rest of the oppressed community (Horsley: 140). According to this theory, that the community begged Jesus to leave after they saw the former demoniac in

---

2. The action of the story takes place just off the eastern coast of the Sea of Galilee in the country or territory of the Gerasenes (Γερασηνων), presumably near a city with that same name (5:1). Geographically, however, none of the known cities to which this could refer—Gergesa, Gadara, and even Gerasa—is as close to the coast as this story narrates. Thus, the historical setting of the story is ambiguous.

his right mind (5:17) demonstrates their frustration with Jesus for removing their indirect form of protest against the Roman military.

However, debate remains regarding the portrait of the Roman military in these discussions. Just how unwelcome the Roman military was in the Decapolis, where the story takes place, is unclear. Alexander the Great likely founded Hellenistic cities in the region. However, because the specific term "Decapolis" is found in later literature, the loose league or federation of ten of these cities may have formed after Pompey's successful campaigns in 64–63 B.C.E. to take back the cities that had fallen to Jewish incursions when Seleucid control waned (Rey-Coquias). Far from resisting Roman intervention, cities in this region, such as Gadara and Gerasa, welcomed it and even celebrated it by instituting new eras, sometimes minting new coins that read "year 1 in the liberty of Rome." Establishing a legion in the area in 66 C.E. came partly as a result of these cities complaining to the Roman emperor that Jews were harassing and ransacking the villages. The specific mention of "legion" makes it difficult not to examine historical aspects of the Roman military, although Mark's Gospel may simply have wanted to use it as a reference point to understand the enormity of the possession: the demon states his name and then explains, "for we are many" (ὅτι πολλοί ἐσμεν) (5:9).

Nevertheless, this theory rightly highlights how environmental stressors significantly influence the ways that people view and respond to the world around them and may contribute to the development of mental illness. However, mental illness can strike regardless of social status; it does not afflict just those who are marginalized or oppressed by society. Moreover, such theories seem to suggest that mental illness is a rational reaction, choice, or strategy. Severe mental illness is not experienced as a rational choice or conscious strategy, as if one can turn it on and off.

Regardless of the degree to which environmental stressors cause demon possession, Mark's Gospel describes how, once inside, the demon had taken control of the man's speech and behavior to such a degree that he was nearly unrecognizable as a human being: like a wild animal, the demoniac broke shackles and chains meant to subdue him (5:4), was apparently unclothed (5:15), and continually wandered isolated places howling (5:5). The demon within the man—not the man himself—responded to Jesus' question and commands (5:7–12).

Those who experience severe mental illness often describe, too, that something descends into their bodies and takes control of them, often resulting in uncharacteristic human speech and behavior. Stewart Govig describes the almost animal-like language that regularly emitted from his son John, who was diagnosed with schizophrenia: he would make "urgent, high-pitched, strange subvocal sounds. At times what seemed like a dog's muffled bark broke through the stormy monologue" (35). These episodes were often accompanied by hyperactive, disorganized activity, which is also associated with some forms of severe mental illness. Once, during an episode of these voices, John demanded that his father stop the van he was driving, and the moment it did, "the grimacing youth burst out the side door to commence a rapid, circular, jerky pace" (36). As quoted by Kay Redfield Jamison, a close friend of Drew Sopirak poignantly describes similar characteristics of Drew during one of his hospitalizations for a severe form of bipolar disorder:

> I remember when [Drew] was hospitalized in D.C. and I went to visit him. His mom left to get dinner, and he laid his head in my lap, curled up in the fetal position. I saw with my eyes the man's face I knew as Drew, but my ears heard another creature. Something else seemed to live in his shell. Someone other than Drew brought words to his lips or created his awkward, disturbing actions. As he rubbed his head, as though to bring his thoughts to some sort of sanity, I looked at him and wondered where my friend had disappeared to. This monster had taken over. He was gaunt and had not shaved in weeks. His skin was sallow and his cheeks sunken; each movement appeared painful. I did not know this person he had become. The more he talked the more my fear for him grew. (1999:62–63)

Like the demoniac in Mark 5, Drew seemed completely controlled by something else that pulled him further and further away from anything recognizably human.

The precipice of death loomed in the life of the demoniac as described in Mark 5. To emphasize its constant presence, the text states three times that the tombs (μνημεῖον) were the possessed man's haunt, away from society and community (5:2, 3, 5). In fact, he "had a home" there (τὴν κατοίκησιν εἶχεν) (5:3), perhaps among tombs designed to resemble small houses and temples (Evans: 17). However, the Greek verb used is the imperfect form of ἔχω and may express the sense that though the man has come habitually to live among the tombs, he has not truly found a home there. Death, though close, has not yet settled. That the demoniac continually bruised/cut himself with stones surely brought him closer to death's door over time (5:5). He literally and spatially occupied the liminal state of being "the living dead"—alive, but for all practical, social purposes already dead.

Similarly, death can be precariously close at hand for those with severe mental illness. A friend of mine recalls how her brother, struggling with bipolar disorder, lingered in that "living dead" state so long that she never knew if, on any given day, she was going to find him dead or alive when she turned the handle to his apartment door. Severe mental illness carries dramatically increased chances of suicide attempts, completions, and, in fewer cases, violence towards others (1999:117; Hendershott: 42). Robert Bayley, as quoted by Jamison, describes how his schizophrenia regularly and uncontrollably brought on suicide attempts: "[The voices'] commands are abrasive and all encompassing. . . . I have run in front of speeding cars and severed arteries while feeling this compulsion to destroy my own life. As their tenacity gains momentum, there is often no element of choice which leaves me feeling both tortured and drained" (1999:119–20). The persistence and pervasiveness of these episodes do not remotely correspond with the trivializing comment that "we all have our 'bad' days." Jamison explains: "To be frightened of the world; to be walled off from it and harangued by voices; to see life as distorted faces and shapes and colors; to lose constancy and trust in one's brain: for most the pain is beyond conveying" (1999:119). Isolation from community, due either to one's own withdrawal or to the attrition of friends and family, invariably worsens the situation. Sometimes even if others succeed at making connection, the nature of the connection can exacerbate the struggle, which I explain next.

The Demoniac, the Severely Mentally Ill, and Community Response

How the community deals with the demoniac is highlighted by a singular action, "No one could restrain (δῆσαι) him" (5:3). This action is then intensified in the text by its developed description of means, frequency, and intent of that restraint: "not even with a chain (ἀλύσει); for he had often (πολλάκις) been restrained with shackles (πέδαις) and chains . . . to subdue (δαμάσαι) him" (5:3b–4).

For this community, restraining the demoniac may not have only kept the man from the place of death—the tombs—but also possibly from death itself. The tombs were places for the dead, places where demons were believed to lurk (Collins: 46). Restraining the demoniac may signal that the community valued his life by keeping him away from the potentially dangerous influence of the very spirits by which he was possessed. Hellenistic culture allowed regular visits to the tomb of a loved one as an acceptable funerary practice (McCane: 11), and self-mutilation—possibly tattooing—was associated with pagan funerary rites (Lev 19:28; 21:5; Deut 14:1). However, because the demoniac was doing these things "always, night and day" (διὰ παντὸς νυκτὸς καὶ ἡμέρας) (5:5), community members may have begun to worry about the outcome of his self-destructive action. Thus, it is conceivable that they would have used restraints to keep this man from taking his own life.

Alternatively, the community may have repeatedly attempted to restrain the possessed man to end his public nuisance, for he was constantly "howling" (κράζων) among the tombs and on the mountains (5:5). While graveyards were typically in isolated areas away from the boundaries of a community, the shrieking of the demoniac may have echoed across the land, preventing the community from forgetting about the man's presence. His noises may have been a public nuisance that restraint (and gagging) could temper.

Similarly, the restraints may have also represented insurance of community protection from the man. The text details the extent to which the man was apparently self-destructive. Was it just a matter of time before he would lash out at others? Had he, indeed, already done so? While the text suggests that the demoniac kept to the tombs and mountains, the Greek verb δέω ("to restrain or bind") was often associated with imprisonment (5:3–4). Were the villagers trying to arrest the man for prior assaults on individuals in the community? Or was just the fear that he might descend on the villagers in a violent rage so great that they wanted to remove that possibility altogether and to control or limit his range? After all, the Greek word for "subdue" (δαμάσαι) suggests taming the unpredictability of a wild animal in order to gain control of and then to manipulate its behavior. Bound and gagged the demoniac could pose no danger to the community, and he could be punished for any past crimes.

Even today, restraints are a common approach to dealing with the severely mentally ill. Before the mid–twentieth century in the United States, institutionalization of those deemed mentally ill was guided by the principle of paternalism: in order to prevent harm or to provide benefit for the mentally ill person, intervention was justified (Janet R. Nelson: 181). Unfortunately, this often meant involuntary and arbitrary commitment of persons to asylums. Those committed were typically restrained with chains and shackles, just as the demoniac had often been. Treatment focused on behavior control and modification primarily through egregious use of radical and invasive psychosurgery and electroconvulsive therapy (181).

As the worst of the horrors of mistreatment within asylums came to light in the 1950s, '60s, and '70s under the watchful eye of civil rights and social reform movements, both deinstitutionalization as policy and the closing of those institutions gained momentum. E. Fuller Torrey writes,

> In effect, approximately 92 percent of the people who would have been living in public psychiatric hospitals in 1955 were not living there in 1994. . . . [This means] that approximately 763,391 severely mentally ill people (over three-quarters of a million) are living in the community today who would have been hospitalized 40 years ago. That number is more than the population of Baltimore or San Francisco. (8–9)

Supporting deinstitutionalization, the community health movement and social service initiatives emerged at this time, and federal programs officially recognized mental illness as a disability. The disability rights movement also fueled deinstitutionalization because it argued against the principle of paternalism and for the principle of autonomy. "Freedom from restraint" for the mentally ill legally came to mean that unless they posed an immanent danger to others, the mentally ill needed to be treated in the "least restrictive setting possible," living life as they wished (Hendershott: 35). The laws and initiatives regarding deinstitutionalization made this hope a reality, and many of those with mental illnesses previously institutionalized thrived and had more fully independent lives outside institutions.

However, adequate funding, coordination of, and commitment to the community-based mental health care system were only sporadic, if existent at all. Long-held social stigmas that link violence with the mentally ill led not only to decreases in community funding for the very programs the mentally ill desperately needed, but also to refusals to allow group homes to be developed in stable residential neighborhoods (Black: 165). Thus, fear of the mentally ill forced agencies to build or establish their centers and group homes in out-of-the-way, difficult-to-reach industrial parks or in crime-ridden neighborhoods that do not have the power to protest such development, all contributing to the alienation and isolation of the mentally ill (Janet R. Nelson: 185). Moreover, the medicines that worked to restore proper chemical balance in the brain were not effective for everyone. Autonomy and independence remained elusive for a substantial number of people with severe forms of mental illness; hence, the lack of consistent access to and connection with care coupled with societal stigma and alienation spiraled many into further mental deterioration.

Under these conditions, the fate of those deinstitutionalized with severe mental illness or those with more recently developed mental illness is oftentimes bleak. Deinstitutionalization, for these people, has been what Torrey calls "a psychiatric Titanic." He explains: "Their lives are virtually devoid of 'dignity' or 'integrity of body, mind, and spirit.' 'Self-determination' often means merely that the person has a choice of soup kitchens. The 'least restrictive setting' frequently turns out to be a cardboard box, a jail cell, or a terror-filled existence plagued by both real and imaginary enemies" (11). Not dissimilar to the experience of the Gerasene demoniac restrained time and again (Mark 5:4), the usual pattern for those with severe mental illness is a revolving door of reinstitutionalization, from asylums to jails and prisons across the country, with no end clearly in sight. Chains and shackles have shape-shifted into prison cells and sometimes, worst of all, isolation boxes. The helplessness of the situation cries out for any measure of hope.

Jesus' Exorcism—
Its Message for Those Dealing with Severe Mental Illness

The last part of the narrative describes Jesus' exorcism, aspects of which are reminiscent of the medical model within disability studies in that the exorcism, almost like a miracle drug, restored the man to functionality and to "normalcy." As if to emphasize that no sane stunt double stepped in to trick bystanders, the text states, "the very man who had had the legion" was found in his "right mind" (σωφρονοῦντα), "sitting" (καθήμενον), and "having been clothed" (ἱματισμένον) (5:15), whereas before he continually wandered, howled, bruised or cut himself, and in so doing presumably tore his clothes off (5:5). His restoration to "normal" again allowed the former demoniac to be reincorporated into society: Jesus sent him back home to his own people (5:19). The recovery is nothing short of miraculous. This exorcism makes for a great story: the one accused of having a demon (Jesus, 3:21–22) now controlled a legion of demons; the one oppressed/possessed who was on the brink of death (the demoniac) now was rid of his oppressor, found life and community again, and watched his oppressor's destruction in the sea (5:13)!

These details can be satisfying to those not actually dealing with severe mental illness, but spiritually alienating to those whose lives are affected by it. What of the mentally ill person who has been taken to exorcisms and feverishly prayed over more times than she could count, all to no avail? Had she not been "good enough"? Did she, or her parents, not have (strong enough) faith, itself a prerequisite for successful healings in Mark's Gospel (5:36; 9:22–24)? What of the person for whom the latest "miracle drug" does not provide the cure he expected and hoped for? Also echoing a limitation of the minority group model within disability studies, would the man in this story really survive on his own, autonomous and in dependent in the community but far from the one who brought healing to him? And what if Jesus had arrived an hour later, a day later—would that have been too late to save the man from his constant cutting of himself, his legion of demons? After recovering from a suicide attempt, Jamison asked, "Where *had* God been?" (1999:311). As she spiraled further and further to death's edge, no Jesus arrived on her shore of utter despair to keep her from the jumping-off point.

However, other aspects of the story may attest to the complexity of living with mental illness and reveal signs of hope. First, an overlooked aspect of the exorcism points to the long, arduous struggle for understanding and perhaps even for life itself among the mentally ill. Recall that the man had apparently struggled for a substantial amount of time with a legion of demons within him: the community had "often" (πολλάκις) restrained him (5:4), but with time found this increasingly difficult, and eventually no one could restrain him "any longer" (οὐκέτι) (5:3). When the legion of demons was exorcised from the man, they separated and individually entered a herd of about two thousand pigs (5:13). Whereas the man had endured an entire legion of demons within him for quite some time, significantly one pig could not even for a moment struggle with one demon, and all two thousand of them immediately rushed to their destruction over the cliff and into the sea (5:13). This story may help others understand the enormity of the battle within that the mentally ill are forced to take up, oftentimes with strength of will and courage that goes unacknowledged. For some this battle may be with voices they hear or images they see. Literally trying to stay sane in this context is a massive undertaking on a daily basis. Similarly, many struggle long and hard with their necessary dependency on pharmacological regimens that "flatten" or "age" them seemingly beyond recognition.

The story line of the Gospel follows Jesus, so when Jesus leaves the community, the story of the demoniac ends. We are not privileged to see how the man fared over time and whether he ever became possessed again. Nevertheless, the second point is that the text emphasizes community. "Home" is not in isolation from society, among the tombs, but a family, friends, a neighborhood, a people, even a region: in response to Jesus' command to "go to your home to your people/friends" (ὕπαγε εἰς τὸν οἶκόν σου πρὸς τοὺς σούς), the man went to the Decapolis—a region of ten loosely federated Hellenistic cities (5:19)! Connection with others reinforces the healing that Jesus provided. Time and again, those whose lives are affected by severe mental illness assert that medicines alone often do not work as effectively as when they are combined with human interaction via psychological services, jobs, or visits and communication with friends and family (Jamison 1995; Neugeboren). This approach seems to address the complexity that severe mental illness presents.

Third, with community come stories. Significantly, Jesus commands the man to "Go tell" (ἀπάγγειλον), and the man complied: "he went away and began to proclaim" (κηρύσσειν) (Mark 5:19–20). The command is significant in the context of Mark's Gospel for it is related to the word for "the good news" of God (εὐαγγέλιον, 1:1, 14–15) that both John the Baptist and Jesus "proclaim" (κηρύσσων, 1:4, 14, 38–39; 3:14). Therefore, the text asserts that the demoniac's story is vitally—not marginally—important to the mission and ministry of the gospel (1:39; 3:15; 9:38–41). Similarly, the command to go and tell others contrasts starkly with Jesus' earlier commands given to those whom he healed *not* to tell anyone about him (1:44; 3:12). For those struggling to heal, telling the story of one's release from terror and horror can reinforce the initial healing, foster connections between people, bring awareness to others about one's experiences, and can even create deeper peace.

Fourth, the telling of the story ultimately becomes a lesson of compassion, an opportunity for connection. Whatever else the man might say about his experience, he must tell others "what the Lord has done (πεποίηκεν), what mercy (ἠλέησέν) he has shown" him (5:19). The aorist tense of the verb "to have mercy" denotes a one-time act, yet the perfect tense of the verb "to do" denotes lasting effects. Any single act of compassion makes a deep impression. Donald Capps states:

> [Love's] medicinal effect is to expand our very sense of life's connections, enabling us to view our own fragile connections in relation to the whole of all that exists. We can see that gentle deeds of love lead inexorably to connections our wintry minds could not have contemplated, for they were hampered and curtailed by visions of life as stable and unchanging. . . . Mental illness is one of the vicissitudes of life that threatens the connections—within and between selves—that are essential to human

life itself. Love is a balm that salves the frayed connections and creates new connections that were heretofore beyond our capacity to contemplate. (254)

Compassion, this quote suggests, changes the perspectives of everyone involved and allows us to move beyond ourselves, our walls, into uncharted territory.

Finally, there is no greater uncharted territory than that wherein one's assumptions about identity are challenged. As the exorcism begins, the demons ask Jesus quite literally, "What is there to us/ours and (at the same time) to you/yours?" (τί ἐμοὶ καὶ σοί), which could be translated more smoothly as "What do we have in common?" (Mark 5:7). Having, or establishing, common ground appears to have a part in the exorcism, in the healing.

It is only after Jesus learns the name of the demon—"Legion"—that he is able to exorcise it from the man (5:9). Knowing and speaking someone's name constituted power in the ancient world. Neugeboren knows something of this power, too, in relation to dealing with severe mental illness: He begins, "In some ideal village of my imagination . . ." and then proceeds to take readers through a scenario of how individual community members would respond to his severely mentally ill brother Robert on one of his bad days (327–32). In this ideal imaginary community, each person who encounters Robert calls him by name, does not bring undue attention to his agitation, but talks to him about ordinary things they might have in common. In this way, those who help Robert gently guide him through a difficult day that easily could have been disastrous. The story of the Gerasene demoniac may help to emphasize the need for community—people who know each other, or at least people who are willing to reach into the world of another to discover how they are similar. Capps poignantly writes, "Perhaps the vocation of these 'strangers in our midst' [loved ones who are severely mentally ill] is to witness to the stranger who lives, unacknowledged and unrecognized, in all of us. Recognition of our own self-alienation is the first step on the difficult journey of making peace with ourselves" (199).

The story of the Gerasene demoniac offers numerous and more richly complex possibilities for addressing the alienation surrounding severe mental illness than what, at first glance, seems possible from a simple miraculous healing story. Through narrative, readers are invited to (1) honor the enormity of the battle of mental illness; (2) create communities, strong networks of care that foster mental health; (3) tell and listen to the stories of struggle and victory with mental illness; (4) be compassionate; and (5) to find and name the numerous commonalities between people regardless of mental status.

10

"For Whenever I Am Weak, Then I Am Strong"

Disability in Paul's Epistles

Martin Albl

This essay attempts to explicate the understanding of disability in Paul's letters. I hope to show that disability is not a peripheral or incidental topic in Paul's thought; rather, it is one that brings us to the very heart of Paul's central beliefs about the human and divine.

I begin with a few remarks about my approach. I restrict my study to the epistles regarded by a consensus of scholars as authentically written by Paul (Dunn: 13). In particular, my focus is on the Letter to the Galatians and, most especially, on Paul's Corinthian correspondence.

In seeking to explicate Paul's understanding of disability, I will, to the extent possible, use Paul's own language and concepts. As Dale B. Martin warns, modern conceptions of "physical," "mental," and "spiritual," influenced by Cartesian dualism, do not correspond well with ancient ways of understanding the body (3–6). As with any study of the past, we must try to avoid reading our contemporary concepts into an ancient text.

My understanding of the modern term "disability," however, must be clarified at the outset. In this essay, of course, I cannot do justice to the complex contemporary debates in disability studies. I shall simply follow David Wasserman by referring to two basic aspects of disability: (1) disability conceived as a kind of natural impairment or functional limitation (a biomedical condition) and (2) disability construed as the social stigma or limitations placed by a society on certain groups who are labeled as "disabled" (219–22). Both aspects are evidenced in Paul's thought.

Paul wrote in a bicultural context, and, in order to comprehend his thought, one must consider both the ancient Jewish and the ancient Hellenistic background. I assume that both are important and make no attempt to disentangle the influence of one or the other in particular cases (compare Dunn: 54–55).

The essay falls into three major sections: (1) Paul's general understanding of disability; (2) Paul's view of disability in the context of his gospel message; and (3) analysis of Paul's personal experience with disability as related in Gal 4:13–14 and 2 Cor 12:1–10.

Paul's Terminology of Disability: "Weakness" and "Flesh"

Perhaps the closest ancient Greek parallel to the modern term "disability" is the word ἀσθενής ("weak") and its correlates. Within the New Testament, this word grouping refers to a variety of what modern Western observers would call "physical" disabilities or illnesses (Stählin: 492; see Luke 10:9; John 5:5; Acts 28:9; Jas 5:14). Paul echoes this use; in 1 Cor 11:30, ἀσθενής is paralleled with ἄρρωστος, a common term for those who are physically ill (BAGD, s.v.). Below I shall study two further passages (Gal 4:13–14 and 2 Cor 12:1–10) that are also generally understood as references to physical limitations.

In other cases, however, ἀσθενής clearly refers to something more than a "physical" disability. In Rom 14:1, Paul employs a verbal form of ἀσθενής to describe someone "weak in faith" (cf. 1 Cor 8:9).[1] Ἀσθενής can also refer to the weakness of the human condition in general, including mental or emotional faculties: "I am speaking in human terms because of your natural limitations" (διὰ τὴν ἀσθένειαν τῆς σαρκός: literally, "because of the weakness of your flesh"; Rom 6:19). Paul contrasts our present human body (σῶμα ψυχικόν), "sown in weakness" (ἀσθένεια), with the resurrected spiritual body (σῶμα πνευματικόν), "raised in power" (δύναμις; 1 Cor 15:43–44).

This sense of the weakness of human nature is also reflected in Paul's use of the term σάρξ (flesh). Following classical Greek usage, Paul at times can use the term to refer to the physical body as a whole (e.g., 1 Cor 15:39; Schweizer, Baumgärtel, and Meyer: 99–101). But in a more extended sense, it refers to the fragility and temporality of all human life; in this sense, it commonly translates the similar conceptual range of the Hebrew term בשׂר (Schweizer, Baumgärtel, and Meyer: 105–7). Thus Paul speaks of "mortal flesh" (θνητὴ σάρξ) and holds that flesh and blood, because they are essentially weak and perishable, "cannot inherit the Kingdom of God" (1 Cor 15:50; Dunn: 64).

At times, Paul associates σάρξ with the power of sin and sees it as opposed to God: "the mind that is set on the σάρξ is hostile to God" (Rom 8:7). But I agree with Dunn that Paul does not think of σάρξ as evil or sinful in itself; rather, because it is weak and focused on transient earthly reality, σάρξ is vulnerable to the influence of sin and evil (66–67). Paul also uses

---

1. Unless otherwise noted, all biblical translations are NRSV.

the terms σάρκικος ("fleshly") and κατὰ σάρκα ("according to the flesh") to describe a way of thinking and acting based on human weakness.

In contrast to ἀσθενής, Paul uses the terms ἰσχυρός (strong) or δυνατός (powerful). The term δυνατός is especially interesting for our current discussion, since its range of meaning includes not only the sense of "powerful," but also carries the broader sense of the ability to perform certain functions or tasks (BAGD, s.v.). Most often, the term δυνατός and its cognates are applied directly to the divine: God, Christ, and the Spirit (e.g., 1 Cor 2:5; 1 Cor 5:4; and Rom 15:13). Quite telling for Paul's understanding is 2 Cor 4:7, "But we have this treasure in clay jars, so that it may be made clear that this extraordinary power (ἡ ὑπερβολὴ τῆς δυνάμεως) belongs to God and does not come from us." A human, in his or her fragile "clay jar," is only powerful or "able" to the extent that the divine works through him or her.

The "Disabled" Christ and the Glorified Christ in Paul's Gospel

Paul's letters, as well as his ministry itself, were focused on his presentation of the "gospel" (εὐαγγέλιον)—the "good news" of God and Jesus Christ (see, e.g., Rom 1:16; 1 Cor 15:1; Gal 1:6–7). In order properly to understand Paul's conception of disability, then, we must set the above terms and concepts within the overall framework of Paul's gospel.

Paul describes Christ as both "disabled" and "powerful." He preached not only "Christ crucified," the "disabled" Christ ("crucified in weakness, 2 Cor 13:4), but also the glorified, powerful Christ—the Christ beyond all disabilities and limitations, including the limitation of death itself (e.g., Rom 6:9). It is the paradoxical connection between the two that is the center of Paul's message.

The key to the paradox is Paul's "Adam Christology": Paul's understanding of Christ as a representative of all humanity (Dunn: 200–204). Just as Adam represents humans in their weak nature, characterized as ἀσθενής and σάρκικος, so Christ represents a human nature that is freed of those "disabilities." The comparison is explicit in two passages: Rom 5:12–21 and 1 Cor 15:21–22, 45. "For if the many died through the one man's [i.e., Adam's] trespass, much more surely have the grace of God and the free gift in the grace of the one man, Jesus Christ, abounded for the many" (Rom 5:15). "For as all die in Adam, so all will be made alive in Christ" (1 Cor 15:22). "The first man, Adam, became a living being; the last Adam [Christ] became a life-giving spirit" (1 Cor 15:45).

What connects Christ as the representative of a renewed humanity with the crucified Christ? In Paul's gospel, God sent the divine Christ in order to save humanity from its condition of sin and death, a salvation effected through Christ's sharing in the weak human condition. Thus, God sent "his own Son in the likeness of sinful flesh, and to deal with sin, he condemned sin in the flesh" (Rom 8:3; cf. 2 Cor 5:21; Dunn: 202–3).

The ultimate sharing in human weakness included a sharing in death. It is clear that in Paul's thinking, Christ's death was a sacrifice that made atonement for human sins (see Dunn: 212–23). "They are now justified by his grace as a gift, through the redemption that is in Christ Jesus, whom God put forward as a sacrifice of atonement by his blood" (Rom 3:24–25). The same thought is conveyed in phrases that refer to the atoning "blood" of Christ (e.g., Rom 5:9: "now that we have been justified by his blood"). Dunn sums up Paul's thinking, "In short, to say that Jesus died as representative of Adamic humankind and to say that Jesus died as sacrifice for the sins of humankind was for Paul to say the same thing" (223).

The Participation of the Followers of Christ in His "Disability" and His "Ability"

In the "Adam Christology," however, Christ did not die as a "substitute" for sinful humans. Rather, again in Dunn's words, "Christ's sharing *their* death makes it possible for them to share *his* death" (223, emphasis original). As representative human, Christ shares in human weakness, suffering, and death; but as followers of Christ, humans also share in his death—they are "interchanged" with Christ (Morna D. Hooker: 42–55). Christ's death can atone for the sins of his followers, because they "participate" in Christ's death. Passages reflective of this interchange between Christ and the believer are numerous:

> Do you not know that all of us who have been baptized into Christ Jesus were baptized into his death? (Rom 6:3)

> We suffer with him. (Rom 8:17)

> [We are] always carrying in the body the death of Jesus. (2 Cor 4:10)

> I have been crucified with Christ. (Gal 2:19)

> I want to know Christ and the power of his resurrection and the sharing of his sufferings by becoming like him in his death. (Phil 3:10; see also Dunn: 482–87)

Paul's language is not merely metaphorical: Christ and his followers share suffering and death in a real, if unspecified, manner (Hooker: 42–43; Proudfoot).

But here is the paradox: Jesus' humiliating, shameful death in ultimate weakness on the cross is the key that unlocks the potential for all followers of Christ to live a life of limitless "ability"—a life of power and glory. The thought is apparent in reading the fuller context of the above passages:

> For if we have been united with him in a death like his, we will certainly be united with him in a resurrection like his. (Rom 6:5)

> If only we suffer with him so that we may also be glorified with him. (Rom 8:17)

[We are] always carrying in the body the death of Jesus, so that the life of
Jesus may also be made visible in our mortal flesh. (2 Cor 4:10)

So it is by sharing in the disability of Christ, including his atoning
death, that the followers of Christ will be able, ultimately, to overcome all
disability by sharing Christ's resurrection and glorification.

The Paradox of the Gospel at Corinth: The "Disabled" God

At the heart of Paul's gospel, of course, are God and Jesus Christ (e.g., Rom
1:1: "gospel of God"; Gal 1:7: "gospel of Christ"). For present purposes, I
must prescind from any discussion of Paul's precise understanding of the
relationship between God and Jesus Christ; it is enough to note that both
God and Christ (together with the Spirit) belong to the divine realm.

At Corinth, Paul presented his gospel as a direct challenge to common ancient expectations regarding the divine and disability. "For Jews
demand signs and Greeks desire wisdom" (1 Cor 1:22): in this brief phrase,
Paul alludes to a conception, held by both Jews and Greeks, that the divine
is overwhelmingly powerful and intelligent.

The Greek word for "signs" is σημεῖα, a word that in a Jewish theological
context would most readily call to mind the phrase σημεῖα καὶ τέρατα—the
"signs and wonders" with which God brought the Hebrew people out of
Egypt (see, e.g., LXX Exod 7:3; 11:9–10; Deut 6:22; 7:19): turning the Nile
to blood, sending thunder and hail, and slaughtering the firstborn. From
within this Jewish tradition, the concept that the divine could be mani-
fested through a crucified person would appear as a "stumbling block"
(literally a "scandal": σκάνδαλον; 1 Cor 1:23).

The second half of Paul's phrase alludes to a Greek conception of the
divine as the ultimate source of wisdom (σοφία), pointing toward the great
Greek tradition of seeking ultimate reality through philosophical thought.
In the eyes of this Greek tradition, the concept of a crucified divine figure
would have been μωρία—a word that Martin Hengel rightly points out
would have meant not merely "foolishness," but something more like an
inconceivable madness (1, 7).

In the ancient world, a crucified person was the ultimate example of
"disability." On the one hand, a crucified person was the ultimate symbol
of "functional limitations"—a person stripped of all ability to do anything
for him or herself. With regard to the second aspect of disability, a crucified
person bore the ultimate in social stigmatization.

In ancient Roman society, Roman citizens or persons with social status
were on occasion crucified (Hengel: 39–45). But, for the most part, the pen-
alty was reserved for criminals, rebels, and slaves (46–63), so much so that
Roman authors such as Tacitus and Livy refer to it simply as the "slaves'
punishment" (*servile supplicium*; Hengel: 51). Hengel describes those who
were crucified as "primarily people who had been outlawed from society
or slaves who on the whole had no rights" (88). "By the public display of

a naked victim at a prominent place—at a crossroads, in the theatre, on high ground, at the place of his crime—crucifixion also represented his uttermost humiliation" (87).

So Paul's message defies all social expectations, "but we proclaim Christ crucified, a stumbling block to Jews and foolishness to the Gentiles" (1 Cor 1:23). It is precisely this crucified Christ who is "the power of God and the wisdom of God" (1 Cor 1:24). "For God's foolishness is wiser than human wisdom, and God's weakness is stronger than human strength" (1 Cor 1:25). Paul completely reverses standard categories of thought, speaking of the "foolishness" (τὸ μωρόν) and "weakness" (τὸ ἀσθενὲς) of the ultimate source of wisdom, strength, and power.

Two Ages and the Overlap of the Ages

Paul's thought here depends on a conception of reality as divided into "two ages." The first age is dominated by sin and death, and in it humanity is characterized as ἀσθενής and σάρκικος. But after the death and resurrection of Christ, a new age has begun, one characterized by spirit (πνεῦμα) and power (δύναμις). But this schema is too simplistic: the followers of Christ in Paul's generation are living in the overlap between the two ages; the spirit and power of the new age are active among them, but they still experience the limitations, the "disabilities" of the old age until Christ returns. This "eschatological tension" is often given the shorthand description "already—not yet": followers of Christ are already experiencing the new life in Christ, but the full experience is "not yet" (Dunn: 461–72).

The "two ages" schema structures Paul's presentation of the gospel in 1 Cor 1. Paul contrasts the values and thinking of "this age" (αἰὼν οὗτος; a reality he also calls "the world"—ὁ κόσμος; 1:20) with the divine values and thinking that characterize the coming age. Paul describes the thinking of the "world" as κατὰ σάρκα—a human orientation "based on the flesh," oriented toward the transitory "age" dominated by sin and death.

In the following table, I summarize Paul's understanding of the two ages. One should note especially the middle column, as it explains Paul's paradoxical use of language. "Christ crucified" signifies foolishness and weakness from the κατὰ σάρκα perspective, but from the divine perspective it signifies power and wisdom.

Worldly values (Social status) Viewed κατὰ σάρκα	Divine values viewed κατὰ σάρκα (Social stigma of disability)	Divine values (Disability transformed into power)
"Wisdom of the wise" (1:19)	Foolishness of the cross (1:18)	Christ crucified: the power of God and the wisdom of God (1:24)
The wise one, the scribe, the debater of "this age"	Christ crucified: stumbling block and foolishness (1:23)	
"Wisdom of the world" (1:20)	"God's foolishness" (1:25)	
Signs and wisdom (1:22)	"God's weakness" (1:25)	

The "Disabled" Paul and the "Disabled" Corinthians

Paul, as a follower of Christ, is "interchanged" with Christ and thus shares the "disabilities" of Christ. Paul recalls that when he first came to the Corinthians,

> I did not come with sublimity of words or of wisdom. For I resolved to know nothing while I was with you except Jesus Christ, and him crucified. I came to you in weakness (ἀσθένεια) and fear and much trembling, and my message and my proclamation were not with persuasive [words] of wisdom, but with a demonstration of spirit and power, so that your faith might rest not on human wisdom but on the power of God. (1 Cor 2:3–5).

Again the paradoxical language: Paul came in weakness (perceived κατὰ σάρκα), but from the divine point of view, his words were accompanied by "a demonstration of spirit and power." Both aspects of disability are in view here: Paul regards his own fear, trembling, and unpersuasive speech as functional disabilities, and no doubt his readers would have agreed in defining Paul as "disabled," from the κατὰ σάρκα perspective. But this very weakness allows the divine power to work through Paul.

At least some of the Corinthians share this sense of human disability. Paul writes, "Consider your own call, brothers and sisters: not many of you were wise by human standards (κατὰ σάρκα), not many were powerful (δυνατοί), not many were of noble birth. But God chose what is foolish in the world to shame the wise; God chose what is weak (τὰ ἀσθενῆ) in the world to shame the strong" (τὰ ἰσχυρά) (1 Cor 1:26). God's purpose is fulfilled by the "disabled" of the world.

In Paul's view, God chooses to reveal himself through the weak and "disabled" of the world so that it might be clear that true power is from God alone. Consider the following:

1 Cor 2:5: God uses Paul's "weak speech" to proclaim the faith, "so that your faith might rest not on human wisdom but on the power of God."

2 Cor 1:9: Paul suffers life-threatening afflictions "so that we would rely not on ourselves, but on God who raises the dead."

2 Cor 4:7: "But we have this treasure in clay jars, so that it may be made clear that this extraordinary power belongs to God and does not come from us." Here, the very fragility of human life is a reminder that true power comes only from the divine.

Yet human disabilities are not only a reminder that true power comes from God; they are also an occasion to participate in the "disability" and atoning death of Christ—the very means that God has employed to raise humans to a life beyond disability and death. Thus Paul recognizes two divine purposes in functional disabilities: (1) they allow the person to realize that true power and ability are not human, but come only from God; (2) they allow the follower of Christ to be "interchanged" with Christ in his suffering and atoning death—and thus open opportunity for the definitive overcoming of all disability in the age to come.

I turn now to consider two further passages, Gal 4:13–14 and 2 Cor 12:1–10, that provide glimpses into Paul's personal experience of disability.

The "Disabled" Paul in Galatians 4:13–14

As his Galatian audience had turned to a "different gospel" from the one he had preached to them (1:6), Paul was concerned to defend the credibility of his message and his own authority. In Hans Dieter Betz's rhetorical analysis, our passage falls in the *probatio* section: Paul's "proofs" of his case. Betz understands 4:12–20 as Paul's fifth "argument"—an emotional appeal to his close bonds of friendship with the Galatians (220–26).

Paul reminds the Galatians of how they had first met, and of the Galatians' initial deep affection for him. "You know that it was because of a physical infirmity that I first announced the gospel to you; though my condition put you to the test, you did not scorn or despise me, but welcomed me as an angel of God, as Christ Jesus" (Gal 4:13–14).

The phrase translated as "physical infirmity" is ἀσθένεια τῆς σαρκός, literally "a weakness of the flesh." As we have seen, ἀσθένεια may refer to any human weakness, "physical" or "mental," while the meaning of σάρξ ranges from the strictly "physical" body to the human condition in general. The precise nature of the disability must thus remain unknown, although the majority of commentators hold that Paul refers to an illness of the physical body (e.g., Betz: 224; Bruce: 208; Schweitzer: 125).[2]

---

2. Based on Paul's following comment, "For I testify that, had it been possible, you would have torn out your eyes and given them to me" (Gal 4:15), some commentators attempt to specify Paul's disability as some sort of eye disease, arguing that the Galatians' affection for him was such that they would have been

What is clear, however, is that Paul's condition involved some sort of functional disability that gave occasion for Paul to preach his gospel to the Galatians. Perhaps the most plausible scenario is that Paul, passing through Galatia on his way to another destination, was forced to stay there due to an illness and thus took the opportunity to preach the gospel to them (Martyn: 420).

Social Stigma and Paul's Disability

Paul writes that "though my condition put you to the test, you did not scorn or despise me" (Gal 4:14). The Greek of the first part of the phrase, καὶ τὸν πειρασμὸν ὑμῶν ἐν τῇ σαρκί μου, is laconic almost to the point of obscurity, reading literally, "your test [or trial] in my flesh." Ancient copyists of Galatians also had trouble with the exact meaning; several manuscripts have the alternative reading, τὸν πειρασμόν μου—"my test [or trial]." But Paul's general meaning is clear enough: his ἀσθένεια τῆς σαρκός presented some kind of a trial for the Galatians (Betz: 224–25). (On the alternative reading, the illness is conceived as a trial for Paul himself; the two alternatives are of course not mutually exclusive.) The key word is πειρασμός, some kind of a trial or test. I identify this πειρασμός with the temptation to attach a social stigma to Paul's disability.

Some commentators speculate that Paul's disability caused him to have a "repulsive physical appearance," which may have been a "trial" for the Galatians (e.g., Wilkinson: 212). Others hold that the Galatians were "tempted" to reject Paul as sinful or demon-possessed, since disabilities were closely connected with sin and evil in both ancient Jewish and ancient Greco-Roman thought (Betz: 225; Martyn: 421). In either case, we are clearly dealing with a negative social definition placed on a disabling condition.

In saying "you did not scorn or despise me" (ἐξουθενήσατε οὐδὲ ἐξεπτύσατε), Paul alludes to this expected social stigma. Of particular interest is Paul's choice of the verb ἐκπτύω. Although by Paul's time the word certainly carried the metaphorical sense of "despise," its original, more literal meaning was "to spit out" (Betz: 225). Possibly, Paul alludes to that more literal meaning here (Schlier: 448).

Even if Paul did not intend a literal reference, a consideration of the

---

willing to replace his diseased eyes with their healthy ones (discussion in Bruce: 209). This speculation is sometimes further connected with the tradition of Paul's temporary blindness recorded in Acts 9:9 and parallels (Wilkinson: 201–2). Betz, however, is doubtless correct to identify this phrase as a standard rhetorical expression of friendship that should not be pressed literally. From a rhetorical standpoint, however, it is remarkable that the Galatians' positive acceptance of Paul and his disability is itself expressed in the metaphorical terms of an impaired condition: the Galatians would have been willing to give up their condition of health and accept a disabling condition in order to restore Paul to health.

original meaning of ἐκπτύω is instructive for shedding light on the ancient stigmatization of disability. The act of spitting carried a wide range of cultural meaning in ancient Jewish and Hellenistic societies. One major sense was an apotropaic one: spitting as a means of keeping a disability away from oneself (see examples in Wilkinson: 218). Thus the first-century Roman writer Pliny says, "We spit on epileptics in a fit, that is, we throw back infection (*contagia*). In a similar way we ward off witchcraft and bad luck which follows meeting a person lame in the right leg" (*Nat.* 28.7, Jones). The playwright Plautus describes epilepsy as *morbus qui insputatur* ("the disease that is spat upon"; *Capt.* 3.4, 550, Nixon). The custom was doubtless connected with the belief that saliva had healing qualities (e.g., Mark 7:33; 8:23; John 9:3; Wilkinson: 117).

Schlier notes that the purpose of spitting could include efforts to ward off the demon that possessed the person with a disability, and indeed demon possession was a common ancient Jewish and Hellenistic etiology of illness. The canonical Gospels, for example, describe a spirit (πνεῦμα) that makes a boy mute and fall to the ground in a seeming epileptic fit (Mark 9:14–29) and portray a woman as "crippled by a spirit (πνεῦμα) for eighteen years" (she is also said to be bound by Satan [Luke 13:11, 18]) (see Avalos 1999:62–63; Pilch: 68–70, 104–6).

Another common ancient etiology held that sin caused disability (e.g., Deut 28; John 9:2; Avalos 1999:64–65). On this view, the Galatians may have been tempted to reject Paul as someone who had been punished by God for his sins (Thomas: 58).

The expected social stigma attached to disability could thus be based on a variety of reasons, ranging from negative reactions to Paul's appearance to beliefs that disability indicated divine displeasure or demonic possession.

Paul commends the Galatians for not accepting these widespread attitudes toward disabilities. Rather than rejecting him as sinful or demon-possessed, the Galatians accepted him "as an angel of God, as Christ Jesus" (Gal 4:14). Again, Paul's language is not merely metaphorical here, as he alludes to the concept of "interchange" between Christ and himself. In accepting Paul's gospel of the crucified Christ, the Galatians also accepted a positive interpretation of his disability. This disability was no longer an occasion to reject Paul, but rather an invitation to recognize the unity between the disabled Paul and the divine Christ—a unity effected by the very disability itself (sharing Christ's atoning death). The disability is thus interpreted not within the context of the demonic, but in the context of the divine.

2 Corinthians: Disability, Social Stigma, and Apostolic Authority

As he was in Galatians, in 2 Corinthians Paul again is at pains to defend his authority as an apostle.[3] In 2 Cor 10–13, Paul is responding to an explicit attack on his apostolic authority by a group he sarcastically labels the "super-apostles" (e.g., 1 Cor 11:5).[4] Amongst other criticisms, the "super-apostles" argued that Paul's disabilities disqualified him as an apostle. Paul quotes their own words: "His letters are weighty and strong, but his bodily presence is weak (ἡ δὲ παρουσία τοῦ σώματος ἀσθενής), and his speech is contemptible" (ἐξουθενημένος; 2 Cor 10:10).

The key phrase, ἡ παρουσία τοῦ σώματος ἀσθενής, may be translated literally as "the presence of [his] body is weak." In common with the passages studied above, Paul's opponents use ἀσθενής for "weak," but instead of σάρξ, use the word σῶμα for "body."

Though the semantic range of σῶμα and σάρξ are distinct, they can at times be used synonymously (Bultmann: 1:233). The term σῶμα can refer specifically to the "physical" body (e.g., Gal 6:17), but it also has the wider meaning of one's "self"—the whole person (e.g., 1 Cor 6:15; Rom 12:1; Bultmann: 1:193–95). In this wider semantic range, Dunn rightly suggests translating σῶμα with a term such as "embodiment"—the whole person, especially in his or her concrete relationships with other persons—as embodied in his or her physical existence (55–58). These points imply that when Paul's opponents say that the presence of Paul's σῶμα is weak, they criticize not only the weakness of his "physical" body, but also his whole person.

The "weakness" of Paul's speech is singled out for special attention. This accusation recalls a similar situation described in 1 Cor 1–2, where Paul admits that he does not speak with "eloquent wisdom," or in "lofty words of wisdom" (1:17; 2:1–4), especially in contrast to the polished "debater of this age" (1 Cor 1:20). In 2 Corinthians, too, Paul admits that he is "untrained (ἰδιώτης) in speech" (11:6). The opponents describe his speech as "contemptible" (ἐξουθενημένος)— a verbal form of the same word Paul uses to describe the expected negative reaction to his disability in Gal 4:13. The opponents thus impugn Paul's authority by pointing out his overall weakness: his physical body, his speech, his whole person is weak.[5]

Martin has shown that this attitude was prevalent in the ancient Greco-Roman world. The "science" of physiognomy claimed the ability

---

3. The literary integrity of 2 Corinthians is commonly questioned; many scholars consider it to be a composite letter (Murray J. Harris: 8–51). For present purposes, however, it is sufficient to note that 2 Cor 10–13 is generally accepted as a coherent literary unit.

4. On the identity of Paul's opponents in 2 Corinthians, see Murray J. Harris: 67–87; Thrall: 2:926–45.

5. This connection between "weak" speaking ability and the authority to speak for the divine has a fascinating parallel in the case of Moses (Exod 4:10).

to read a person's inward character by an analysis of his or her outward body (18–20). Ancient rhetoricians in particular strove to improve their own physical appearance in order to enhance the power of their speeches and used the "science" to point out the weakness of their opponents' bodies as proof of their weakness of character (Martin: 35).[6]

Paul's Response to His Opponents: Reevaluation of Disability

Paul's response to his opponents' attacks once again focuses on the re-evaluation of the meaning of "disability." So anxious is Paul to defend his authority, however, that he begins by defending himself κατὰ σάρκα—on the basis of the "worldly standards" that he no longer accepts (2 Cor 11:18). Paul "boasts" of his descent κατὰ σάρκα: just as his opponents are Israelites, descendants of Abraham, so too is Paul (2 Cor 11:22).

But Paul quickly changes his rhetorical strategy. Instead of continuing, as expected, with a list of his strengths κατὰ σάρκα, Paul presents a long list of his sufferings as an apostle: imprisonments, floggings, beatings, enduring hunger, thirst, cold, and various life-threatening situations (11:23–28). In 11:30, Paul summarizes his approach, "If I must boast, I will boast of the things that show my weakness" (ἀσθένεια). Even in relating his own extraordinary visionary experiences (he "was caught up into Paradise and heard things that are not to be told, that no mortal is permitted to repeat" [12:4]), Paul distances himself from the claim that these events occurred due to his own power or ability: "On behalf of such a one I will boast, but on my own behalf I will not boast, except of my weakness" (12:5).

Paul's "Thorn in the Flesh"

Again alluding to the visionary experiences, Paul comments further, "Therefore, to keep me from being too elated (ὑπεραίρομαι), a thorn (σκόλοψ) was given me in the flesh, a messenger of Satan to torment me, to keep me from being too elated" (12:7). The nature of the "thorn" has been much debated. Thrall sums up the major options: "(i) an internal psychological state, whether of temptation or grief; (ii) external opposition; (iii) physical illness or disability" (2:809–18). As with Paul's condition described in Gal 4:13–14, however, the evidence does not allow a precise identification of the disability. The qualifying phrase "in the flesh" provides little help, as

---

6. J. Albert Harrill shows persuasively that the opponents' attack on Paul's "weak bodily presence" (2 Cor 10:10) falls within a well-established Greco-Roman rhetorical tradition. Based on physiognomic analysis, this sophistic tradition associated physical weakness with slaves and claimed that physical disabilities evidenced one's unfitness for leadership positions. Harrill further shows that in its rejection of the logic of physiognomy, Paul's response shows connections with similar critiques by philosophers in the "Cynic-Socratic" tradition. For a recent study relating physiognomy to a healing narrative in Acts 3–4, see Parsons 2005.

we have seen that σάρξ carries a broad range of meaning, physical and non-physical, and the word σκόλοψ itself could refer to an infinite variety of unpleasant or painful states (Murray: 857–58).[7]

For our purposes, however, the precise nature of the disability matters little. What is clear is that Paul describes it as a condition that "torments" (κολαφίζω) him and from which he asked three times to be freed (12:8). Paul himself experienced this condition as a disability, some kind of functional limitation. And indeed, Paul associates it with the demonic realm in identifying it as a "messenger [or angel] of Satan" (ἄγγελος Σατανᾶ).

But Paul qualifies this view in the very same phrase: "a thorn [messenger of Satan] was given (ἐδόθη) me." Commentators rightly recognize this as an example of the "divine passive"—a way of obliquely referring to divine activity (Lambrecht: 202; Thrall 2:806). Thus, although Paul sees Satan's messenger as the instrumental cause of the disability, the ultimate cause is the Lord.[8]

In response to his triple request to be relieved of the disability, Paul notes that the Lord replied, "My grace is sufficient for you, for power is made perfect in weakness" (2 Cor 12:9). Paul's own response was to conclude, "So I will boast all the more gladly of my weaknesses, so that the power of Christ may dwell in me. Therefore, I am content with weaknesses, insults, hardships, persecutions, and calamities for the sake of Christ; for whenever I am weak, then I am strong" (2 Cor 12:9–10).

One may perhaps detect a movement in Paul's own thought. He at first stigmatized the disability as a demonic force, a "messenger of Satan," and he sought to be free from it. But after his revelation from the Lord, Paul interprets the disability as a condition about which he will be content and even "boast." He sees that the disability, even if instrumentally associated with the demonic, is ultimately of divine origin and has a divine purpose.

Conclusion

The study of Paul's thought on disability takes us to the very heart of his gospel message. Paul preached "Christ crucified"—the ultimate symbol of

---

7. Although "thorn" is doubtless the best translation for σκόλοψ, it should be noted that the word was also used to refer to a stake used in crucifixion, and possibly Paul had this connection between his own suffering and Christ's crucifixion in mind when selecting this word. While Paul himself uses only σταυρός (cross) and σταυρόω (crucifixion) in reference to Christ, his contemporary Philo uses the verbal form of σκόλοψ, ἀνασκολοπίζω, to refer to crucifixion (*Flacc.* 84; *Somn.* 2.213; *Post.* 61), and the satirist Lucian applies this verb specifically to Christ's crucifixion (*Pereg.* 11, 13). Σκόλοψ is used for Christ's cross in Origen *Cels.* 2:55, 68–69. See Hengel: 24; Delling; BAGD s.v.

8. For a discussion on beliefs about different causes of illness in non-Western cultures, including instrumental and ultimate causes, see George M. Foster: 778.

disability, whether disability is considered as functional limitation or as social stigma. Paul's gospel called for nothing less than a radical rethinking of the whole concept of "disability." For it is precisely through this ultimate symbol of weakness and disability that divine power, strength, and "ability" is revealed.

Nor is this only a message about Christ. Through the notion of "interchange," Paul argues that Christ shares the disability and limitations of humans; followers of Christ, in turn, share in his suffering and atoning death. But it is precisely in this shared disability that the way is opened to a completely new way of life, free of disability, sin, and even death itself.

Paul's thought challenged, in a fundamental way, the accepted understanding of disability in his day, removing it from the realm of social stigma and from its close association with sin and the demonic. Rather, disability was seen as an occasion for a person to allow true divine power, the power of the crucified and resurrected Christ, to manifest itself in his or her own life.[9]

---

9. This essay has benefited from the editorial comments of Hector Avalos.

Responses

11

Enabling the Body

Janet Lees

This essay explores ways in which ordinary people, including those with disabilities and communication difficulties, interpret the Bible and how they could use this material. As a speech therapist, pastoral minister, and socially committed biblical scholar I have been engaged in interpreting the Bible with people with disabilities including communication difficulties, and I illustrate my responses to the work presented here with examples from that work carried out over the past decade.

Ordinary People Interpret the Bible

Just imagine—Easter is approaching. You've sat through most of Lent and the final week is almost here. It is Palm Sunday once more with its stories of donkeys and hosannas. You go to church as usual. It is time to receive the palm crosses. Everyone goes up to the front of the church to receive a palm cross: everyone except you. They say you must stay where you are. There's not enough room for your wheelchair to go around the church along the aisles. Someone will bring you one: you just stay there.

It is perhaps not too surprising a scene in the UK, in which those adults, of whatever ability, attending mainstream churches have largely learnt to be passive. Many will not have thought it unreasonable that you in your wheelchair should remain there, out of the way. They will have their own explanations: "He can't do it"; "She doesn't understand anyway"; "It will be easier for everyone else." Few will be thinking about the Palm Sunday story in quite the same way as you.

Thus when it comes to role models in the gospel story they will each have her or his own.[1] It is perhaps not too surprising that a group of white not yet disabled ministers remembering some gospel stories together said: "We saw ourselves as Jesus" (Lees 1997:189). Similarly it may not be too unusual to hear that women identified with some of the women mentioned in the Gospels. Mary, a deaf woman said, "I identify with the widow," because she had recently lost her job and her home and left the country of her birth (Lees 1997:147).[2]

For the disabled person, a whole host of anonymous, often silent, people exist on the edges of the gospel story. The twelve named male disciples are usually presented as a robust gang of young adults, called away from earning their various livings. What impairments did they live with? Fishing was a dangerous occupation then as now. How many fingers did Peter have? Living in occupied territory was a dangerous business then as now. How many scars did Andrew have? Leaving your job was risky then as now. How much stress did Matthew or Thomas have? If these people were living with impairments then the church does not portray them in that way.

We each have faith and imagination. If we could use that imagination to inform faith how might discipleship challenge all of us again? But what Bible shall we use, those of us who cannot speak, read, or turn over the pages?

We will use the authentic Bible of the people: a remembered Bible. Bible study participants with communication impairments say they use remembered versions of the Bible rather than written ones. Robin, a professed religious woman who has dyslexia, said, "From my point of view the Bible stories come alive when they're told," and, "If it's read in chapel it goes right over my head. I don't really hear it." Furthermore, "It's more in my body, in my heart, in my gut, than in my head" (Lees 1997:79–82).

It is a combination of remembered Bible and remembered experience that Andrew, who has cerebral palsy, used for his interpretation of the Palm Sunday story:[3]

> JAL: Can we think about that Palm Sunday story? When you were in the crowd how did it feel?
>
> AS: Jerusalem.

---

1. The work discussed here, both Lees (1997) and more recent work (Lees 2007a, 2007b), has been based on studies with people of all ages and abilities using material from the Gospels.

2. Both of these Bible study groups, the ministers and the women, were discussing the story of the widow in the temple, who places two small coins in the offertory: Luke 21:1–4.

3. A conversation between Andrew (AS), his mother (CS), and the author (JAL). Andrew, who has cerebral palsy, uses a voice-output communication aid and nonverbal communication.

CS: Like when you were in Jerusalem? Do you remember being there? Wasn't it a bit scary with the crowds pushing against your wheelchair?

AS: Because people welcomed him into Jerusalem and Hosanna to him who comes in the name of the Lord.

JAL: That's what you said as a member of the crowd. And how did it feel to be a member of the crowd?

AS: Cross, because when everybody went up on Sunday I felt that I should go up with them. Did you have them [palm crosses] in your church like us as well?

JAL: Yes we did. We also had a big tree—an Easter tree—and lots of crosses made by children and young people. Some were made of wood, to plant in our gardens, to remember this week that Jesus died. Now that first Palm Sunday: if there was a boy like you in the crowd—how would he have felt?

CS: Like when we were at the church of the Beatitudes and you were lying on the ground with the crowd all around you?

AS: Do your children get bored?

JAL: Yes I expect so—it can get boring.

CS: Are you saying that people who would be lying on the ground and couldn't see things would get bored?

AS: Sometimes.

CS: Being disabled can be like being like a small child and being ignored.

AS: [*nods*]

Remembered versions of the Bible are used by many people, including those with communication difficulties and disabilities. Gerald O. West (1999) says "ordinary African interpreters work with a remembered as well as a read Bible" (96). He reviews the work of a number of African biblical scholars on this issue and concludes that remembering the Bible is "a communal process" in which the read Bible and the remembered version "reside side by side" (96). It is this joint process that formed the basis of the contextual Bible studies in Janet A. Lees (1997 and 1998) and has, more recently, been developed with marginalized groups in two small urban churches (one a multiracial inner-city church and the other a church on a housing estate) over a five-year period and described as "a critical pedagogy of the oppressed" in the Freirian tradition (Lees 2007a, 2007b). Limited literacy and communication impairments will influence the way people interact with the Bible. An oral method of using the Bible means that remembering and interpreting the text occur in close proximity, because our interpretation probably affects what we remember as much as what we remember influences our interpretation. Putting the process of remembering and interpreting into the hands of ordinary people, including those with disabilities such as communication difficulties, will open up the potential for a whole new range of public understandings of the Bible.

Trained Biblical Scholars Interpret the Bible

Even trained biblical scholars start off as ordinary interpreters of the Bible. In this volume, Fontaine describes herself as belonging to "a handicapped female elite," referring to the medical care, work, and status that are available to her, recognizing that these may not be available to many ordinary people with disabilities. It is well recognized that people with disabilities are among the most socioeconomically disadvantaged in the UK, and access to inclusive education is a recent, and still contentious, aspect of government policy.

Research about disability has also been criticized by disabled people. The move toward including people with disabilities as research partners rather than the object of research is quite recent. G. Zarb (1992) discusses the difference between participatory and emancipatory research in respect to disabled people.[4] Asking "who controls what the research will be about and how it is carried out" (128) and drawing on his experiences of doing research and evaluation work for organizations of disabled people and other work in what he describes as a "framework of 'user's perspectives' on services and policy" (125), he proposes some criteria for evaluating research practice in order to change "the relations of research production" (137). These include:

- making the research accountable to disabled people
- critical scrutiny by researchers in order to learn from mistakes and avoid repeating them
- "making skills and knowledge available as resources to disabled people who may want to use them" (137)

It is therefore pertinent to ask what part will biblical scholarship of the sort presented in this volume play in the process of interpreting the Bible with people with disabilities. How will it work?

Consider this conversation (Lees 1997:219), about the Gospel story of the boy with epilepsy, with a parent of a disabled child:[5]

JAL: I expect you've heard that story before or even read it yourselves before. When you heard it read this time and in view of the things we

---

4. Zarb's paper is entitled "On the Road to Damascus." He uses the phrase to refer to a life-changing experience that causes an oppressor to change sides. It is not clear whether he is using a remembered Bible.

5. Paula (P) is the mother of a girl with cerebral palsy, JAL is the author. The story is found in Mark 9:14–29.

said before we read it—were there any things that particularly surprised you?

P: Well I rather get the feeling that his lack of faith is why the son's not been healed.

JAL: You think the story comes across as if the father's lack of faith being the thing that's contributed to his son having this difficulty?

P: So that's why he's frightened of, and thinks Jesus doesn't love him, and that's why we all believe that sort of thing, because of that sort of story. My daughter has a hip problem which has caused her lots of difficulty and I've prayed long and hard for this problem to be healed and it never has and I'm very angry about this.

JAL: I see.

P: And then I feel guilty because I'm angry, in fact.

JAL: And do people interpret that to you as you having a lack of faith?

P: Well no, it's just that when you read it you think well that's what Jesus is saying; it's because I haven't got enough faith.

JAL: So you actually agree that it says that?

P: Yes, I think it says that.

A conversation (Lees 1997:226) about the same text with professionals who work with children and young people went like this:[6]

JAL: Can you identify with the boy at all?

J: No, I can't. I don't see the point: we don't know anything about him.

JAL: Well, could we imagine what he might be like, his age, his circumstances?

J: No, I don't know if he's a child or a teenager. Anyway, we shouldn't try to guess. If it's not there then we're not supposed to know. God has told us all we need to know about this story already.

L (to JAL): But you know him already, don't you?

JAL: Oh yes, I do, I work with children like him every day.

L: That's right, me too. I know this boy. And I'm not surprised by the way things are put here, the language of spirits and the like. That kind of language is used in some places, like when I visited my daughter who is a missionary in Kenya. People there would talk about spirits causing illnesses. It's not for us to disagree with because there are many kinds of medicine, not just Western medicine. After all, if I give a child Epilim or something [a commonly used anticonvulsant in the UK] then it stops the

---

6. John (J) is a church youth worker, Leslie (L) is a pediatrician, JAL is the author.

fit but it doesn't necessarily cure him. But this child was cured completely.
I wonder why?

What arises from these conversations is that although the people are highly experienced, either as carers or workers, their experiences as biblical interpreters are less developed. The normative interpretation of this story, concerning lack of faith, is the one that dominates the conversation. Ordinary people are not used to contest interpretations of biblical texts, probably because they do not think of themselves as trained readers. West (1999) says this is because they read the Bible "precritically" because "they have not been trained in the critical models of reading that characterise biblical scholarship" (90), and, indeed, as we have seen many are not readers at all but "retellers." He points out that the notions "critical" and "precritical" are not value judgments: one is not better or worse than the other. Rather, they are about the ways in which the Bible is read by different groups, the questions that are asked about the text, the parts of the text that are read and why. In the Bible studies reported by Lees (1997), ordinary people with disabilities and communication difficulties did want to ask questions about the text and were interested in parts of the Bible they had previously overlooked. For example:

> E: I have never seen that significance of that story which you asked me to read: the Canaanite woman. I've never before understood the significance of this story: I hadn't paid much attention to it. What a marvelous lady . . . and a wonderful answer to that particular question. She deserved her reward.[7]

There are a number of issues discussed in this volume that would be of interest to ordinary biblical interpreters. Comments on sensory criticism, gender, and socio-cultural reconstruction will be illustrated with further examples from contextual Bible studies with people with disabilities and communication difficulties (Lees 1997, 1998, 2007a, 2007b).

Sensory Criticism

In this volume, Avalos discusses sensory criticism: the way in which the senses are represented in biblical texts. There are high incidences of impairments of sight and hearing in the population: about two million people in the UK have sight impairments, nearly nine million have hearing impairments (in both cases this is proportionally higher in those over 70 years of age).[8] People with visual and hearing impairments are likely to be common in the aging congregations of our churches but not all will consider

---

7. Edward (E) has mental health problems and was talking about Matt 15:21–28 (Lees 1997:268–69).

8. Figures from the Royal National Institute for the Blind and the Royal National Institute for the Deaf—two UK voluntary organizations working with people with visual and hearing impairments, respectively.

themselves disabled. Neither will they necessarily think it at all odd that hearing and visual impairments are often linked to sin in the talk that goes on in churches, both prayers and hymns. Avalos argues that sensory criticism will help us to get a better idea of how biblical writers understood the human body. He analyses various texts from the Hebrew scriptures from this perspective. Working with people of all ages and abilities on Gospel texts could also be done from a sensory perspective. Using remembered texts could mean inviting participants to remember stories about sensory experiences: healing a deaf and speechless man, for example, or using senses to "consider the lilies of the field." Avalos goes on to argue that initial studies suggest that all senses are not given equal value. A hierarchy of value also operates in respect of disabilities in our society today, and some people with what might be termed "hidden disabilities" report that their impairments attract less attention or greater misunderstanding.

Gender

Several authors in this volume discuss gender: either gender in the text or the gender of the interpreter/s. Fontaine describes being female and disabled as "a potent 'double whammy' " of cultural constructions. Awareness of gender issues varies among ordinary interpreters of the Bible. This conversation, about Jesus healing the woman with a hemorrhage,[9] with a group of retired older women, some of whom had acquired mobility or sensory impairments, illustrates some of the changes in gender understanding that the majority group (older women outnumber all other groups in mainstream UK churches) has had to accommodate over the last fifty years (Lees 1997:236):[10]

JAL: So what do you think the passage is about?

P: The woman's faith and her belief.

D: The woman's suffering.

E: She was trying to help herself.

ES: It's a healing story.

B: It could be about faith or suffering. Jesus feels the power going out of him.

P: It seems to be a special experience to this woman—it's not mentioned anywhere else.

---

9. Mark 5:23–61.

10. Doris (D) has hearing and mobility impairments, Eva (E) has a hearing impairment and is originally from Eastern Europe, Pat (P) cared for her disabled husband until his death. Estelle (ES), Barbara (B), and JAL (the author) are the other group members.

E: Women aren't mentioned much. There's just all those female relatives wailing in the background.

P: Well Jesus seems to have a special relationship with this woman. She touched him.

E: How did she know to do that?

ES: It can't have been easy, going up and touching such a powerful man.

E: Yes, she was considered unclean. Like after a woman had a baby and before she'd had been "churched," as they used to say. I remember that from my childhood.

D: Well even not touching some things, or not bathing, during your period: that was common in my childhood.

B: Yes, and you didn't talk about sanitary towels, like they have these adverts for them on the TV now. It was all very hush-hush, and your mother wrapped some things up for you in newspaper, and you had to get rid of it with no one looking.

JAL: So it seems more acceptable now?

ES: Women are accepted as equals, not like when we were first married.

P: Girls today get more chances, but it's still hard bringing up children equally.

JAL: Because our society still isn't equal?

ES: Well men just think of one thing at a time! [*Group laughs.*]

On the whole there are fewer men in the churches, and less attention is paid to changes in understanding masculinity. Some male characters have attracted attention in contextual Bible studies using remembered texts. These comments on the character of Lazarus come from a Bible study with people with learning and communication difficulties in Glasgow (Lees 2007a, 2007b):

Mary said: My house is different. My brother is different. He lets me be different. He lets me learn and listen.

He was useless and he went and died.

I was not a well man. My name was never mentioned because I was never there.

Lazarus said: I've not said a lot. My sisters keep the family on an even keel. I went and died. I'm a bloke with not many choices in life.

I don't think much was said about the brother.

These participants revealed important insights about the part Lazarus, a silent man, played in the story:

Beginning of the story:	Middle of the story:	End of the story:
Silence from and about Lazarus	Lazarus dies	Silence from and about Lazarus

People often assumed to be silent could identify with the huge silences in this story about the presence and role of a key character in the story—the silent Lazarus. In this volume, Hentrich suggests that a man like Lazarus might be part of the story because he is a *disabled* man, rather than because he is a disabled *man*. By going to Lazarus's tomb Jesus also challenges the purity restrictions to allow the real Lazarus to emerge.

These examples indicate that ordinary biblical interpreters can use their own experiences as a starting point for discussing gender issues.

Socio-Cultural Reconstruction

Another aspect of the work in this volume is the reconstruction of the socio-cultural context of disability that lies behind the biblical text. This is something that ordinary interpreters are interested in and recognize that they may have limited knowledge of.

Andrew (see the conversation on pp. 162–63) used his experiences of visiting some of the places mentioned in the Gospels to interpret the Palm Sunday story from the perspective of people with disabilities. When he was a pilgrim in Jerusalem, he felt very vulnerable in the crowds in his wheelchair. In some places on this journey, he sat out of his wheelchair on the ground, in the dust looking at people's legs. Andrew reminds us that this is the main view people with severely impaired mobility would have had of Jesus' ministry in first-century Palestine: just the legs. This could have been quite frightening. It is therefore not surprising that people might have shouted out as a way of drawing attention to themselves so that people did not step on them.

Andrew's view of what these early Christian communities looked like to disabled people is from the floor. The Palm Sunday story is not told from the perspective of disabled people. Two thousand years later it is not so different, as Andrew is unable to take an active part in the celebrations when the church building fails to meet his needs.

Andrew wanted to know more about the lives of people with disabilities in the first century in Palestine. His experience of pilgrimage in the twentieth century sets the scene for some basic observations about what that must have been like. Andrew uses a wheelchair for mobility, although he can also move around on his hands and knees or walk short distances with the support of one or two other people who can walk. In his interpretation of the boy in the Palm Sunday crowd, Andrew placed him on the floor. He had experienced this and also found the use of wheeled transport in a crowd frightening. It is likely that a person with impaired mobility in first-century Palestine would have used a number of means. Handmade carts and buggies are found in most societies and communities that do not have access to factory-made high-technology transport systems.

The Gospel texts rarely describe how people with impaired mobility moved around. In the story of the healing of the paralyzed man, Mark has him carried on a mat (Mark 2:1–4) and Luke on a bed (Luke 5:17–20). Most of the time walking seems to have been the assumed method of getting from place to place. The text makes almost no consideration of how this was accomplished by those who found walking difficult or impossible.

There is, then, a huge silence in the text about the contribution of people with disabilities to the Easter story. If so many people with disabilities followed Jesus (Mark 1:32–34)—and crowds in which people with disabilities were present are recorded (Mark 5:24–34)—then some are likely to have been present on Palm Sunday and the rest of Holy Week. This is a contradiction, as they are not mentioned. Sermons on gender (the place of the women who followed Jesus) or race (black followers like Simon in Mark 15:21) in the Passion narratives have become a feature of some Holy Week celebrations. Andrew used his experiences to open up discussion on the role of disabled people in the Easter story. This could be developed by reference to research into socio-cultural reconstruction of disability such as that provided in this volume.

Interpreting the Bible Together

The contextual Bible studies described here have, like those described by West (2004), been not so much about reading the Bible for research but reading "with local communities as a resource for social development and transformation" (211). "We must learn to work together," says John M. Campbell (2003), advocating a shared creative process of biblical interpretation when he says: "We do not need calm solitude to approach a text, we need a clamour of diverse voices, a cacophony of competing insights, but with a real chance for the disparate whispering voices to be heard as well as the loud confident ones" (41). This is particularly important for people with disabilities, including communication difficulties, who have long been silenced by church and society.

Interpreting the Bible with people with disabilities including communication difficulties has led to some practical considerations for those wanting to do similar work (Lees 1997):

- create a safe place;
- begin by using remembered texts;
- use an informed facilitator;
- encourage the repositioning of silent characters;
- make links between the many layers of silence.

A safe place is one in which people of all abilities are able to take the risks associated with working together. West (2004) agrees with the need for a safe space—one in which traditional power imbalances have been set aside and those most often marginalized are able to meet as equals with elite, more powerful groups. Facilitating such space requires careful consideration, training, and evaluation.

Remembered texts are those chosen by people with communication difficulties themselves. Trained readers may have to put written texts aside sometimes and be prepared to use the remembered versions of ordinary people when working together.

An informed facilitator uses the social model of disability and, where possible, works from it via their lived experiences. In this volume, Toensing does this when she positions her interpretation of the story of the demoniac in the light of her own experience as the sibling of a person with severe mental illness. She recognizes, as we all must, that we cannot impose Western twenty-first-century understandings of well-being on a text about the first-century Mediterranean culture. Like most of the authors in this volume she examines the claims of the social model of disability. She also uses the story of a person hospitalized with bipolar disorder to further illuminate the text. Toensing concludes that the process of interpretation is a complex one and has many different layers. Describing these layers is part of the process of developing critical interpretation skills for ordinary biblical interpreters.

Silent and often anonymous characters at the edges of the texts are often good places to begin to see the text from the perspective of people with communication difficulties and disabilities. As these examples have shown, biblical interpretation by and with people with disabilities involves many layers of silence: historical, cultural, sociological, and ideological. Resources such as those presented in this volume can help to uncover these layers and could be used to enable us, as a body, to come out of silence together. As Toensing says, "Biblical texts are living traditions that are challenged and renewed by lived experiences of ongoing generations of Christians." It is to the challenge of interpreting texts with people with disabilities for the purposes of social transformation that I hope we will all continue to commit ourselves.

12

"Jesus Thrown Everything Off Balance"

DISABILITY AND REDEMPTION IN BIBLICAL LITERATURE

David Mitchell
Sharon Snyder

"That Old Dream of Similitude"

In *The Sacred and the Profane*, Mircea Eliade argues that the sacred can only be understood as "wholly other" and "wholly familiar" at the same time. Disability studies, as an academic field of critical inquiry, has wrestled with variations on Eliade's thesis as a key understanding of responses to corporeal, sensory, and cognitive difference for nearly four decades. Not in the sense of puzzling over the status of disability in ancient texts (although it has done some of that) (Garland 1995; Stiker 1999; Rose 2003); but, rather, in that disabled people find themselves historically in sites of cultural abjection while also performing as objects of intense scrutiny (Bogdan 1990; Thomson 1996; Snyder and Mitchell 2006). Perhaps one of the key insights brought by disability studies centers on the critique of this socially created paradox as decidedly non-paradoxical. One can be thoroughly "inside" a context in the midst of experiencing utter depreciation (Mitchell and Snyder 1997). Consequently, the nature of the sacred within biblical literature presents an important opportunity for undertaking further analyses of disabled peoples' foundational status in culture.

Much of our previous work has tried to illuminate the nature of this contradiction in secular contexts because we find that disabled peoples' situation remains largely misunderstood with respect to the nature of their social exclusion. Unlike the beginnings of other identity-based area studies, wherein social exclusion was explained by an absence of representations about life in the oppressed group, disability engenders a different representational fate. Likewise, whereas studies of race, gender, and class all work to unveil a lack of attention by medicine, rehabilitation, and even the social

sciences to the specifics of de-privileged populations as biological citizens,
disabled people have formulated their subjugation in terms of over-medi-
calization, rampant pathology, and perpetual objectification. Paradoxically,
disability discrimination takes place in the midst of its continual address.
Across the modern academy, entire research domains have been devoted
to the pathologization and, subsequently, normalization of disability as
deviance. The eugenics period (1880–1939), for instance, invested a half-
century of research in the belief that all social inequities—namely, poverty,
crime, unemployment, vice, prostitution, delinquency, disease, and so
on—were perpetuated by inferior existences that could be eradicated with
the institution of rigorous social engineering programs (Trent 1995; Snyder
and Mitchell 2006). This is a belief that the French feminist theorist Luce
Irigaray once referred to as "that old dream of similitude" (1985: 139)

Dreams of similitude underwrite the social debasement of disabled
people. The essays in this volume emphasize variations on this thesis with
respect to biblical narratives: gender ambiguity; the likeness of humanity
made in God's image; the economically abject's location on the outskirts
of biblical society; bodily incapacity as expression of divine disapproval;
the use of disabled people as a defensive frontline to ward off intruders;
disability as a marker of tainted priesthood or moral failing; mental illness
as satanic possession; the perfect body of Christ as the approximation of
godliness; physical disability as loss of claim to hereditary kingship; sexual
infidelity as source of childhood deformity; excessive vulnerability as the
definition of impairment; among others. The catalog features an alarming
array of ways in which disability prompts cultural disavowal. One almost
has to admire the "flexibility" of thought inaugurated by disabled people
in response to the crises they provoke in biblical traditions. This recognition underscores the skepticism with which disability-studies scholars
have traditionally approached religious frameworks of interpretation. Not
the clinic alone, but religious locales provoke suspicion among those who
have traveled to a variety of meccas only to find themselves treated as abject supplicants. Their bodily, cognitive, and sensory differences continue
to provide opportunities for exclusion rather than embrace.

Significantly in line with this view, the scholars in this volume assist
modern-day audiences in comprehending the degree to which disability
functions as, what we have elsewhere called, "a master trope of human
disqualification" (Snyder and Mitchell 2006: 125). Disabled bodies are
marked bodies, fully socialized, and over-analyzed in their significance
to the destiny of nations, monarchies, communities, families, individuals, and corporealities. They embody the impossibility of similitude across
human organisms as dynamic expressions of embodiment. In the illusion-
ary pursuit of homogeneity across time, human communities have failed
to adequately recognize difference as the architect of variation on which
dynamic organisms thrive for survival. Similitude closes down variety,

whereas difference prompts the need for creativity in the press to adapt to perpetually shifting circumstances—social, environmental, political, economic, bodily, and otherwise. Eugenics offered a form of redemption that would solve social crises through the eradication rather than accommodation of human variation. There is a marked depreciation toward the human when disabled people are so routinely treated as if they were outside the scope of necessary social provisions.

This Abled Body: Re-thinking Disability in Biblical Studies

The title of this volume recognizes the degree to which narrow formulas of ability serve to exclude people with disabilities. Disability represents a largely undertheorized aspect of human experience despite the fact that estimates place the percentage of disability in most cultures near 20 percent. Likewise, as Anna Borsay points out in this collection, the "cultural history [of disability] remains a lacuna." Because of this defining neglect, disability studies unveils the coordinates of philosophies, beliefs, and practices that affect disabled people socially—across periods, cultures, and traditions. In doing so, disability studies not only demonstrates the prevalence of what we recognize today as congenital and acquired impairments, but, more importantly, attending to common practices towards disabled people yields significant social insights. Disability-studies-based analysis challenges our understanding of "pragmatism" by demonstrating the extent to which the most supportive systems often operate at the expense of the population they have presumably evolved to accommodate. Because disability crosses all cultural, social, economic, and political divisions, it often proves revelatory of the ways in which naturalized attitudes toward variations in human capacities, appearances, and/or functions distort our understanding of ourselves as social and biological animals.

Thus we are not just interested in the exposé of stereotypes or prejudices toward disabled people, but rather the systemic inequities that beliefs about disability maintain. Consequently, it is not enough, as Nicole Kelly argues, to explicate the portrayal of the crook-footed god Hephaistos's cuckolding on the basis of his disability by Mars and Venus. Instead, analysis of disability-based plots promises to yield access, however tentative, into the ideological atmosphere characteristic of a time and place, into belief systems that may or may not have recognized disabled people as significant social actors. Thus, the ancient Greeks and Romans may have practiced infanticide by exposure against disabled infants. Such a practice assists us in understanding the degree to which classical aesthetics infiltrated public policy.

Disability-studies scholars have also observed that the presence of disability often impairs the normative expectations of other foundational social roles such as gender. Wherein a patriarchal structure may be posited as the primary mode of social interaction in biblical writings—the stories are primarily about men's relationships, activities, prowess, failings, and so on—disability overshadows masculinity as a gendered identity. In fact, as Thomas Hentrich underscores, disability may even upset one's relationship with God. While the Hebrew Bible consistently represents God's image as masculine, disability enjoins purity laws against male priests as prohibitive of one's ability to engage in meaningful communication with the divine: "[The purity laws] essentially turned them [disabled priests] into outsiders and second-class citizens, at least where temple worship is concerned." Such an analysis of disability in purity laws helps explain scholarly assertions that Jesus' willingness to approach those with illnesses and disabilities challenges purity based discrimination statutes. A contemporary, yet similar, version of the purity laws also infuses Holly Joan Toensing's essay, wherein she finds herself needing to reject Christianity's teaching about her brother's mental disability (paranoid schizophrenia) as a scourge more in need of treatment than community receptiveness, understanding, and support.

As instances of cognitive and physical disability surface in biblical texts and elsewhere (due to a shift in the methodological lens that disability studies provides), we allow ourselves to contemplate mechanisms of stigma. Yet, perhaps even more importantly, we also provide ourselves with the opportunity for changing perceptions and alternative ways of comprehending disabled lives today. Here is the key pragmatic goal of disability studies scholarship, one that operates while attempting to be appropriately suspicious of simply overlaying contemporary beliefs upon ancient social contexts. However, as the analysis in this volume of Paul's attitudes about disability in the epistles makes clear, the experience of disability can significantly influence one's understanding of the intersection between social and biological realms. Paul, who began his career as an apostle with a speech impediment, claimed a better understanding of the power of devalued communities as they fought against oppressive social structures as a result of his own communicative marginalization.

While this particular analysis of Paul's developing prowess as an orator of God's message occurs strictly within a theological context, Jeremy Schipper employs his analysis of disability in the Deuteronomistic History as a transitional device for understanding changes in Israelite leadership. While Paul's disability experience provides him with a vantage point on social disempowerment, most images of disability function as metaphorical equivalents for other social conflicts. Disability is rarely explored as an experience in its own right; rather, like prosthetics themselves, disabled bodies substitute for inadequacies in the larger social body. According to Schipper, Moses' depiction as a hyper-able-bodied religious leader, even at the end of his life, contrasts sharply with the use of disability as a marker of the decline of other leadership regimes in biblical Israel.

The Deuteronomistic History also provides an opportunity for contrast with the book of Job on the basis of sensory privileging, according to Hector Avalos. Rhetorical and metaphorical reliance on hearing or sight unearths ways in which biblical cultures value human capacities. Such hierarchies of sensory experience help to reveal ways in which sense-based disabilities such as deafness or blindness devalue some communities more severely than others. Attention to this facet of narrative further underscores how disability functions as an elastic category of social meaning. The overdetermination of one sense's value above another demonstrates the degree to which some disabilities prove more or less stigmatizing at various points in history. The malleable nature of stigmatization exposes the degree to which disabilities are socially constructed and, thus, amenable to revision.

Yet within the parameters of biblical narratives, revision of the meaning of disability remains an exclusive province of divinity. For example, Melcher examines metaphors of impairment as the subject of passages that depict God as a restorer/healer—one whose restorative powers can alleviate as well as devastate populations and individuals alike. Disabilities visited upon a people by YHWH function as forms of divine retribution. Melcher quotes one revealing example from Isaiah, who identifies cognitive slowness, deafness, blindness, and incapacity to empathize as forms of punishment meted out from the heavens. In nearly every case, disability denotes a form of social devaluation wherein those punished with disability find themselves banished to the lowest rungs of social existence. Individual injuries can also be experienced as punishment on behalf of a sinful community—that is, a scapegoat who suffers the fallout in order to deflect more wide-ranging disciplinary action upon others. Likewise, in a more promising political inversion, lives marked by impairment and severe need will undergo redemption withheld from the powerful. These final two metaphorical references to disability offer up, according to Melcher, the potential beginnings of a biblically based liberation ethic in that "God chooses the shape of every person so that every type of person should be valued, as she or he is."

Perhaps what most consistently comes to light in these analyses is that disability may be identified with individuals whose bodies, minds, and/or senses inhibit them (or are believed to inhibit them) in performing socially prescribed tasks. Walls's essay explains one approach to disability as the community model. The community model highlights roles as socially prescribed, and, as a result, an individual's value to a community is often determined by an ability to fulfill such roles adequately. Interpreting disability from this perspective may offer an opportunity to consider the impact of impairments (particularly in more ancient societies) in a more nuanced manner. The community model of disability recognizes that not all "medically based" conditions today may be retroactively applied to an earlier period/culture as a reason for social exclusion. A disability that does not interfere with the performance of a socially prescribed duty, for instance, may not hinder an individual's ability to participate actively. Consequently, disability, like all socially derived categories of identity and experience, neither remains static nor fully deterministic of one's recognition as a contributing cultural participant.

In fact, as Walls explains, it becomes imperative to keep in mind that disability operates in decidedly different ways in other cultural contexts. For instance, ancient Mesopotamian stories describe disabled people assigned to specific roles according to their capacities, in addition to the rejection of some infants as less than fully human according to their birth status. A disabled person could find him or herself entirely abandoned by friends, family, and colleagues *or* elaborately cared for and accommodated over the course of a long life with a chronic condition. In either case one must conclude that in ancient Mesopotamia as in biblical Israel, functions, appearances, and capacities considered abnormal are recognized as part of the organization of the world—rather than simply excessive to it. Yet we want to return in the last section of this afterword to a point with which this section began: in addition to analyzing meanings ascribed to human differences, disability studies also provides opportunities that may expose seemingly benign systems of treatment as anathema to disabled peoples' well-being.

Disability and the Limits of Redemption Narratives

In order to further analyze social longings for similitude in Christianity, allow us a final excursion into recent critiques of redemption narratives as a gloss on contemporary social conflicts. While others in this volume share affinities with this critique, no essay provides a sustained reading of Christ's acts of miracle healing as the erasure rather than acceptance of disability. Of course, the reasons for this omission appear relatively easy to explain: miracle cures and raisings of the dead seem too fantastical as happenings to offer much in the way of sociological insight. As compensation for their faulty verisimilitude, many biblical scholars now treat such events in a metaphorical manner, wherein "cure" denotes social tolerance. Yet, for us, often the most telling sociological episodes about disability occur where the mundane and miraculous meet. The elusive materiality of corporeal life finds a more palatable ideological referent in these fantastical discursive episodes.

While we do not want to make an equation between disability and death (that is, that a disabled life is tantamount to dying), we intend to suggest that the restoration of bodies to normative health through acts of faith healing ultimately devalues our commitments to the demands of embodiment overall. Miracles of the body (that is, disability cures, the alleviation of chronic illness, resuscitation of the organism from non-being, etc.) function as a form of *deus ex machina* in stories hard-pressed to resolve corporeal crisis in any other way. If a community of disabled people finds itself excluded from a temple or other site of cultural privilege, then an accommodation is in order—even in biblical times. One could lift the prohibition, eradicate a structural obstacle, or, as in many New Testament stories, remove disability through cure so the access barrier in question no longer hinders participation. In the last instance, one alters an individual or group biology in order to secure inclusion. Jesus as a prophet engaged in faith healing treats disability as any other socially made obstacle in that bodies may be revised into less cumbersome experiences. Whereas the removal of social barriers delimits the environment as the target of intervention, in cure/resurrection/redemption scenarios bodies are fixed to fit an unaccommodating environment.

Perhaps Nietzsche pursued an analysis of the degradation of the Christian redemption narrative most vehemently in Western philosophy. He recognized redemption as a form of social cleansing—one that dismissed what was most difficult in human relations with the superficial, and impossible, gloss of transcendence. The concept of afterlife, as the staple story of salvation, promoted social contempt toward the demands of earthly existence—including the ability to accommodate lives that, at least outwardly, appear lacking in social utility. Ironically for Nietzsche, such individuals excluded from mainstream community found themselves and their fellow outsiders inoculated from what he viewed as the bankrupt morality of popular culture. Their expulsion functioned as the agent of their cultural salvation. It freed them up to pursue alternative value systems less susceptible to the debasements of "ordinary" lives.

Not only does the New Testament cultivate social contexts that expect the eradication of disability as a resolution to human-made exclusion, it does so by depicting disabled people as the agents of their own curative ambitions. As the prophet Jesus wanders on the outskirts of biblical society, disabled bodies materialize and seek out the opportunity to experience his healing touch. From a representational standpoint, disabled people are characterized in mass as pushing their own cure agenda. These biologically rejected hordes seek cures even to the point where, in popular culture renditions of the Bible such as *Jesus Christ Superstar* (1973), Christ tires of their persistent requests. The son of God narrates his experience as victimized by disabled peoples' maniacal allegiance to the promise of eradication, a promise he has purposefully introduced as a preeminent sign of his own divine powers. This becomes one of the strangest narrative inversions in the New Testament wherein disabled people fulfill their social roles as sycophants and Jesus secures allegiance to his status as prophet while claiming to be overtaxed by those whose bodily fates he depends on for evidence of his own divinity.

Just as the hordes of cripples on the outskirts of the biblical mainstream seek alleviation of their corporeal fates through miracle cures rather than

social accommodation of their differences, the healing touch of Christ devalues disability as that to be alleviated rather than valued. One of the key
scenes in Nietzsche's *Thus Spake Zarathustra* parodies such biblical stagings
by turning the tables on cure requests (2005:119). Rather than offer a false
salvation of bodily fix, the prophet/philosopher Zarathustra addresses a
group of cripples at a bridge, who argue that he must demonstrate his
divine status by curing their conditions. In his response Zarathustra emphasizes the value of their bodily situations as the foundation of their
characters. The erasure of disability would not prove his divine qualities
but rather thrust them into commerce with a mainstream culture that is
devoid of worth. Healing a hunchback, blindness, or mobility impairment would destroy their uniqueness and return them to participation in
a bankrupt cultural belief system. For Nietzsche moral vision depends on
the understanding that the promise of bodily overcoming degrades the
experience of corporeality. Any doctrine that promises to undo this experience ultimately depreciates difference, mutability, and even suffering as
manifestations of "the human experience."

Along a similar line of thought, Flannery O'Connor's celebrated
story "A Good Man Is Hard to Find" offers readers insight into Christian
formulas of similitude as part and parcel of a catastrophic post-eugenic/
post-Holocaust depreciation of bodies. Whereas the standard biblical interpretation recognizes miracle cures and raisings from the dead as evidence
of increased tolerance toward the "unfortunate," "afflicted," or "disempowered," disability studies approaches body intervention strategies
(real or imagined) with significant trepidation. Contemporary medical,
pharmaceutical, surgical, and rehabilitation techniques notwithstanding,
bodies appear least malleable when it comes to adapting to barriers that
are ultimately social in nature.

O'Connor's macabre tale, originally published in 1955, provides a window into the genocidal fallout following World War II in the southern U.S.
A lower-middle-class Southern family leaves on a planned family vacation.
Along the way they unwittingly run into a nightmarish meeting with an
escaped serial killer from a local maximum-security facility. The character
allegorically called "The Misfit" kidnaps the family and takes them off into
the woods, where he plans to shoot them one at a time. Just prior to doing
so, he lectures the pious family matriarch, Granny, on the devaluation of
human life occasioned by the biblical concept of raising the dead:

> "Jesus thrown everything off balance . . . Jesus was the only one that ever
> raised the dead," The Misfit continued, "and he shouldn't have done it.
> He thrown everything off balance. If He did what He said, then it's noth-
> ing for you to do but throw away everything and follow Him, and if He
> didn't, then it's nothing for you to do but enjoy the few minutes you
> got left the best way you can by killing somebody or burning down this
> house or doing some other meanness to him. No pleasure but meanness,"
> he said and his voice had become almost a snarl. (131–32)

   While the story is significantly nuanced and open-ended, we want to focus on The Misfit's argument that Jesus' raising of the dead "thrown everything off balance." Despite the fact that the character's name references a notorious social identity, his delivery of this rant against New Testament philosophy may be easily discounted. Instead, the argument underscores the degree to which a seemingly benign act can disguise disastrous social consequences—particularly when it comes to intervening in bodily life as a source of social renewal.

   O'Connor's participation in the southern grotesque allows her to trade in a thoroughly modern use of irony, in which the most corrupt characters deliver insightful revelations. In literature one often finds, as Fredric Jameson explains, "that the purest sensation can only be rendered through a mingling of its opposites in language" (1974: 318). Such is the case in "A Good Man Is Hard to Find." The Misfit becomes a powerful social commentator—one who has literally come back from his own experience of social death in prison—in order to disquisition on the falsity of this doctrine of redemption in resurrection. Within the redemption story, death and disability lower to equivalent states of non-being in need of rescue. They represent conditions of human existence so undesirable that their eradication supports one of Christianity's major tenets: the afterlife's removal of all that is imperfect and burdensome in earthly existence.

   By following the New Testament in its claims to singularity for one of Christ's acts of ultimate love ("Jesus was the only one that ever raised the dead"), The Misfit turns the story of redemption into its corrupt obverse. By raising the dead Jesus lessened the value of human life. The sanctity of life is effectively "thrown off balance" because, if Christian afterlife promises a superior life of the spirit, then material existence serves as a mere way station of intolerable suffering on the road to another form of perfected existence. Such logic abounds in euthanasia stories that depict disability as pure suffering and death as the merciful alleviation of the pain of corporeal existence. In O'Connor's canon disabled characters abound. Her social experiments in fiction test those whose lives already exist on the margins of human value. Disability, as a synecdoche for human vulnerability, becomes more than an experience on a continuum of existence: its representation presses the boundaries of a truly inclusive humanity—one that recognizes disability not only as integrable, but, more importantly, as *integral* to embodied experience.

   The Misfit's logic, admittedly twisted but revelatory nevertheless, rationalizes the raising of the dead as the source of humanity's degradation rather than salvation. The corporeal world, now exposed as shadow and light, harbors no inherent value, and, therefore, "it's nothing for [Granny] to do but throw away everything and follow Him" with the help of the murderous Misfit. In fact, The Misfit recognizes himself within this perverse scenario as an agent of God, more speedily helping God's subjects along on the path to grace. If humanity finds itself redeemed upon the alleviation of disability or after death, then the eradication of some lives becomes a potentially productive, merciful expression of social will toward individuals whose social utility seems in doubt. Why not hasten the demise of corporeal existence in order to get on with eternal reward and the transcendence of bodily life?—particularly when disability exposes individuals to levels of suffering that presumably render existence unlivable.

Of course, the real insight here is not The Misfit's sadistic rationale of "[n]o pleasure but meanness." Rather, the story poses a Nietzchean transvaluation of all value as its antidote to the perverse death drive inspired by Christian stories of redemption. The Misfit's argument rests on an "if-then" premise: *if* the world functions according to a logic of perfection in afterlife *then* embodied lives (that include a range of disability) are less meaningful *and* overly subject to the vagaries of worldly existence. Such a formula suggests that extinction provides a way out of the conundrum of socially devalued forms of being.

The Misfit's genocidal mania (perhaps a characterization method based on popular stereotypes of psychiatric conditions) allows the post-Holocaust context of "A Good Man Is Hard to Find" to surface most fully at this moment. In the wake of a world war that witnessed the death of more than 260,000 people with psychiatric diagnoses as well as six million Jews, Romany, gay, Russian, and political dissidents, we become less capable of the outrage necessary to sustain our devotions to a vulnerable materiality. Instead, vulnerability becomes less easy to rationalize as a worthy state of being. O'Connor's story contemplates the degree to which ideologies of eradication—the erasure of certain kinds of people from the planet—cheapen commitments to the value of bodily life in general. Death proves no longer a state of non-being but an extension and improvement upon earthly life free of the conflicts that commonly beset human beings. Likewise, disability's need for social supports and accommodations can be bypassed once the promise of cure alleviates communities of responsibility to reimagine a more accessible world. The active exclusion of some bodies ultimately devalues our investment in all bodies as dynamic, vulnerable, and mutating in their capacities over a life span.

Finally, if we underscore O'Connor's own disability experience of lupus over her creative career as one impetus for this story, then we may come full circle to an understanding of her significant argument with the New Testament and other biological engineering campaigns. In one of her collected essays, O'Connor connects the relationship between genocide and redemption narratives by commenting on the cultural "sentimentality" that surrounds childhood and disability (Snyder and Mitchell 2006: 168). The first mass eradication campaign undertaken by the Nazis was the children's program that sent disabled kids to their deaths in psychiatric institutions. Their deaths were rationalized as the alleviation of suffering and the destruction of lives unworthy of life.

As a disabled author herself, O'Connor relentlessly seeks to establish a connection between seemingly benign social institutions and ideologies that degrade people with disabilities. Her work exposes the means by which tragic embodiment and contempt for difference underlie practices of exclusion while posing as their opposites (that is, meaningful empathy and embrace of human difference). Neither religion nor charity nor pathos leads to justice in O'Connor's fictional contexts—instead, injustice is covered up by superficial investments in disability as unlivable embodiment.

The essays in this volume demonstrate the invalidity of treating disability as an ontological category of experience. Taken together as a collective scholarly endeavor these works play witness to a multiplicity of perspectives on disability as biological difference, rhetorical figure, and body image. They avoid the pathologizing arguments of medicine, rehabilitation, and other traditional views of disability as a form of embodied victimization. The critical evaluation of Christian narrative traditions on health, illness, and bodily difference expose consistent views of disability as moral failing, a punishment for generational waywardness from Christian teachings, violent tests of divine affliction, and non-disabled charity opportunities.

A liberatory theology of disability involves what Nancy Eiesland identifies as the evolution of new forms of resistance that topple models of devaluation (1994:86). In doing so, disability-studies-based analyses can guide reform-minded readers to alternative applications of Christian narrative traditions—perspectives that often lead beyond tinkering around the edges of theological orthodoxy and, like Nietzsche and O'Connor, into full-scale incursions on beliefs that operate in an oppressive manner. The acceptance of disabled people can no longer be predicated on the perverse interests that underwrite fantasies of erasure, cure, or elimination of bodily difference. Such longings for human similitude ultimately avoid rather than engage the necessity of providing provisions for our meaningful inclusion in social life.

13

Impairment as a Condition
in Biblical Scholarship
A RESPONSE

Bruce C. Birch

Impairment comes in many forms.[1] In truth, no person is without impairment in some form because none manifests the fullness of the image of God in which we are created. If, as Sarah J. Melcher notes, impairment implies a departure from an "ideal" construct, at least when that construct is the God who created us, all depart from it rather than only some socially defined group of us. Such an awareness might help level the playing field in a society that labels persons as "abled" or "disabled" for purposes of social categorization and frequent stigmatization.

These essays reminded me of some of my own impairments, particularly those I have experienced as a biblical scholar. I have been trained in biblical scholarship with a limited awareness and understanding that has allowed me to spend decades in studying and teaching the Bible without noticing or paying any particular attention to the large number of references to impairment/disability in the biblical witness. The invisibility of these texts to my notice is, in my opinion, akin to the invisibility persons defined as disabled by our society experience in the regard and treatment given to them by the wider community. It is socially easier not to notice such persons, and I suppose it has been easier for biblical scholars to give texts referencing impairment/disability only the general descriptive treatment accorded to a disabled character that enters the story or the minimal explanation given to a reference to impairment that crops up in a text. I have,

---

1. It is clear from the essays in this volume that there is as yet no consensus on the use of the terms "impairment" or "disability." Each seems to have its nuances. I will use both terms in this response, often keying my usage to that chosen by the author to whom I am responding at that point.

myself, written a commentary on the books of Samuel and in the course of comment dealt with the references to "the lame and the blind" in the story of David's capture of Jerusalem and with the character of Mephibosheth in David's story. But it did not occur to me nor to other commentaries I have read that interpretation of such characters and references might need to be explored against fuller backdrops of ancient societal attitudes and practices toward the disabled or that particular methodologies out of disability studies might inform the way such texts have been read and used.

This sense of my own impairment as a biblical scholar is somewhat ironic in my case. I have been the father for twenty-six years of a daughter with significant developmental disabilities that place limits on her possibilities for independent life in the wider social community. I have learned about conditions, systems, attitudes, and barriers faced by persons like my daughter to a degree that I never anticipated. I know about IEPs and the Americans with Disabilities Act (ADA) legislation; the heartbreak that comes from watching my daughter become aware of her limitations and the pride that comes from her achievements within them; the crucial difference in social attitudes when she is referred to as developmentally disabled or labeled retarded. I have been a cheerleader, a comforter, an advocate, and a negotiator of problems. I have come to a deep respect for her and her friends as children of God's creation.

This experience of parenting a child with such impairments has had beneficial fallout in other parts of my life. As the administrator of a theological school I have fought for the accommodations needed to open access to theological education and worked with and taught many students who came through the doors that were opened. It has been my privilege to see them enter ministries to which they were once denied.

But none of this personal consciousness raising experience really affected the way I work as a biblical scholar until I was approached by a group of scholars, including the editors and many of the contributors to this volume, to lend my support to the formation of a group within the Society of Biblical Literature on Disability and Biblical Studies. I was pleased to advocate for such a group and honored to preside at the first section of papers read at the Annual Meeting, but I was there to learn. Perspectives and methodologies for understanding biblical texts that referenced impairment/disability were new discoveries for me and for others who attended those sessions and subsequent sessions of that group at the Annual Meeting. I now read texts that I have known for many years and interrogate them with new questions. I have some clues from these scholars on where I might go to find a wider literature with perspectives and methods unfamiliar to me but very helpful in opening familiar texts in new ways.

Now this collection of essays will begin to make this growing discussion on disability and biblical studies available to a wider group of colleagues and fellow scholars. Having read these essays I know that they are in for some genuine discoveries of method, contextualization, exegesis, and theological meaning related to texts familiar but seldom read in this way. My assigned task is to respond to the essays in this volume, and I do so out of deep gratitude that this conversation has begun, and that I can listen in on it, learn from it, and hopefully join it.

Introducing a New Context

In the last half of the twentieth century there began a significant shift in interpretive method for biblical studies. Even in the decade of the 1960s biblical studies were dominated by methodologies that focused on the construction of the text and to some degree on its ancient context to the degree that could be discovered. These were the methods associated with historical criticism (literary criticism, form criticism, tradition history, redaction criticism, and others). Popular textbooks and reference tools published in the '60s were still suggesting that one could first find out what the text meant (in its ancient context) and then consider what the text means (interpretation for present meaning and insight). Obviously some of the tools and approaches for these methodologies remain important and helpful, but the last decades of the century into the first of the new century saw a dramatic shift in the methodological framework within which interpretation of biblical texts takes place. Scrutiny of the text and its ancient context was matched by attention to the context and social location of the interpreter. Attention was now also focused on the reader of the text or on communities with a common social identity within which texts were read. Interpretation was seen as emerging from an interaction of text and reader, each carrying with itself important contextual information that had to be critically considered in advancing interpretive opinions. Genuinely objective opinions became widely considered impossible and undesirable, although it remained important that both text and reader be considered critically and dialogically. A glance at the program for the SBL Annual Meeting from the '80s to the present would document this change. Groups consciously sought to read texts as women (feminists and womanists), African Americans, or scholars from particular global contexts (Asia, Africa, Latin America), among others. The result has been a new valuing of interested reading of biblical text (as opposed to disinterested). What do we see about a given text if we read it through the experience of a particular, consciously articulated context rather than from the assumed "normate" context that Kerry H. Wynn reminds us in his essay was usually "able-bodied, white, Protestant, male and heterosexual"?

The essays in this volume introduce a new context for interpreting biblical texts and entering into conversation with those texts. It is the context of those who have been labeled by the wider society to be disabled or impaired. It is the context of a growing critical attention in various academic disciplines to disability and impairment and a conviction that these wider academic discussions have something to offer the work of biblical interpretation. The hope of this volume is that this relatively new conversation in biblical studies might become more widely known and its insights and methods more widely appropriated.

There are reasons why this conversation is only now in its early stages.

- It required the consciousness of a new group of interpreters. These interpreters are appearing out of the ranks of persons defined by our society as "disabled" in some way or those with family members so labeled. This has been slow to happen because theological schools and graduate schools have been slow to make their programs open and accessible even as they began to open their doors to women, ethnic groups, and international candidates. Because scholarship on disability studies is still relatively unknown in the biblical guild of scholars there has often been little encouragement to explore dissertation and publication topics in this area. The scholars represented in this volume are beginning to change that reality.

- I believe the essays in this volume reflect a wider change in the social climate in North America. There is a greater public awareness of the contributions and needs of those persons traditionally labeled as disabled or impaired. The ADA has provided new access for education, social services, and employment opportunities to a group of citizens treated as invisible by many in the communities they are a part of. Although biblical studies may have been a bit slower, this volume matches similar developments in fields such as psychology, sociology, anthropology, history, community planning, management, and business. The bibliographies and footnotes in these essays show that biblical scholars are learning from colleagues across disciplinary lines, and these references can provide helpful sources for readers of this volume who may want to join the conversation. These new conversations in various settings in our society are welcome but have been slower to develop than those of gender, race, class, culture, and sexual orientation.

This volume is a landmark contribution to biblical studies and opens a new and broader conversation. It introduces new categories and methods; it surveys the literatures related to biblical studies with a new and revealing lens; it gives us surprising and rich new encounters with old, familiar texts.

New Categories and Methods

All who read this volume will have to make room in their consciousness for a new set of categories and methodologies.

Most foundational will be the simple addition of the words "disability" and "impairment" to one's vocabulary along with a new awareness of how difficult it is to define the content of these words. Readers new to this arena will be surprised at the range of issues the mere defining of these terms raises. Although the two terms are often used interchangeably, as in much of this volume, the semantic range seems to be somewhat different. Melcher, in declaring her preference for the term "impairment," suggests that "disability" evokes judgments about lack of ability, whereas "impairment" links to a much broader range of limitations, some more and some less serious, that do not seem as negative in defining a person's ability.

What may be surprising to many readers is how fluid and dynamic these terms can be. Ancient conceptions of disability/impairment were often very different than our own. The essays of both Walls and Kelley make clear that the ancient world made few distinctions among disease, injury, and disability, even though some conditions may be permanent and others not. Ancient lists of those with disabilities often include, to our minds, some surprising categories. Infertility was almost always listed as a major disability for women because the ancient social stigma was so great when a woman's major role was defined as contingent on childbearing. Modern women may experience such a condition as a major sorrow but would not usually consider themselves disabled, at least in societies with expanded opportunities for women.

This leads into what seems to be a major agreement among the contributors to the volume. All contributors seem to prefer a social model for considering disability rather than a medical model (although some acknowledge a role for the medical framework). Although most of the essays indicate this preference, Walls, Wynn, and Melcher discuss their reasons for this choice at greater length. They indicate a growing opinion in the literature of disability studies that disability should be considered a social construction that may take different forms in different cultural and historic situations. Such a social model emphasizes the importance of disability as defined by the social order as opposed to a medical model that simply observes disability as a bodily condition (Wynn, Toensing). Walls calls this a community model and emphasizes the importance that attaches to the community's judgment on ability to perform social functions rather than the mere existence of medical or physical conditions. Melcher indicates how broadly current social structures are willing to define disability, ranging from physical differences to mental conditions to diseases and illness to injuries or undesirable body characteristics. Walls and Kelley make clear how different this list could be in ancient cultures, obviously including the biblical communities. I suspect that this shift from medical to social models of disability will be one of the most helpful learnings for those new to this discussion. This, however, is bound to create some confusion since many teach in schools with disability accommodation programs that are still greatly influenced by medical models of understanding and responding to disability.

The essays of this volume also introduce us to some new methodologies that may prove effective additions in approaching the work of biblical interpretation. Hector Avalos introduces sensory criticism based on observation of the differential evaluation given to the senses in various biblical texts. He posits that this may affect the way these texts value persons in defining disabilities and applies his method to the Deuteronomistic History and the book of Job as examples. Wynn introduces us to the category of the "normate" to give nuance to the use of the social model in looking at biblical texts involving disability. This refers to a socially constructed ideal image used to measure the degree to which persons are understood by themselves or others as definitive human beings. This actually seems a concept useful in evaluating attitudes of the social order to any who deviate from the ideal norm, whether because of disability, race, gender, or sexual preference. Melcher draws upon metaphor theory in analyzing prophetic use of disability metaphors. This technique is well known in contemporary literary criticism and poetics, but is not widely used in biblical studies. Fuller treatments of these methodologies should be left to the reading of the essays, but suffice it to say that readers will be stimulated to think beyond the usual array of analytical tools common to biblical interpretation.

New Perspectives to Survey the Literature

One of the contributions of a volume such as this is that it usually includes some essays that helpfully survey broad expanses of material viewed through a new interpretive lens. Such essays are both programmatic and suggestive. They are like roadmaps that suggest new paths for scholars to travel, perhaps stopping along the way to explore an idea more deeply or to take a suggestive side path to a new insight. This volume is rich in such essays.

Two of the most obvious open the volume as Neal Walls and Nicole Kelley explore the concept of disability in the ancient Near East and the Greco-Roman world respectively. Obviously the literature is vast and can only be sampled, but both essays succeed in introducing us to a new landscape in which our assumptions about disability and impairment are not shared by the ancient world, and we begin to see more clearly that such assumptions are socially constructed. I am particularly grateful to Walls for introducing me to the text of Enki and Ninmah. The attitude that bodies formed with "otherness" are capable of productive occupations in the social order and therefore are not to be considered "good or bad" (as does

Ninmah) gives us in Enki a model to emulate from a most unlikely source. That otherness in some particular form labeled a disability may limit the activity or occupation of a person is no different than the reality for every person, none of whom is gifted for every activity or occupation. Both Walls and Kelley provide us with avenues into vast ancient literatures in productive ways that it is hoped will encourage others to follow and explore further.

Other essays in the volume similarly explore particular bodies of biblical material in a broad fashion to expose a range of biblical perspectives on disability/impairment. Avalos looks at the broad sweep of the Deuteronomistic History with attention to the privileging of hearing in this broad corpus. The essay succeeds in provoking us to new ways of thinking about this great sweep of literature. Does the prophetic influence reflected in the Deuteronomistic History and its emphasis on Word privilege the auditory and to what effect? I would caution against using every use of the verb "to hear" as auditory in character. For example, the Shema (Hear, O Israel . . .) may carry the meaning of "obey" rather than simple sensory reception. Jeremy Schipper also takes the Deuteronomistic History as his field of investigation, sweeping across its breadth to show convincingly that disability is being used as a tool for social commentary rather than as comment on lived experience. Particularly significant is his observation that images of disability surface regularly at key points of leadership transfer.

Melcher surveys disability metaphors in the Latter Prophets to excellent effect, linking metaphors of impairment to prophetic views of God as healer/restorer. Of course, more problematic are prophetic references to God as using impairment to punish moral deficiency. Such texts strike me as having something in common with the problems discussed in feminist treatments of the prophetic use of abuse images in the punishment of Israel as Yahweh's wife. Disability studies of biblical literature will have to face the problems of such texts squarely, and Melcher has made a good beginning. I did find some of the texts used to discuss impairment to suggest Israel is willfully rebellious rather than impaired, for example Ezek 12:1–16.

Martin Albl in a broad-ranging treatment of Pauline texts discusses Paul's theology of both a disabled and a glorified Christ and Paul's summons to participate in Christ's disability (cross) and glorified ability (resurrection). I found most provocative his treatment of Paul's own physical infirmity ("weakness of the flesh") in Galatians and his "thorn in the flesh" in 2 Corinthians.

The essays of Fontaine and Hentrich deserve special mention for their employment of a double lens of interpretive perspective. To the intent of looking at ancient and biblical literature from the perspective of disability is added the perspective of gender. Fontaine's work suggests that being female itself is considered an impairment. In ancient art, enemies and captives are depicted as feminized. Women who do manage to rise to power are painted as men. Philistines are taunted in 1 Samuel with becoming a woman in order to urge them to courage in battle. Her work suggests that interesting additional work might be done on race or sexual orientation as socially defined impairment. Fontaine and Hentrich both note that most depictions of the disabled or impaired in the Bible are men, except for the stories of women as infertile. Hentrich helpfully focuses a vast range of references to men as disabled or impaired on the question of whether disability affects human interaction with God. The answer seems to be that this is more problematic for kings and priests, who to some degree represent God, than for the average Israelite.

New Encounters with Familiar Texts

Some essays have chosen less to survey a broad range of texts and references than to look at particular texts in order to demonstrate the benefits of new disability perspectives on the work of biblical interpretation. Even some of the broader-sweep essays pause for deeper exegetical work on selected texts. The result is that this volume is filled with interpretive gems. Texts are looked at through new and different lenses, and the effect is rich and sometimes astonishing. There is a danger here that I could find myself summarizing treatments that are much more fruitfully enjoyed in their full text within the essays, so I will content myself with simply indicating some of the exegetical discussions that I found especially insightful.

Holly Joan Toensing's essay deserves special mention because she has chosen to focus entirely on a single text, the story of Jesus and the demon-possessed man in Mark 5:1–20. She has interwoven her treatment of this passage with comment on historic and current treatment of persons with mental illness, and the conversation between her exposition of the text and her experience of the contemporary context is genuinely illuminating. She is convincing in making connections between the ancient language of demon possession and testimony by those struggling with mental illness of experiencing a seizure of control by something other and beyond their own selves. The role of community in the Markan story is brought out much more clearly in both positive and negative ways than in previous treatments I have read. This in turn begins to suggest some connection to the role community has played, both in its presence and absence, as large numbers of the mentally ill have been deinstitutionalized to live among us. There is more that could be said, but it is enough to be grateful for the modeling of such a strong connection between textual exposition and contemporary experience. One wishes there were a few more essays in the collection that probed deeply into a single text.

There are, however, ample examples of thought-provoking and insightful treatments of particular texts throughout the essays in this volume.

- Wynn focuses on two Jacob stories that involve disability: the blindness of Isaac when Jacob takes the blessing from Esau (Gen 27) and the disabling of Jacob in the wrestling with the night visitor (Gen 32). His careful readings take us to interesting conclusions. In Gen 27, he suggests that Isaac is not powerless or near death simply because he is blind. His disability is the context for the deception of Jacob and not its cause. In Gen 32, Wynn surprisingly and convincingly sees Jacob's limp as a sign of the covenant and of the blessing he gained, not a shame or a curse.

- In Schipper's treatment of texts in the Deuteronomistic History, already mentioned above, I felt his recasting of the story of Michal in 2 Sam 6 was especially helpful. He treats Michal's childlessness as infertility but makes a convincing case that time should not be spent seeking the cause for this in an individual body when the function of the story is as an ideologically charged metaphor for the end of the Saulide house.

- Melcher helpfully surveys a wide range of prophetic texts, but her notion that Isa 45:9–12 could be used in a disability liberation ethic is inspired and provocative. The free sovereignty of God as Creator who creates all persons in forms and purposes that suit divine intentions is an idea worth exploring. Melcher deserves our thanks for making clear that specific categories of disability or characters with disabilities do not need to appear in order to make texts worth exploring in constructing a biblical disability theology/ethics.

- Avalos couples his broad survey of auditory images in the whole of Deuteronomistic History with a closer look at visual images in a single book, Job. He makes a strong case that the text of Job especially values visual imagery. I do think images of light, darkness, seeing, and visions play a dominating role, and Job acknowledges in 42:5 that he has been transformed by "seeing" God. However, I do think we should not overstate this case when the theophany, though face to face, has the content of Yahweh's speeches to Job, an audio experience with a content agreed by most commentators to be key in interpreting the book.

- Albl's closer comment on Gal 4:13–14 and 2 Cor 10–13 has been mentioned above, but these are especially strong expositions of key texts in understanding the nature of Paul's self-admitted bodily impairments.

Remaining Agenda

The nature of collections such as this is that, when well done as this one is, they actually generate as many new issues as they resolve. Reading these essays should stimulate many to think in new categories and to pursue ideas down new pathways. It was part of the intent of those who initiated this volume.

I will only share two brief issues that lodge in my mind after reading these essays. The first is that it seems to me more work needs to be done on distinguishing between conditions that reflect diversity in creation and conditions that exist because of acts of personal will. This is where "disability" seems to be better able to make such a distinction than the term "impairment." I can choose to do things that seriously impair my ability to function in relationships, responsibilities, and general citizenship in the community, but I would seldom speak of these as disabilities. Theologically I can be a sinner, and this has consequences. I might speak of being impaired by my willful acts of sin that create brokenness, but I do not think that we should speak of this broken condition as a disability. This seems particularly urgent since some biblical texts and many religious attitudes through the ages have suggested sin as a cause or explanation of disability. It does seem to me that, whatever terms we use, some further discussion is necessary to make clear distinctions between conditions that reflect the diversity of persons by genetic or acquired characteristics that are socially construed by the community as disability and acts of human will that disrupt our full functioning and capacity in human community. This is applicable to biblical interpretation in which the effects of human sin are often part of the story but seem different than the appearance of characters and categories that reflect the otherness that the stories and texts themselves seem to regard as disability. Cain is treated as a sinner, not as a man with disabilities, but his life becomes significantly impaired. I fully appreciate the complexity of these questions but urge continuing conversation on them.

A second thought was raised after a full reading of these essays. Do we not need both medical and social models for speaking of disability? Both Toensing and Albl suggest that we do. The two models seem like alternative and needed perspectives that do not require a hard either-or choice. In the story of the man in Mark 5 the community was required to respond to the medical symptoms of the man's condition because he may have been a danger to the community, but, of course, the methods they chose were socially conditioned by the attitudes and practices of their time. I return to my own daughter mentioned at the start of this essay. Medications assist her to function in a manner that allows her an independence she could not otherwise enjoy. I am grateful every day for the careful diagnosis and treatment of her bodily condition by many caring medical personnel. But the shift in social attitude and social policy has also allowed her to construct an independent life when I know she would have been warehoused in an institution not too long ago. Surely, even in the work of biblical interpretation we need both of these lenses to look most fully at biblical understandings of disability.

The Goal of Interpretation

Finally let me acknowledge my gratitude to the contributors that in this entire volume they operate out of an interpretive perspective that is not defined by a disinterested effort to expand human knowledge. Interpretation in this volume has a vested interest in reading the texts of Jewish and Christian scriptures in ways that might help make a difference in the lives of those defined by bodily realities and social categories as disabled. There is a context for such interpretation that lies in compassion and advocacy for those children of God whose particularity is still often rendered invisible or objectionable by the communities within which we function. The community of biblical scholarship has been impaired by the largely absent witness of the disabled/impaired and those who know and value their presence as a part of the richness of the human family. Perhaps this volume helps signal the end of that era.

Conclusion

Hector Avalos
Sarah J. Melcher
Jeremy Schipper

The very title of our work, *This Abled Body*, invites readers to think in new ways about texts. The title encourages vocal and auditory dissonance insofar as it can be heard and voiced as "disabled body." Yet we mean the opposite. The realization that texts can mean the opposite of what we have thought them to mean lies at the very heart of our mission for the book. We want readers to think in new ways about what it means to be abled-bodied or disabled in the Bible and the ancient Near East. In so doing, we discover more about what it means to be disabled and abled of body today, and how those ancient texts have influenced, for better or for ill, our present embodied experience.

I. The Future

This Abled Body is, of course, not the last word on disabilities in the Bible. We have presented it as a starting point for a larger interdisciplinary conversation. In fact, it is exciting to think of what is coming over the horizon in the field of disability studies in the ancient world. We need not be over-confident in our augury to state that what we will experience in the next decade will be a proliferation of books on disability. We take it as a good sign for the state of this field that this volume was not able to reflect all of the talented scholars, the theories, or the methods that are emerging at the time of publication. By way of conclusion, we would like to reflect briefly on some of the promising avenues of research that disability studies will pursue in the years to come. We also note some additional scholarly works that may help move this field in these directions.

Unlike many biblical disciplines that focus on the purely formal features of textual and archaeological objects, disability studies is first and foremost about people and how we value them. As such, it follows in the traditions of the humanities and the social sciences. The differential valuation of persons, based on their perceived mental or physical features, is a persistent aspect of our human history. Everything from race to gender is associated with differential valuations, and so it is imperative that we understand the mechanisms by which those differential valuations come into existence.

Along these lines, disability studies will probably interact more intimately with physiognomy, the study of how bodily features were perceived as expressions of character, including moral character. We already see this in the work of Mikeal Parsons on the Bible. Physiognomy has undergone quite a revival within the study of the Greco-Roman period and Late Antiquity, especially as new editions of texts have been published recently (see Boys-Stones et al.). Within Assyriology, major studies by Barbara Böck have also appeared. So already emerging is a new or enhanced set of data for the study of physiognomy from Mesopotamia to the Mediterranean and beyond.

Still not so widely recognized are the interesting insights emanating from the study of embryology in the Near Eastern and Mediterranean worlds. How human beings develop in the womb has been linked to how they will be valued after birth and what sorts of disabilities they are likely to experience. Important new editions of such embryological treatises are being published (e.g., Cilliers). Within biblical studies, Lourdes Garcia Ureña argues that the enigmatic Hebrew word *nasakti* (NRSV: "I have set") in Ps 2:6 is actually an embryological description that is best translated as "I have woven [my king]." The notion of "weaving" human beings adds another dimension to how biblical authors thought about the divine crafting of the human body.

Disability studies will continue to be an integral part of, and contributor to, what might be best described as "corporeal criticism," which would treat the human embodied experience. Such studies can shed much light not only on disabilities but on how our modern world constructs the embodied experience from the cellular level (e.g., Henry Harris) to the highest embodied collectivities. As such, corporeal criticism already has a vigorous existence in the study of cultures and religions outside of Judaism and Christianity (see Beck; Desjarlais). Such investigations are important in light of the increasing attention to how technology and the cyber-age may change our concept of human nature itself (Baillie and Casey; Baldi)

Within biblical studies, scholars have become increasingly sensitive to the theological or ideological perspectives encoded in the imagery of the Bible and its cognate literature. Scholars have produced many highly nuanced works that treat biblical images such as kingship, covenant, Zion, and land, to name a few. Such works also show how these images help "map out" the theological or ideological landscape of the Bible and its cognate literature. Nonetheless, until recently, scholarly treatments of disability have remained relatively un-nuanced and assumed that the social meanings and experience of disability are basically stable and transparent. Yet a disability studies perspective shows how ancient writers employ disability as a literary motif with a great deal of sophistication. This use invites the same amount of critical inquiry as other more traditionally acknowledged biblical motifs. Monograph-length studies are beginning to address this need. In addition to *This Blemished Body* (Dorman) and *Disability Studies and the Hebrew Bible* (Schipper), which are now in print, we look forward to the publication of further important monographs along these lines (Olyan; Raphael).

As we continue to "map out" the literary use of disability in the Bible and its cognate literature, we will not simply create yet another sub-discipline within biblical or Near Eastern studies. Rather, as such work helps us better appreciate the poetics of ancient texts, it will make substantive contributions to the more traditional set of critical issues within biblical studies, including questions of textual history, production, and redaction. As this research progresses, disability studies will help scholars interested in traditional-critical issues approach them with greater methodological and exegetical rigor.

Over the past several decades, many biblical scholars have gained a renewed appreciation for the history of interpretation. Among other things, this history has further sensitized contemporary scholars to the poetics of the Bible by noting what details their early counterparts highlighted, puzzled over, or filled in. We may learn much about the "meanings" encoded in biblical images of disability by studying closely how early exegetes read such images. Recently, Scott Cason has written a dissertation dealing with the images of disability in the *Testament of Job* (Cason). Such promising works on the history of interpretation help us explore not only textual poetics but how texts and their interpreters reflect and reinforce the differential valuation of persons.

As seen in this volume, the vast majority of work on disability and ancient texts has focused on those texts that contain images of disability. In the coming years, more thorough studies of the poetics of disability may also help us better understand ancient texts that do not deal directly with images of disability. For example, we may ask what would happen if one applied a disability studies perspective to a reading of the creation accounts in the Bible or other ancient Near Eastern sources. Such a project may help explain further how ancient cultures constructed their theological or anthropological systems.

Furthermore, while this volume has focused on images of disability in ancient texts, future studies likely will explore the ethical implications of such texts for cognitively and physically impaired persons today. The essays in this volume represent a prolegomena of sorts—innovative research into the depiction of disability in ancient literature. Future research could dig more deeply into the relevance of these depictions for current attitudes toward persons with physical and cognitive impairments.

The contributors in this volume surely differ on the place of these texts in their lives. Some are members of faith communities, in which biblical texts are normative for practice to varying degrees. Others do not see these texts as normative and are concerned about the possible impact the texts' devaluation of disabled persons can have on those who read them. Whatever the authors' personal commitments and perspectives, they would likely agree that the Bible has had a prominent role historically in shaping readers' attitudes.

Because of the Bible's influence in Western culture and its role in shaping readers' attitudes and actions, future work will wrestle with the ethical ramifications of representations of disability in ancient texts and artwork. Perhaps, if the authors of this volume were pressed for an answer, they would concede that at the heart of research into disability in ancient texts is a desire to be advocates for those contemporaries who have experienced disability. Exploration into ancient perspectives about disability can help us to confront current attitudes toward those perceived to be disabled by their culture. By confronting these attitudes, perhaps they can be changed.

Leaders in the field of biblical studies have urged others in the biblical guild to consider the public impact of their interpretations. Biblical scholars do consider the relevance of their work. If the work reflected in this volume is indeed relevant, its significance lies in what it can do in confronting and changing the devaluation of those who are characterized as disabled. The studies undertaken here are a first step to discern the various perspectives toward physical and cognitive impairment imbedded in some ancient texts.

As the study of disability moves forward, it will possibly reflect a variety of approaches. Perhaps some interpreters will develop a kind of disability criticism that resembles feminist criticism in its goals and practices. In some cases, scholars will search for texts that will serve as a source for an emancipatory perspective for disabled persons today. Others will reject the ancient perspectives toward disability encoded in texts and juxtapose an inclusive perspective from secular sources. Whatever the multitude of approaches toward the study of disability in the Bible and the ancient Near East, they will probably share in common a concern to improve conditions for living persons. *This Abled Body*, in that sense, is an expression of hope for the improvement of the life of every body on our fragile planet.

Bibliography

Abusch, Tzvi. 2002. *Mesopotamian Witchcraft: Toward a History and Understanding of Babylonian Witchcraft Beliefs and Literature.* Ancient Magic and Divination 5. Leiden: Styx.

Achtemeier, Paul J. 1996. *The HarperCollins Bible Dictionary.* Rev. ed. New York: HarperCollins.

Ackerman, Diane. 1990. *A Natural History of the Senses.* New York: Random House.

Ackroyd, Peter R. 1979. *The Second Book of Samuel. The Cambridge Bible Commentary. New English Bible.* 2d ed. Cambridge: Cambridge University Press.

Albl, Martin C. 1999. *"And Scripture Cannot Be Broken": The Form and Function of The Early Christian Testimonia Collections.* Leiden: Brill.

———. 2002. "Are Any Among You Sick?" The Health Care System in the Letter of James. *JBL* 121:123–43.

———. 2004. *Pseudo-Gregory of Nyssa: Testimonies against the Jews.* Atlanta: Society of Biblical Literature.

Albrecht, Gary L., Katherine D. Seelman, and Michael Bury, eds. 2001. *Handbook of Disability Studies.* Thousand Oaks, CA: Sage Publications.

Alster, Bendt. 1997. *Proverbs of Ancient Sumer: The World's Earliest Proverb Collections.* 2 vols. Bethesda, MD: CDL.

———. 2005. *Wisdom of Ancient Sumer.* Bethesda, MD: CDL.

Amundsen, Darrel W. 1987. Medicine and the Birth of Defective Children: Approaches of the Ancient World. Pages 3–22 in *Euthanasia and the Newborn: Conflicts Regarding Saving Lives.* Edited by R. McMillan, H. Tristram Engelhardt Jr., and Stuart F. Spicker. Dordrecht, Germany: D. Reidl.

Andersen, Arnold A. 1989. *2 Samuel.* Word Biblical Commentary 11. Dallas: Word.

Arnheim, Rudolf. 1957. *Film as Art.* Berkeley: University of California Press.

Arnold, Dorothea. 1996. *The Royal Women of Amarna: Images of Beauty from Ancient Egypt.* New York: Metropolitan Museum of Art/Harry Abrams.

Asher-Greve, Julia M. 1998. The Essential Body: Mesopotamian Conceptions of the Gendered Body. Pages 8–37 in *Gender and the Body in the Ancient Mediterranean.* Edited by Maria Wyke. Oxford: Blackwell.

Avalos, Hector. 1995a. *Illness and Health Care in the Ancient Near East: The Role of the Temple in Greece, Mesopotamia, and Israel.* HSM 54. Atlanta: Scholars.

———. 1995b. Ancient Medicine: In Case of Emergency Contact Your Local Prophet. *BR* 11 (June): 26–32, 34–35, 48.

———. 1995c. Epilepsy in Babylonia. *JCS* 47:119–21.

———. 1998. Disability and Liturgy in Ancient and Modern Religious Traditions.

Pages 35–54 in *Human Disability and the Service of God*. Edited by Nancy L. Eiesland and Don E. Saliers. Nashville: Abingdon.

———. 1999. *Health Care and the Rise of Christianity*. Peabody, MA: Hendrickson Press.

———. 2007a. Redemptionism, Rejectionism, and Historicism as Emerging Approaches in Disability Studies. *Perspectives in Religious Studies* (spring): 91–100.

———. 2007b. *The End of Biblical Studies*. Amherst, NY: Prometheus Press.

Bail, Ulrike, et al., eds. 2003. *Körperkonzepteim Ersten Testament: Aspekte einer Feministischen Anthropologie*. Bonn: W. Kolhammer.

Baillie, Harold W., and Timothy Casey. 2005. *Is Human Nature Obsolete? Genetics, Bioengineering, and the Future of the Human Condition*. Cambridge: MIT Press.

Baines, John. 1995. Origins of Egyptian Kingship. Pages 109–21 in *Ancient Egyptian Kingship*. Edited by David O'Connor and David Silverman. Leiden: Brill.

Baldi, Pierre. 2001. *The Shattered Self: The End of Natural Evolution*. Cambridge: MIT Press.

Barton, Carlin A. 1993. *The Sorrows of the Ancient Romans: The Gladiator and the Monster*. Princeton: Princeton University Press.

Bauer, Walter, et. al. 1979. *A Greek-English Lexicon of the New Testament and Other Early Christian Literature*. 2nd ed. Chicago: University of Chicago Press.

Bazopoulou-Kyrkanidou, Euterpe. 1997. What Makes Hephaestus Lame? *American Journal of Medical Genetics* 72:144–55.

Beare, Francis Wright. 1981. *The Gospel according to Matthew: A Commentary*. Oxford: Basil Blackwell.

Beck, Guy L. 1993. *Sonic Theology: Hinduism and Sacred Sound*. Columbia: University of South Carolina Press.

Becking, Bob. 1996. Touch for Health . . . Magic in II Reg 4, 31–37 with a Remark on the History of Yahwism. *ZAW* 108:34–54.

Benito, Carlos. 1969. "Enki and Ninmah" and "Enki and the World Order." Ph.D. diss., University of Pennsylvania.

Berger, Maurice, Brian Wallis, and Simon Watson, eds. 1995. *Constructing Masculinity*. New York: Routledge.

Berlin, Adele. 1994. *Zephaniah: A New Translation with Introduction and Commentary*. AB 25A. New York: Doubleday.

Berquist, Jon L. 2002. *Controlling Corporeality: The Body and the Household in Ancient Israel*. New Brunswick, NJ: Rutgers University Press.

Betcher, Sharon V. 2001. Rehabilitating Religious Discourse: Bringing Disability Studies to the Theological Venue. *RelSRev* 4:341–48.

Betz, Hans Dieter. 1979. *Galatians*. Hermeneia. Philadelphia: Fortress.

Biggs, Robert D. 1967. *ŠÁ.ZI.GA: Ancient Mesopotamian Potency Incantations*. TCS 2. Locust Valley, NY: Augustin.

———. 1995. Medicine, Surgery, and Public Health in Ancient Mesopotamia. *CANE* 3:1911–24.

Birch, Bruce C. 1971. The Development of the Tradition of the Anointing of Saul in 1 Sam 9:1–10:16. *JBL* 90:55–68.

———. 1976. *The Rise of the Israelite Monarchy: The Growth and Development of 1 Samuel 7–15*. Missoula, MT: Scholars.

———. 1985. *What Does the Lord Require? The Old Testament Call to Social Justice*. Philadelphia: Westminster.

————. 1991. *Let Justice Roll Down: The Old Testament, Ethics, and Christian Life*. Louisville: Westminster John Knox.

————. 2003. Integrating Welcome into the Seminary Curriculum. Pages 23–31 in *Graduate Theological Education and the Human Experience of Disability*. Edited by Robert C. Anderson. Binghamton, NY: Haworth.

Birch, Bruce C., and Larry Rasmussen. 1989. *The Bible and Ethics in the Christian Life*. Minneapolis: Augsburg.

Black, Kathy. 1996. *A Healing Homiletic: Preaching and Disability*. Nashville: Abingdon.

Bloch, Raymond. 1963. *Les prodiges dans l'antiquité classique (Grèce, Étrurie et Rome)*. Paris: Presses Universitaires de France.

Boaz, Noel T., and Alan J. Almquist. 2002. *Biological Anthropology: A Synthetic Approach to Human Evolution*. Upper Saddle River, NJ: Prentice Hall.

Böck, Barbara. 2000. *Die babylonisch-assyrische Morphoskopie*. AfOB 27. Vienna: Institut für Orientalistik der Universität Wien.

————. 2004. Weitere Texte physiognomischen Inhalts. *Sefarad* 64:289–314.

Bogdan, Robert. 1990. *Presenting Human Oddities for Amusement and Profit*. Chicago: University of Chicago Press.

Boswell, John E. 1988. *The Kindness of Strangers: The Abandonment of Children in Western Europe from Late Antiquity to the Renaissance*. New York: Pantheon.

Bottéro, Jean, and Samuel Noah Kramer. 1989. *Lorsque les dieux faisaient l'homme: Mythologie mésopotamienne*. Paris: Gallimard.

Boys-Stones, George, et al. 2006. *Seeing the Face, Seeing the Soul: Polemon's Physiognomy from Classical Antiquity to Medieval Islam*. New York: Oxford.

Braddock, David L., and Susan L. Parish. 2001. An Institutional History of Disability. Pages 11–68 in *Handbook of Disability Studies*. Edited by Gary L. Albrecht, Katherine D. Seelman, and Michael Bury. Thousand Oaks, CA: Sage.

Braude, William G., trans. 1959. *The Midrash on Psalms*. Vol. 1 of 2. New Haven: Yale University Press.

Brink, Edwin C. M. van den, and Thomas E. Levy, eds. 2002. *Egypt and the Levant: Interrelations from the Fourth through the Early Third Millennium BCE*. London: Leicester University Press.

Brown, Christopher G. 1989. Ares, Aphrodite, and the Laughter of the Gods. *Phoenix* 43:283–93.

Brown, Michael L. 1995. *Israel's Divine Healer*. Grand Rapids: Zondervan.

Bruce. F. F. 1982. *The Epistle to the Galatians*. NIGTC. Grand Rapids: Eerdmans.

Brueggemann, Walter. 1982. *Genesis*. Interpretation. Atlanta: John Knox Press.

————. 1998. *A Commentary on Jeremiah: Exile and Homecoming*. Grand Rapids: Eerdmans.

Brunet, Gilbert. 1979. Les aveugles et les boiteux jébusites. *VTS* 30. 65–72.

Bultmann, Rudolf. 1951. *Theology of the New Testament*. 2 vols. New York: Charles Scribner's Sons.

Burkert, Walter. 1985. *Greek Religion: Archaic and Classical*. Translated by J. Raffan. Oxford: Blackwell.

Butler, Judith. 1990. *Gender Trouble: Feminism and the Subversion of Identity*. New York: Routledge.

Buxton, R. G. A. 1980. Blindness and Limits: Sophokles and the Logic of Myth. *The Journal of Hellenic Studies* 100:22–37.

Calvin, John. 1992. *Sermons on 2 Samuel: Chapters 1–13*. Translated by Douglas Kelly. Edinburgh: Banner of Truth Trust.

Campbell, John M. 2003. *Being Biblical: How Can We Use the Bible in Constructing Ethics Today*. London: United Reformed Church.

Caplice, Richard. 1974. *The Akkadian Namburbi Texts: An Introduction*. SANE 1. Los Angeles: Undena.

Capps, Donald. 2005. *Fragile Connections: Memoirs of Mental Illness for Pastoral Care Professionals*. St. Louis: Chalice.

Cason, Scott. 2007. " 'Gird Your Loins Like a Man': The Interplay of Disability and Masculinity in the Testament of Job." Ph.D. diss., Florida State University.

Cassin, Elena. 1987. La droit et le tordu—II. Handicapés et marginaux dans la Mésopotamie des IIe-Ier millénaires. Pages 72–97 in *Le semblable et le différent: Symbolismes du pouvoir dans le Proche–Orient ancien*. Paris: Découverte.

Chapman, Cynthia R. 2004. *The Gendered Language of Warfare in the Israelite-Assyrian Encounter*. HSM 62. Winona Lake, IN: Eisenbrauns.

Childs, Brevard S. 2001. *Isaiah*. OTL. Louisville: Westminster John Knox.

Chillers, L. 2004. Vindicianus' *Gynaecia* and Theories on Generation and Embryology from the Babylonians to Graeco-Roman Times. Pages 343–67 in *Magic and Rationality in Ancient Near Eastern and Graeco-Roman Medicine*. Edited by H. E. J. Horstmanshoff and M. Stol. Leiden: Brill.

Classen, Constance.1993. *Worlds of Sense: Exploring the Senses in History and Across Cultures*. London: Routledge.

Classen, Constance, David Howes, and Anthony Synott, eds. 1994. *Aroma: The Cultural History of Smell*. London: Routledge.

Clines, David J. A. 1989. *Job 1–20*. Dallas: Word Books.

———. 1995. David the Man: The Construction of Masculinity in the Hebrew Bible. Pages 212–41 in *Interested Parties: The Ideology of Writers and Readers of the Hebrew Bible*. JSOTSup 205: Gender, Culture, Theory 1. Sheffield: Sheffield Academic Press.

Coats, George W. 1977. Legendary Motifs in the Moses Death Reports. *CBQ* 39:34–44.

Collins, Adela Yarbro. 1992. *The Beginning of the Gospel: Probings of Mark in Context*. Minneapolis: Augsburg Fortress.

Dalley, Stephanie. 1991. *Myths from Mesopotamia: Creation, the Flood, Gilgamesh, and Others*. Oxford: Oxford University Press.

Dasen, V. 1993. *Dwarfs in Ancient Egypt and Greece*. Oxford Monographs in Classical Archaeology. Oxford: Clarendon Press.

Davies, Vivian, and Renee Friedman. 1998. The Narmer Palette: A Forgotten Member. *Nekhen* 10:22.

Davis, Lennard J. 1995. *Enforcing Normalcy: Disability, Deafness, and the Body*. London: Verso.

———. 2002. *Bending Over Backwards: Disability, Dismodernism, and Other Difficult Positions*. New York: New York University Press.

Davis, Whitney. 1989. *The Canonical Tradition in Ancient Egyptian Art*. Cambridge: Cambridge University Press.

———. 1992. *Masking the Blow: The Scene of Representation in Late Prehistoric Egyptian Art*. Berkeley: University of California Press.

Delcourt, Marie. 1938. *Stérilités mystérieuses et naissances maléfiques dans l'antiquité classique*. Paris: Belles Lettres.

———. 1957. *Héphaistos ou la légende du magicien*. Paris: Belles Lettres.

Delling, Gerhard. 1971. σκόλοψ. Pages 409–13 in vol. 7 of *Theological Dictionary of the*

New Testament. Edited by Gerhard Kittel and Gerhard Friedrich. Translated by Geoffrey W. Bromiley. 10 vols. Grand Rapids: Eerdmans, 1964–76.

den Boer, W. 1979. *Private Morality in Greece and Rome: Some Historical Aspects.* Leiden: Brill.

Desjarlais, Robert. 2003. *Sensory Biographies: Lives and Deaths among Nepal's Yolmo Buddhists.* Berkeley: University of California Press.

Dille, Sarah J. 2004. *Mixing Metaphors: God as Mother and Father in Deutero-Isaiah.* London: T & T Clark International.

Dille, Sarah J., and Sarah J. Melcher. Forthcoming. *Discerning the Body: Metaphors of the Body in the Bible.* Guest volume for *The Classical Bulletin.* Wauconda, IL: Bolchazy-Carducci.

Dodds, E. R. 1965. *Pagan and Christian in an Age of Anxiety.* Cambridge: Cambridge University Press.

Dorman, Joanna. 2007. *The Blemished Body: Disability and Deformity in the Qumran Scrolls.* Groningen: Rijksuniversiteit.

Dunn, James D. G. 1998. *The Theology of Paul the Apostle.* Grand Rapids: Eerdmans.

Durrant, Michael, ed. 1993. *Aristotle's De Anima in Focus.* New York: Routledge.

Edwards, Martha Lynn. 1995. "Physical Disability in the Ancient Greek World." Ph.D. thesis, University of Minnesota.

———. 1996. The Cultural Context of Deformity in the Ancient Greek World. *AIIB* 10.3–4: 79–92.

———. 1997. Constructions of Physical Disability in the Ancient Greek World: The Community Concept. Pages 35–50 in *The Body and Physical Difference: Discourses of Disability.* Edited by David T. Mitchell and Sharon L. Snyder. Ann Arbor: University of Michigan Press.

Edwards, Timothy C. 2006. *Cultures of Masculinity.* New York: Routledge.

Eiesland, Nancy L. 1994. *The Disabled God: Toward a Liberatory Theology of Disability.* Nashville: Abingdon.

———. 1998. Barriers and Bridges: Relating the Disability Rights Movement and Religious Organizations. Pages 200–229 in *Human Disability and the Service of God: Reassessing Religious Practice.* Edited by Nancy L. Eiesland and Don E. Saliers. Nashville: Abingdon.

Eiesland, Nancy L., and Don E. Saliers, eds. 1998. *Human Disability and the Service of God: Reassessing Religious Practice.* Nashville: Abingdon.

Eilberg-Schwartz, Howard, ed. 1992. *People of the Body: Jews and Judaism from an Embodied Perspective.* Albany: State University of New York Press.

———. 1994. *God's Phallus and Other Problems for Men and Monotheism.* Boston: Beacon.

Eliade, Mircea. 1968. *The Sacred and the Profane.* New York: Harvest Books.

Ellenius, Allan, ed. 1998. *Iconography, Propaganda, and Legitimation.* European Science Foundation. Oxford: Clarendon Press.

Evans, Craig A. 1997. A Note on the Targum 2 Sam 5:8 and Jesus' Ministry to the "Maimed, Halt, and Blind." *JSP* 15:79–82.

———. 2003. *Jesus and the Ossuaries: What Jewish Burial Practices Reveal about the Beginning of Christianity.* Waco, TX: Baylor University Press.

Evelyn-White, Hugh G., trans. 1914. *The Homeric Hymns and Homerica.* LCL. Cambridge: Harvard University Press.

Exum, J. Cheryl. 1993. *Fragmented Women: Feminist (Sub)versions of Biblical Narratives.* Valley Forge, PA: Trinity Press International.

Faraone, Christopher A. 1992. *Talismans and Trojan Horses: Guardian Statues in Ancient Greek Myth and Ritual*. New York: Oxford University Press.

Farber, Walter. 1985. Akkadisch "blind." *ZA* 75:210–33.

———. 1995. Witchcraft, Magic, and Divination in Ancient Mesopotamia. *CANE* 3:1895–909.

Fincke, Jeanette. 2000. *Augenlieden nach keilschriftlichen Quellen*. Würzburger medizinhistorische Forschungen 70. Würzburg, Germany: Königshausen & Neumann.

Finkel, Irving L. 1998. A Study in Scarlet: Incantations against Samana. Pages 71–106 in *Festschrift für Rykle Borger zu seinem 65. Geburtstag am 24. Mai 1994*. Edited by Stefan M. Maul. Cuneiform Monographs 10. Groningen: Styx.

Finkel, Irving L., and Markham J. Geller, eds. 2007. *Disease in Babylonia*. Cuneiform Monographs 36. Leiden: Brill Academic.

Fleming, Daniel. 1993. The Etymological Origins of the Hebrew *nabî*: The One Who Invokes God. *CBQ* 55, no. 2: 217–24.

Fontaine, Carole R. 1996. Disabilities and Chronic Illness in the Bible: A Feminist Perspective. Pages 286–301 in *A Feminist Companion to the Hebrew Bible in the New Testament*. FCB 10. Edited by Athalya Brenner. Sheffield: Sheffield Academic Press.

———. 2002. *Smooth Words: Women, Proverbs, and Performance in Biblical Wisdom*. New York: Continuum.

———. 2005. Visual Metaphors and Proverbs 5:15–20: Some Archaeological Reflections on Gendered Iconography. Pages 185–202 in *Seeking Out the Wisdom of the Ancients*. Edited by Ronald L Troxel, Kelvin G. Friebel, and Dennis R. Magary. Winona Lake, IN: Eisenbrauns.

Fontaine, Carole R., and Claudia V. Camp, eds. 1993. *Semeia* 61. The theme of the issue is "Women, War, and Metaphor: Language and Society in the Study of the Hebrew Bible."

Foster, Benjamin R. 1995. *From Distant Days: Myths, Tales, and Poetry of Ancient Mesopotamia*. Bethesda, MD: CDL.

———. 1997. The Poem of the Righteous Sufferer. *COS* 1.153:486–92.

Foster, George M. 1976. Disease Etiologies in Non-Western Medical Systems. *American Anthropologist* 78:773–82.

Freedman, H., trans. 1983. *Midrash Rabbah: Genesis*. 1 of 10 vols. London: Soncino.

Freedman, Sally M. 1998. *If a City Is Set on a Height: The Akkadian Omen Series* Šumma Alu ina Mēlê Šakin. *Volume I: Tablets 1–21*. Philadelphia: Samuel Noah Kramer Fund.

Friedman, Richard Elliott. 1987. *Who Wrote the Bible?* New York: Summit Books.

Gallagher, Catherine, and Stephen Greenblatt. 2001. *Practicing New Historicism*. Chicago: University of Chicago Press.

García Ureña, Lourdes. 2004. He tejido mi Rey (Sl 2,6). La importancia del contexto. *Estudios Biblicos* 62:171–184.

Gardiner, Sir Alan. 1957. *Egyptian Grammar: Being an Introduction to the Study of Hieroglyphs* 3rd rev. ed. Oxford: Griffith Institute, Ashmolean Museum.

Garland, Robert. 1994. The Mockery of the Deformed and Disabled in Graeco-Roman Culture. Pages 71–84 in *Laughter Down the Centuries*, vol. 1. Edited by Siegfried Jäkel and Asko Timonen. Turku, Finland: Turun Yliopisto.

———. 1995. *The Eye of the Beholder: Deformity and Disability in the Graeco-Roman World*. Ithaca, NY: Cornell University Press.

Gelb, I. J. 1972. The Arua Institution. *RA* 66:1–32.

———. 1973. Prisoners of War in Early Mesopotamia. *JNES* 32:70–93.

George, Andrew. 1999. *The Epic of Gilgamesh: The Babylonian Epic Poem and Other Texts in Akkadian and Sumerian*. New York: Penguin.

Gerstenberger, Erhard S. 1996. *Yahweh—The Patriarch: Ancient Images of God and Feminist Theology*. Minneapolis: Fortress.

Gilad, Yoav, et al. 2004. Loss of Olfactory Receptor Genes Coincides with the Acquisition of Full Trichromatic Vision in Primates. *Public Library of Science Biology* 2:120–25.

Glendening, K. K. 2005. The Evolution of the Auditory Pathways Underlying Human Hearing. *Mankind Quarterly* 46, no. 1: 3–27.

Goffman, Erving. 1963. *Stigma: Notes on the Management of Spoiled Identity*. Englewood Cliffs, NJ: Prentice Hall.

Goldingay, John. 2001. *Isaiah*. NIBCOT. Peabody, MA: Hendrickson.

Goldwasser, Orly. 1992. The Narmer Palette and the Triumph of Metaphor. *Lingua Aegyptia. JELS* 2:67–85.

Govig, Stewart D. 1994. *Souls Are Made of Endurance: Surviving Mental Illness in the Family*. Louisville: Westminster John Knox.

Grayson, Albert Kirk. 1995. Eunuchs in Power. Their Role in the Assyrian Bureaucracy. Pages 85–98 in *Vom Alten Orient zum Alten Testament: Festschrift für Wolfram Freiherrn von Soden*. Edited by Manfried Dietrich and Oswald Loretz. AOAT 240. Kevelaer, Germany: Butzon & Bercker.

Greenberg, Moshe. 1983. *Ezekiel 1–20: A New Translation with Introduction and Commentary*. AB 22. Garden City, NY: Doubleday.

———. 1987. Job. Pages 283–304 in *The Literary Guide to the Bible*. Edited by Robert Alter and Frank Kermode. Cambridge: Harvard University Press.

Grmek, Mirko D. 1989. *Diseases in the Ancient Greek World*. Translated by Mireille Muellner and Leonard Muellner. Baltimore: Johns Hopkins University Press.

Grønbæk, Jakob H. 1971. *Die Geschichte vom Aufstieg Davids (1. Sam. 15–2. Sam. 5): Tradition und Komposition*. Acta theologica Danica 10. Copenhagen: Munkegaard.

Grosz, Elizabeth. 1994. *Volatile Bodies: Toward a Corporeal Feminism*. Bloomington: Indiana University Press.

Habel, Norman C. 1985. *The Book of Job*. OTL. Philadelphia: Westminster.

Hallo, William W. 1969. The Lame and the Halt. *Eretz–Israel* 9:66–70.

Hamerton-Kelly, Robert. 1979. *God the Father: Theology and Patriarchy in the Teaching of Jesus*. Philadelphia: Fortress.

———. 1981. God the Father in the Bible and the Experience of Jesus: The State of the Question. *Concilium* 17:95–102.

Hanson, Paul D. 1975. Masculine Metaphors for God and Sex-Discrimination in the Old Testament. *The Ecumenical Review* 27:316–24.

Harris, Henry. 1999. *The Birth of the Cell*. New Haven: Yale University Press.

Harris, Murray J. 2005. *The Second Epistle to the Corinthians*. NIGTC. Grand Rapids: Eerdmans; Milton Keynes, England: Paternoster.

Harris, Rivkah. 2000. *Gender and Aging in Mesopotamia: The Gilgamesh Epic and Other Ancient Literature*. Norman: University of Oklahoma Press.

Harrison, Roland K. 1962. Lame. *IDB* 3:59–60.

Hayes, John H., and Carl R. Holladay. 1982. *Biblical Exegesis: A Beginner's Handbook*. Atlanta: John Knox Press.

Heessel, Nils. 2000. *Babylonisch-assyriche Diagnostik*. AOAT 43. Münster, Germany: Ugarit-Verlag.

———. 2004. Reading and Interpreting Cuneiform Texts: Methods and Problems. *Le Journel des Médecines Cunéiformes* 1:2–9.

Heller, Jan. 1965. David und die Krüppel. *Communio viatorum* 8:251–58.

Hendershott, Anne. 2002. *The Politics of Deviance*. San Francisco: Encounter Books.

Hengel, Martin. 1977. *Crucifixion*. Translated by John Bowden. Philadelphia: Fortress.

Hentrich, Thomas. 1986. Das Bilderverbot und die weibliche Gottesvorstellung. M.Th. diss., Universität Bonn.

———. 2000. Die Kritik Hoseas an der kanaanäischen Religion: Eine redaktionsge-schichtliche Analyse. Ph.D. diss., Université de Montréal.

———. 2003. The "Lame" in Lev 21, 5–8 and 2 Sam 5, 6–8. *Annual of the Japanese Biblical Institute* 29:5–30.

———. 2005. Disability in Ancient Israel: The "Lame" (נכה/פסח) in 2 Samuel. *Journal of Christian Studies* 25 (in Japanese).

Hertzberg, Hans Wilhelm. 1964. *I and II Samuel: A Commentary*. OTL. Translated by J. S. Bowden. Philadelphia: Westminster.

Heyes, Cecilia, and Ludwig Huber, eds. 2000. *The Evolution of Cognition*. Cambridge: MIT Press.

Holloway, Steven. 1987. Distaff, Crutch, or Chain Gang: The Curse of the House of Joab in 2 Samuel III 29. *VT* 37:370–73.

Hooker, Morna D. 1990. *From Adam to Christ: Essays on Paul*. Cambridge: Cambridge University Press.

Hooker, Richard. 1996. Gibbor; Hero; Man of Might. http://www.wsu.edu/~dee/HEBREWS/GIBBOR.HTM.

Hornblower, Simon, and Anthony Spawforth, eds. 1996. *The Oxford Classical Dictionary*. 3rd ed. Oxford and New York: Oxford University Press.

Horsley, Richard A. 2001. *Hearing the Whole Story: Politics of Plot in Mark's Gospel*. Louisville: Westminster John Knox.

Houtman, Alberdina. 2000. Sin and Illness in the Targum of the Prophets. Pages 195–206 in *Purity and Holiness: The Heritage of Leviticus*. Edited by Marcel Poorthuis and Joshua Schwartz. Leiden: Brill.

Huehnergard, John. 2000. *A Grammar of Akkadian*. HSS 45. Winona Lake, IN: Eisenbrauns.

Hull, John M. 2001. *In the Beginning There Was Darkness: A Blind Person's Conversation with the Bible*. Harrisburg, PA: Trinity Press International.

Irigaray, Luce. 1985. *This Sex Which Is Not One*. Translated by Catherine Porter with Carolyn Burke. New York: Cornell University Press.

Jacob, Edmond. 1985. Traits féminins dans la figure du Dieu d'Israël. Pages 221–30 in *Festschrift Mathias Delcor*. Edited by André Cacquot, S. Lagassé, and Michel Tardieu. AOAT 215. Neukirchen-Vluyn: Neukirchener Verlag.

Jacobsen, Thorkild. 1987. *The Harps That Once . . . : Sumerian Poetry in Translation*. New Haven: Yale University Press.

Jager, Eric. 1990. Speech and the Chest in Old English Poetry: Orality or Pectorality? *Speculum* 65:845–59.

Jamison, Kay Redfield. 1995. *An Unquiet Mind: A Memoir of Moods and Madness*. New York: Vintage Books.

———. 1999. *Night Falls Fast: Understanding Suicide*. New York: Vintage Books.

Jasper, David. 1990. Siding with the Swine: A Moral Problem for Narrative. Pages 65–74 in *The Daemonic Imagination: Biblical Text and Secular Story*. Edited by

Robert Detweiler and William G. Doty. American Academy of Religion Studies in Religion 60. Atlanta: Scholars Press.

Jeffreys, David, and John Tait. 2000. Disability, Madness, and Social Exclusion in Dynastic Egypt. Pages 87–95 in *Madness, Disability, and Social Exclusion: The Archaeology and Anthropology of "Difference."* Edited by Jane Hubert. London: Routledge.

Kampen, Natalie Boymel, ed. 1996. *Sexuality in Ancient Art: Near East, Egypt, Greece, and Italy.* Cambridge: Cambridge University Press.

Kee, Howard Clark. 1983. The Testaments of the Twelve Patriarchs. Pages 775–828 in vol. 1 of *The Old Testament Pseudepigrapha: Apocalyptic Literature and Testaments.* Edited by James Charlesworth. Garden City, NY: Doubleday.

Kelley, Nicole. 2004. The Cosmopolitan Expression of Josephus's Prophetic Perspective in the Jewish War. *HTR* 97:257–74.

———. 2005. Problems of Knowledge and Authority in the Pseudo-Clementine Romance of Recognition. *JECS* 13:315–48.

———. 2006. *Knowledge and Religious Authority in the Pseudo-Clementines: Situating the Recognitions in Fourth-Century Syria.* Tübingen: Mohr Siebeck.

Kilmer, Anne Draffkorn. 1976. Speculations on Umul, the First Baby. Pages 265–70 in *Kramer Anniversary Volume: Cuneiform Studies in Honor of Samuel Noah Kramer.* Edited by Barry L. Eichler et al. AOAT 25. Kevelaer, Germany: Butzon & Bercker.

Kinnaer, Jacques. 2004. What Is Really Known about the Narmer Palette? *KMT* 15, no. 1: 48–54.

Kinnier Wilson, James V. 1966. Leprosy in Ancient Mesopotamia. *RA* 60:47–58.

———. 1967a. Organic Diseases of Ancient Mesopotamia. Pages 191–208 in *Diseases in Antiquity.* Edited by Don Brothwell and A. T. Sandison. Springfield, IL: Charles C. Thomas.

———. 1967b. Mental Diseases of Ancient Mesopotamia. Pages 723–33 in *Diseases in Antiquity.* Edited by Don Brothwell and A. T. Sandison. Springfield, IL: Charles C. Thomas.

Klein, Jacob. 1990. The "Bane" of Humanity: A Lifespan of One Hundred Twenty Years. *Acta Sumerologica* 12:57–70.

———. 1997. Enki and Ninma. *COS* 1.159: 516–18.

Klein, Lillian. 2000. Michal, the Barren Wife. Pages 37–46 in *Samuel and Kings.* A Feminist Companion to the Bible 2/7. Edited by Athalya Brenner. Sheffield: Sheffield Academic Press.

Köhler, E. Christiana. 2002. History or Ideology? New Reflections on the Narmer Palette and the Nature of Foreign Relations in Pre- and Early Dynastic Egypt. Pages 505–7 in *Egypt and the Levant: Interrelations from the Fourth through the Early Third Millennium BCE.* Edited by Edwin C. M. van den Brink and Thomas E. Levy. London: Leicester University Press.

Kramer, Samuel Noah, and John Maier. 1989. *Myths of Enki, the Crafty God.* New York: Oxford University Press.

Krappe, Alexander Haggerty. 1928. Teiresias and the Snakes. *The American Journal of Philology* 49:267–75.

Kraus, Hans-Joachim. 1972. Hören und Sehen in der althebräischen Tradition. Pages 84–101 in *Biblisch-theologische Aufsätze.* Edited by Hans-Joachim Kraus. Neukirchen-Vluyn: Neukirchener Verlag.

Lakoff, George and Mark Johnson. 1980. *Metaphors We Live By*. Chicago: University of Chicago Press.

———. 1999. *Philosophy in the Flesh: The Embodied Mind and Its Challenge to Western Thought*. New York: Basic Books.

Lambert, Wilfred G. 1998. The Qualifications of Babylonian Diviners. Pages 141–58 in *Festschrift für Rykle Borger zu seinem 65. Geburtstag am 24. Mai 1994*. Edited by Stefan M. Maul. Cuneiform Monographs 10. Groningen: Styx.

Lambrecht, Jan. 1999. *Second Corinthians*. SP 8. Collegeville, MN: Liturgical.

Lattimore, Richmond, trans. 1951. *The Iliad of Homer*. Chicago: University of Chicago Press.

———. 1965. *The Odyssey of Homer*. New York: Harper & Row.

Layton, Scott. 1989. A Chain Gang in Samuel iii 29? A Rejoinder. *VT* 39:81–86.

Lees, Janet. 1997. Interpreting the Bible with People with Communication Difficulties. M.Th. thesis, Department of Theology, University of Natal, South Africa.

———. 1998. Liberation through "Liberator": A Study of Conversation. Paper presented at the European Academy of Child Disability, Lisbon, Portugal.

———. 2007a. Remembering the Bible as a "Critical Pedagogy of the Oppressed." In *Reading Other-Wise: Socially Engaged Biblical Scholars Reading with Their Local Communities*. Semeia Studies. Edited by G. O. West. Atlanta: Society of Biblical Literature.

———. 2007b. *Word of Mouth*. Glasgow: Wild Goose.

Leichty, Erle. 1970. *The Omen Series Šumma Izbu*. TCS 4. Locust Valley, NY: Augustin.

Lemos, T. M. 2006. Shame and Humiliation of Enemies in the Hebrew Bible. *JBL* 125:225–41.

Levy, Thomas E., and Edwin C. M. van den Brink. 2002. Interaction Models, Egypt, and the Levantine Periphery. Pages 3–38 in *Egypt and the Levant: Interrelations from the Fourth through the Early Third Millennium BCE*. London: Leicester University Press.

Levy, Thomas E., et al. 1995. New Light on King Narmer and the Protodynastic Egyptian Presence in Canaan. *BA* 58, no. 1: 26–35

Lichtheim, Miriam. 1997. Instruction of Amenemope. *COS* 1.47: 115–22.

Lindberg, David C. 1978. *Science in the Middle Ages*. Chicago: University of Chicago Press.

Linton, Simi. 1998. *Claiming Disability: Knowledge and Identity*. New York: New York University Press.

Longman, Tremper, III. 1991. *Fictional Akkadian Autobiography: A Generic and Comparative Study*. Winona Lake, IN: Eisenbrauns.

Lundbom, Jack R. 2004. *Jeremiah 21–36: A New Translation with Introduction and Commentary*. AB 21B. New York: Doubleday.

Malul, Meir. 1990. Adoption of Foundlings in the Bible and Mesopotamian Documents. *JSOT* 46:97–126.

Marcus, David. 1980. Euphemisms for Blind Persons in Akkadian and Other Semitic Languages. *JAOS* 100:307–10.

Martin, Dale B. 1995. *The Corinthian Body*. New Haven: Yale University Press.

Martyn, J. Louis. 1997. *Galatians*. AB 33A. New York: Doubleday.

Maul, Stefan M. 1994. *Zukunftsbewältigung: Eine Untersuchung altorientalischen Denkens anhand der babylonisch-assyrischen Löserituale (Namburbi)*. Mainz: Philipp von Zabern.

McCane, Byron R. 2003. *Roll Back the Stone: Death and Burial in the World of Jesus.* Harrisburg, PA: Trinity Press International.

McCarter, P. Kyle. 1980. *I Samuel: A New Translation, Introduction, and Commentary.* AB 8. Garden City, NY: Doubleday.

———. 1984. *2 Samuel.* AB 9. Garden City, NY: Doubleday.

McCarthy, Heather. 2005. Palace of the Beautiful Ones. Pages 14–25 in *Archaeology Odyssey,* March/April.

McCloughry, Roy, and Wayne Morris. 2002. *Making a World of Difference: Christian Reflections on Disability.* London: SPCK.

McLuhan, Marshall. 1962. *The Gutenberg Galaxy: The Making of Typographic Man.* Toronto: University of Toronto Press.

Meekosha, Helen. 2004. Gender and Disability. Draft entry for the *Sage Encyclopaedia of Disability.* Edited by Gary L. Albrecht. Thousand Oaks, CA: Sage. www.leeds.ac.uk/disability-studies/archiveuk/meekosha/meekosha.pdf.

Melcher, Sarah J. 1996. The Holiness Code and Human Sexuality. Pages 87–102 in *Biblical Ethics and Homosexuality: Listening to Scripture.* Edited by Robert Brawley. Louisville: Westminster John Knox.

———. 1998. Visualizing the Perfect Cult: The Priestly Rationale for Exclusion, Pages 55–71 in *Human Disability and the Service of God: Reassessing Religious Practice.* Edited by Nancy L. Eiesland and Don S. Saliers. Nashville: Abingdon.

———. 2002. Kinship and Enculturation: Shaping the Generations in Leviticus 18. *Proceedings Eastern Great Lakes and Midwest Biblical Societies.* 22:63–77.

———. 2003. Lacan, the Phallus, and the Construal of Intergenerational Kinship in Genesis–Numbers. Pages 191–205 in *Relating to the Text: Interdisciplinary and Form-Critical Insights on the Bible.* Edited by T. J. Sandoval and C. R. Mandolfo. London and New York: T & T Clark International.

———. 2004. "I Will Lead the Blind by a Road They Do Not Know": Disability in Prophetic Eschatology. *Society of Biblical Literature Seminar Papers.* http://www.sbl-site.org/PDF/Melcher_Prophetic_Disability.pdf.

Melcher, Sarah J., and Sarah J. Dille, eds. Forthcoming. *Discerning the Body: Metaphors of the Body in the Bible.* Guest volume for *The Classical Bulletin.* Wauconda, IL: Bolchazy-Carducci.

Meskell, Lynn M., and Rosemary A. Joyce. 2003. *Embodied Lives: Figuring Ancient Maya and Egyptian Evidence.* London and New York: Routledge.

Milgrom, Jacob. 1991. *Leviticus 1–16: A New Translation with Introduction and Commentary.* AB 3. New York: Doubleday.

Miller, Patrick D. 1994. *They Cried to the Lord: The Form and Theology of Biblical Prayer.* Minneapolis: Fortress.

Millet, Nicholas B. 1990. The Narmer Macehead and Related Objects. *JARCE* 27:53–59.

Miroschedji, Pierre de. 2002. The Socio-Political Dynamics of Egyptian-Canaanite Interaction in the Early Bronze Age. Pages 39–57 in *Egypt and the Levant: Interrelations from the Fourth through the Early Third Millennium BCE.* Edited by Edwin C. M. van den Brink and Thomas E. Levy. London: Leicester University Press.

Miscall, Peter D. 1993. *Isaiah.* Readings: A New Biblical Commentary. Sheffield: Sheffield Academic Press.

Mitchell, David T. 2002. Narrative Prosthesis and the Materiality of Metaphor. Pages 15–30 in *Disability Studies: Enabling the Humanities*. Edited by Sharon L. Snyder, Brenda Jo Brueggemann, and Rosemarie Garland-Thomson. New York: Modern Language Association.

———. Forthcoming. *Eugenics in America, 1848–1945: A Disability Studies Primary Source Book*. Ann Arbor: University of Michigan Press.

Mitchell, David T., gen. ed. 2005. *Encyclopedia of Disability: A History of Disability in Primary Sources*. Vol. 5. Thousand Oaks, CA: Sage.

Mitchell, David T., and Sharon L. Snyder. 2000. *Narrative Prosthesis: Disability and the Dependencies of Discourse*. Ann Arbor: University of Michigan Press.

Mitchell, David T., and Sharon L. Snyder, eds. 1997. *The Body and Physical Difference: Discourses of Disability*. The Body, in Theory. Ann Arbor: University of Michigan Press.

Montagu, Ashley. 1986. *Touching: The Human Significance of the Skin*. 3rd ed. New York: Harper & Row.

Moore, Stephen D. 1996. *God's Gym: Divine Male Bodies of the Bible*. New York: Routledge.

Mountcastle, Vernon B. 2005. *The Sensory Hand: Neural Mechanisms of Somatic Sensation*. Cambridge: Harvard University Press.

Moyers, Bill. 1996. *Genesis: A Living Conversation*. New York: Doubleday.

Mulack, Christa. 1984. *Die Weiblichkeit Gottes. Matriarchale Voraussetzungen des Gottesbildes*. 3rd ed. Stuttgart: Kreuz.

Münsterberg, Hugo. 1916/1970. *The Photoplay. A Psychological Study*. Mineolla, NY: Dover.

Murray, A. T., trans. 1919. *Homer: The Odyssey*. 2 vols. LCL. Cambridge: Harvard University Press.

Nelson. Janet R. 2003. Bioethics and the Marginalization of Mental Illness. *JSCE* 23:179–97.

Nelson, Richard. 2005. The Double Redaction of the Deuteronomistic History: The Case Is Still Compelling. *JSOT* 29:319–37.

Neugeboren, Jay. 2001. *Transforming Madness: New Lives for People Living with Mental Illness*. Pbk. ed. Berkeley and Los Angeles: University of California Press.

Neusner, Jacob. 1973. *The Idea of Purity in Ancient Judaism*. Leiden: Brill.

Newton, Rick M. 1987. Odysseus and Hephaestus in the *Odyssey*. *The Classical Journal* 83:12–20.

Niditch, Susan. 1987. *Underdogs and Tricksters: A Prelude to Biblical Folklore*. San Francisco: Harper & Row.

Nietzsche, Friedrich. 2005. *Thus Spake Zarathustra*. Translated by Graham Parkes. Oxford: Oxford University Press. (Orig. pub. 1902).

Nissinen, Martti. 1998. *Homoeroticism in the Biblical World*. Minneapolis: Fortress.

Nunn, John F. 1996. *Ancient Egyptian Medicine*. London: British Museum.

O'Connor, David. 2004a. Context, Function, and Program: Understanding Ceremonial Slate Palettes. *JARCE* 39:5–25.

———. 2004b. Narmer's Enigmatic Palette. Pages 16–52 in *Archaeology Odyssey*, September/October.

O'Connor, Flannery. 1971. A Good Man Is Hard to Find. Pages 117–33 in *The Complete Stories*. New York: Farrar, Straus & Giroux.

Olson, Dennis T. 1994. *Deuteronomy and the Death of Moses: A Theological Reading*. Minneapolis: Fortress.

Olyan, Saul. 1998. "Anyone Blind or Lame Shall Not Enter the House": On the Interpretation of Second Samuel 5:8b. *CBQ* 60:218–27.

———. 2000. *Rites and Rank: Hierarchy in Biblical Representations of Cult.* Princeton: Princeton University Press.

———. Forthcoming. *Disability in the Hebrew Bible: Representation and Stigma.* Cambridge: Cambridge University Press.

Parker, Simon B., ed. 1997. *Ugaritic Narrative Poetry.* SBLWAW 9. Atlanta: Scholars.

Parpola, Simo. 1970. *Letters from Assyrian Scholars to the Kings Esarhaddon and Assurbanipal. Part I: Texts.* AOAT 5/1. Kevelaer, Germany: Butzon & Bercker.

———. 1983. *Letters from Assyrian Scholars to the Kings Esarhaddon and Assurbanipal. Part II: Commentary and Appendices.* AOAT 5/2. Kevelaer, Germany: Butzon & Bercker.

Parpola, Simo, and R. M. Whiting, eds. 2002. *Sex and Gender in the Ancient Near East.* Proceedings of the 47th Rencontre Assyirologique Internationale, Helsinki, July 2–6, 2001. Helsinki: Neo-Assyrian Text Corpus Project.

Parsons, Mikeal C. 2005. The Character of the Lame Man in Acts 3–4. *JBL* 124, no. 2: 295–312.

———. 2006. *Body and Character in Luke and Acts: The Subversion of Physiognomy in Early Christianity.* Grand Rapids: Baker Books.

Patterson, Cynthia. 1985. "Not Worth the Rearing": The Causes of Infant Exposure in Ancient Greece. *Transactions of the American Philological Association* 115:103–23.

———. 1998. *The Family in Greek History.* Cambridge: Harvard University Press.

Phillips, Marilynn J. 1993. Straight Talk from Crooked Women. Pages 396–410 in *Feminist Theory and the Study of Folklore.* Edited by Susan Tower Hollis, Linda Pershing, and M. Jane Young. Urbana: University of Illinois Press.

Pilch, John J. 2000. *Healing in the New Testament: Insights from Medical and Mediterranean Anthropology.* Minneapolis: Fortress.

Plautus, Titus Maccius. 1966–80. *Plautus.* Translated by Paul Nixon. 5 vols. LCL. Cambridge: Harvard University Press.

Pliny. 1967–1975. *Natural History.* Translated by W. H. S. Jones et al. 10 vols. LCL. Cambridge: Harvard University Press.

Polzin, Robert. 1989. *Samuel and the Deuteronomist: A Literary Study of the Deuteronomic History. Part Two: 1 Samuel.* San Francisco: Harper & Row.

Pope, Marvin H. 1975. *Job: A New Translation with Introduction and Commentary.* AB 15. Garden City, NY: Doubleday.

Popper, Karl. 2002. *The Poverty of Historicism.* 2nd ed. New York: Routledge.

Porter, Barbara Nevling. 1993. *Images, Power, and Politics: Figurative Aspects of Esarhaddon's Babylonian Policy.* Philadelphia: American Philosophical Society.

———. 2003. *Trees, Kings, and Politics: Studies in Assyrian Iconography.* OBO 197. Fribourg: Academic Press.

Portier-Young, Anathea. 2005. "Eyes to the Blind": A Dialogue between Tobit and Job. Pages 14–27 in *Intertextual Studies of Ben Sira and Tobit.* Edited by Jeremy Corley and Vincent Skemp. The Catholic Biblical Quarterly Monographs Series 38. Washington, DC: Catholic Biblical Association of America.

Proudfoot, C. Merrill. 1963. Imitation or Realistic Participation? A Study of Paul's Concept of "Suffering with Christ." *Int* 17:140–60.

Rackham, H., trans. 1944. *Aristotle: The Politics.* LCL. Cambridge: Harvard University Press.

Raphael, Rebecca. 2004. Things Too Wonderful: A Disabled Reading of Job. *Perspectives in Religious Studies* 31:399–424.
———. 2007. Madly Disobedient: The Representation of Madness in Handel's Oratorio *Saul*. *Perspectives in Religious Studies* 34/1 (Spring).
———. Forthcoming. *Biblical Corpora: Representations of Disability in Hebrew Biblical Literature*. Library of Hebrew Bible/Old Testament Studies. New York: T & T Clark International.
Rautman, Alison E., ed. 2000. *Reading the Body: Representations and Remains in the Archaeological Record*. Philadelphia: University of Pennsylvania.
Ravaud, Jean-François, and Henri-Jacques Stiker. 2001. Inclusion/Exclusion. An Analysis of Historical and Cultural Meanings. Pages 490–513 in *Handbook of Disability Studies*. Edited by Gary L. Albrecht, Katherine D. Seelman, and Michael Bury. Thousand Oaks, CA: Sage.
Reeves, Carole. 1992. *Egyptian Medicine*. Shire Egyptology Series 15. Princes Risborough, England: Shire Egyptology.
Renger, Johannes 1992. Kranke, Krüppel, Debile—Eine Randgruppe im Alten Orient? Pages 113–26 in *Außenseiter und Randgruppen: Beiträge zu einer Sozialgeschichte des Alten Orients*. Edited by Volkert Haas. Das Konstanzer altorientalische Symposion 3, 1989. Constance, Germany: Universitätsverlag.
Rey-Coquias, Jean-Paul. 1992. Decapolis. Translated by Stephen Rosoff. Pages 116–21 in vol. 2 of *The Anchor Bible Dictionary*. Edited by David Noel Freedman. 6 vols. New York: Doubleday.
Ricoeur, Paul. 1976. *Interpretation Theory: Discourse and the Surplus of Meaning*. Fort Worth: Texas Christian University Press.
Robbins, Gay. 1993. *Women in Ancient Egypt*. Cambridge: Harvard University Press.
Roehrig, Catherine H., Renee Dreyfus, and Catherine A. Keller, eds. 2005. *Hatshepsut: From Queen to Pharaoh*. New York: Metropolitan Museum of Art.
Römer, Thomas. 2005. *The So-Called Deuteronomistic History: A Sociological, Historical, and Literary Introduction*. Edinburgh: T & T Clark.
Römer, Willem H. P. 1993. Mythen und Epen in sumerischer Sprache. Pages 351–559 in *Mythen und Epen I. TUAT* III, 3. Edited by Otto Kaiser. Gütersloh: Gütersloher Verlagshaus Gerd Mohn.
Rose, Martha L. 2003. *The Staff of Oedipus: Transforming Disability in Ancient Greece*. Ann Arbor: University of Michigan Press.
Roth, Ann M. 2000. Father Earth, Mother Sky: Ancient Egyptian Beliefs about Conception and Fertility. Pages 199–200 in *Reading the Body: Representations and Remains in the Archaeological Record*. Edited by Alison E. Rautman. Philadelphia: University of Pennsylvania.
Roth, Martha T. 1997. *Law Collections from Mesopotamia and Asia Minor*. 2nd ed. WAW 6. Atlanta: Scholars Press.
Ruether, Rosemary Radford. 1985. *Sexismus und die Rede von Gott: Schritte zu einer anderen Theologie*. Gütersloh: Mohn.
Schaper, Joachim. 2005. Exilic and Post-exilic Prophecy and the Orality/Literacy Problem. *VT* 55:324–42.
Schipper, Jeremy. 2004. "Why Do You Still Speak of Your Affairs?" Polyphony in Mephibosheth's Exchanges with David in 2 Samuel. *VT* 54:344–51.
———. 2005a. Reconsidering the Imagery of Disability in 2 Samuel 5:8b. *CBQ* 67:422–34.

————. 2005b. "Significant Resonances" with Mephibosheth in 2 Kings 25:27–30: A Response to Donald F. Murray. *JBL* 124:51–59.

————. 2006. *Disability Studies and the Hebrew Bible: Figuring Mephibosheth in the David Story*. Library of Hebrew Bible/Old Testament Studies 441. New York: T & T Clark International.

Schlier, Heinrich. 1964. ἐκπτύω. Pages 448–49 in vol. 2 of *Theological Dictionary of the New Testament*. Edited by Gerhard Kittel and Gerhard Friedrich. Translated by Geoffrey W. Bromiley. 10 vols. Grand Rapids: Eerdmans, 1964–76.

Schmidt, Gail Ramshaw. 1982. *De divinis nominibus*: The Gender of God. *Worship* 56:121.

Schorch, Stefan. 2000. Baal oder Boschet? Ein umstrittenes theophores Element zwischen Religions- und Textgeschichte. *ZAW* 112:598–611.

Scurlock, JoAnn. 2005. Ancient Mesopotamian Medicine. Pages 302–15 in *A Companion to the Ancient Near East*. Edited by Daniel C. Snell. Malden, MA: Blackwell.

————. 2006. *Magico-Medical Means of Treating Ghost-Induced Illness in Ancient Mesopotamia*. Studies in Ancient Magic and Divination 3. Leiden: Styx.

Scurlock, JoAnn, and Burton R. Andersen. 2005. *Diagnoses in Assyrian and Babylonian Medicine: Ancient Sources, Translations, and Modern Medical Analyses*. Urbana: University of Illinois Press.

Schweizer, Eduard, Friedrich Baumgärtel, and Rudolf Meyer. 1971. σάρξ. Pages 98–151 in vol. 7 of *Theological Dictionary of the New Testament*. Edited by Gerhard Kittel and Gerhard Friedrich. Translated by Geoffrey W. Bromiley. 10 vols. Grand Rapids: Eerdmans, 1964–76.

Shaw, Ian, ed. 2000. *The Oxford History of Ancient Egypt*. Oxford: Oxford University Press.

Shorey, Paul, trans. 1953. *Plato: The Republic*. 2 vols. LCL. Cambridge: Harvard University Press.

Slanski, Kathryn. 2003. *The Babylonian Entitlement Narûs: A Study in Form and Function*. Boston: ASOR.

Smith, Henry. 1899. *A Critical and Exegetical Commentary on the Books of Samuel*. ICC. Edinburgh: T & T Clark.

Smith, Mark S. 2001. *The Origins of Biblical Monotheism. Israel's Polytheistic Background and the Ugaritic Texts*. Oxford: Oxford University Press.

Snyder, Sharon L., Brenda Jo Brueggemann, and Rosemarie Garland-Thomson. 2002. Introduction: Integrating Disability into Teaching and Scholarship. Pages 1–12 in *Disability Studies: Enabling the Humanities*. Edited by Sharon L. Snyder, Brenda Jo Brueggemann, and Rosemarie Garland-Thomson. New York: Modern Language Association.

Snyder, Sharon, and David T. Mitchell. 2006. *Cultural Locations of Disability*. Chicago: University of Chicago Press.

Stafford, Maria Barbara. 1997. *Body Criticism: Imaging the Unseen in Enlightenment Art and Medicine*. Cambridge: MIT Press.

Stählin, Gustav. 1964. ἀσθενής. Pages 490–93 in vol. 1 of *Theological Dictionary of the New Testament*. Edited by Gerhard Kittel and Gerhard Friedrich. Translated by Geoffrey W. Bromiley. 10 vols. Grand Rapids: Eerdmans, 1964–76.

Stanley, Jean-Daniel. 2002. Configuration of the Egypt-to-Canaan Coastal Margin and the North Sinai Byway in the Bronze Age. Pages 98–117 in *Egypt and the Levant: Interrelations from the Fourth through the Early Third Millennium BCE*. Ed-

216

BIBLIOGRAPHY

ited by Edwin C. M. van den Brink and Thomas E. Levy. London: Leicester University Press.
Stevenson, William Edward III. 1975. *The Pathological Grotesque Representation in Greek and Roman Art.* Ph.D. thesis, University of Pennsylvania.
Stiker, Henri-Jacques. 2000. *A History of Disability.* Translated by William Sayers. Ann Arbor: University of Michigan Press.
Stoebe, Hans Joachim. 1994. *Das zweite Buch Samuelis.* Kommentar zum Alten Testament 8/2. Gütersloh: Gütersloher Verlagshaus.
Stol, Marten. 1986. Blindness and Night-Blindness in Akkadian. *JNES* 45:295–99.
———. 1993. *Epilepsy in Babylonia.* Cuneiform Monographs 2. Groningen: Styx.
———. 2000. *Birth in Babylonia and the Bible: Its Mediterranean Setting.* With a chapter by F. A. M. Wiggermann. Groningen: Styx.
Stol, Marten, and Sven P. Vleeming, eds. 1998. *The Care of the Elderly in the Ancient Near East.* Leiden: Brill.
Strecker, Christian. 2002. Jesus and the Demoniacs. Pages 117–33 in *The Social Setting of Jesus and the Gospels.* Edited by Wolfgang Stegemann, Bruce J. Malina, and Gerd Theissen. Minneapolis: Augsburg Fortress.
Swain, Simon, ed. 2006. *Seeing the Face, Seeing the Soul: Polemon's Physiognomy from Classical Antiquity to Medieval Islam.* New York: Oxford.
Sweeney, Marvin A. 2003. *Zephaniah: A Commentary.* Hermeneia. Minneapolis: Augsburg Fortress.
Tawil, Hayim. 1974. Some Literary Elements in the Opening Sections of the Hadad, Zakir, and Nerab II Inscriptions in the Light of East and West Semitic Royal Inscriptions. *Orientalia* 43:40–65.
Temkin, Owsei, trans. 1956. *Soranus' Gynecology.* Baltimore: Johns Hopkins University Press.
Terrien, Samuel L. 1957. *Job: Poet of Existence.* Indianapolis: Bobbs-Merrill.
Thomas Aquinas. 1947. *The Summa Theologica.* Translated by Fathers of the English Dominican Province. Benziger Bros. www.ccel.org/a/aquinas/summa/home.html.
Thomas, John Christopher. 1998. *The Devil, Disease, and Deliverance: Origins of Illness in New Testament Thought.* Journal of Pentecostal Theology Supplement Series 13. Sheffield: Sheffield Academic Press.
Thomson, Rosemarie Garland. 1996. *Freakery: Cultural Spectacles of the Extraordinary Body.* New York: New York University Press.
———. 1997. *Extraordinary Bodies: Figuring Physical Disability in American Culture and Literature.* New York: Columbia University Press.
Thrall, Margaret. 2000. *II Corinthians.* 2 vols. ICC. Edinburgh: T & T Clark.
Toensing, Holly Joan. 1995. Politics of Insertion: The Pericope of the Adulterous Woman and Its Rhetorical Context at John 7:52. *Proceedings Eastern Great Lakes and Midwest Biblical Societies* 15:1–14.
———. 1997. Assessing Context and Conflict: Two Voices from *Reading from This Place. Proceedings Eastern Great Lakes and Midwest Biblical Societies* 17:129–134.
———. 2005. Women of Sodom and Gomorrah: Collateral Damage in the War against Homosexuality. *JFSR* 21:61–74.
Tolbert, Mary Ann. 1989. *Sowing the Gospel: Mark's World in Literary-Historical Perspective.* Minneapolis: Augsburg Fortress.
Torrey, E. Fuller. 1997. *Out of the Shadows: Confronting America's Mental Illness Crisis.* New York: John Wiley & Sons.
Tougher, Shaun, ed. 2002. *Eunuchs in Antiquity.* London: Duckworth.

Trent, James. 1995. *Inventing the Feeble Mind: A History of Mental Retardation in the United States.* Berkeley: University of California Press.

Tuell, Steven Shawn. 2004. Contemporary Studies of Ezekiel: A New Tide Rising. Pages 241–54 in *Ezekiel's Hierarchical World: Wrestling with a Tiered Reality.* Edited by Stephen L. Cook and Corrine L. Patton. SBL Symposium Series 31. Atlanta: Society of Biblical Literature.

Ugolini, Gherardo. 1995. *Untersuchungen zur Figur des Sehers Teiresias.* Tübingen: Narr.

United Nations Economic and Social Commission for Asia and the Pacific. 2006. Hidden Sisters: Women and Girls with Disabilities in the Asian and Pacific Region. http://www.unescap.org/esid/psis/disability/decade/publications/wwd1 .asp.

Veijola, Timo. 1978. David und Meribaal. *Revue biblique* 85:338–61.

———. 2002. Deuteronomismusforschung zwischen Tradition und Innovation (I). *Theologische Rundschau* 67:273–327.

Viljoen, G. van N. 1959. Plato and Aristotle on the Exposure of Infants at Athens. *Acta Classica* 2:58–69.

Vlaardingerbroeck, Johannes. 1999. *Zephaniah.* Historical Commentary on the Old Testament. Louvain: Peeters.

Vlahogiannis, Nicholas. 1998. Disabling Bodies. Pages 13–36 in *Changing Bodies, Changing Meanings: Studies on the Human Body in Antiquity.* Edited by Dominic Montserrat. London and New York: Routledge.

Von Rad, Gerhard. 1962. *Genesis.* Translated by John H. Marks. OTL. Philadelphia: Westminster Press.

———. 1966. *Deuteronomy.* Translated by Dorothea Barton. OTL. Philadelphia: Westminster Press.

von Staden, Heinrich. 1990. Incurability and Hopelessness: The *Hippocratic Corpus.* Pages 75–112 in *La maladie et les maladies dans la Collection hippocratique.* Edited by P. Potter, G. Maloney, and J. Desautels. Québec: Les Éditions du Sphinx.

Walls, Neal H. 1992. *The Goddess Anat in Ugaritic Myth.* Atlanta: Scholars Press.

———. 2001. *Desire, Discord, and Death: Approaches to Ancient Near Eastern Myth.* Boston: American Schools of Oriental Research.

Walls, Neal H., ed. 2005. *Cult Image and Divine Representation in the Ancient Near East.* Boston: American Schools of Oriental Research.

Walters, Stanley D. 1993. Childless Michal, Mother of Five. Pages 290–96 in *The Tablet and the Scroll: Near Eastern Studies in Honor of William H. Hallo.* Edited by Mark E. Cohen, Daniel C. Snell, and David B. Weisberg. Bethesda, MD: CDL.

Wasserman, David. 2001. Philosophical Issues in the Definition and Social Response to Disability. Pages 219–51 in *Handbook of Disability Studies.* Edited by Gary L. Albrecht, Katherine D. Seelman, and Michael Bury. Thousand Oaks, CA: Sage.

Watson, W. G. E. 1979. An Unrecognized Hyperbole in *Krt. Or* 48:112–17.

Webster, Douglas B., Richard R. Fay, and Arthur N. Popper. 1992. *The Evolutionary Biology of Hearing.* New York: Springer Verlag.

Weeks, Kent R. 1995. Medicine, Surgery, and Public Health in Ancient Egypt. *CANE* 3:1787–98.

Wefald, Eric K. 1995. The Separate Gentile Mission in Mark: A Narrative Explanation of Markan Geography, the Two Feeding Accounts, and Exorcisms. *JSNT* 60:3–26.

Wendell, Susan. 1996. *The Rejected Body*. New York: Routledge.

West, Gerald O. 1999. *The Academy of the Poor: Towards a Dialogical Reading of the Bible*. Sheffield: Sheffield Academic Press.

———. 2004. Artful Facilitation and Creating a Safe Interpretive Site: Analysis of Aspects of a Bible Study. In *Through the Eyes of Another: Intercultural Reading of the Bible*. Edited by Hans deWit et al. Amsterdam: Institute of Mennonite Studies, Vrije Universiteit.

Westbrook, Raymond. 1998. Legal Aspects of Care of the Elderly in the Ancient Near East: Conclusion. Pages 241–50 in *The Care of the Elderly in the Ancient Near East*. Edited by Marten Stol and Sven P. Vleeming. Leiden: Brill.

Westermann, Claus. 1995. *Genesis 12–36. A Continental Commentary*. Translated by John J. Scullion. Minneapolis: Fortress Press.

Wilkinson, John. 1998. *The Bible and Healing: A Medical and Theological Commentary*. Edinburgh: Handsel; Grand Rapids: Eerdmans.

Wright, David P. 1987. *The Disposal of Impurity*. Atlanta: Scholars Press.

Wynn, Kerry. 1999. Sin versus Disability: A Rereading of Mark 2:1–12. Paper presented at the Annual Meeting of the American Academy of Religion, Boston.

———. 2000. The Invisibility of Disability at Qumran. Paper presented at the Annual Meeting of the American Academy of Religion, Nashville, Tennessee.

———. 2001. Disability in Bible Translation. *BT* 52:402–14.

Zarb, G. 1992. On the Road to Damascus: First Steps towards Changing the Relations of Disability Research Production. *Disability, Handicap, and Society* 7:125–38.

Zevit, Ziony. 2001. *The Religions of Ancient Israel: A Synthesis of Parallactic Views*. New York: Continuum.

Zuckerman, Bruce. 1991. *Job the Silent: A Study in Historical Counterpoint*. New York: Oxford.

List of Contributors

Martin Albl is Associate Professor of Religious Studies at Presentation College in Aberdeen, South Dakota, where he teaches courses on health care in the Christian tradition. He is the editor and translator of *Pseudo-Gregory of Nyssa: Testimonies against the Jews* (2004) and other publications that focus on the interpretation of scripture in early Christianity and on early Christian health care.

Hector Avalos is Professor of Religious Studies at Iowa State University. He received his Ph.D. (1991) from Harvard University in Hebrew Bible and Near Eastern Studies. His seven books include *Health Care and the Rise of Christianity* (1999), *Fighting Words: The Origins of Religious Violence* (2005), *Strangers in Our Own Land: Religion in U.S. Latina/o Literature* (2005), and *The End of Biblical Studies* (2007).

Bruce C. Birch (Ph.D., Yale University) is Dean and Miller Professor of Biblical Theology at Wesley Theological Seminary. He has been an advocate of greater attention in theological education to issues of disability in the ministries of the church and of greater access for students with disabilities in theological education. He is currently serving on a task force to draft the first policy statement on disabilities for the Association of Theological Schools. He is the author of numerous books, the most recent co-authored with Lewis Parks, is *Ducking Spears, Dancing Madly: A Biblical Model for Church Leadership*.

Carole R. Fontaine (Ph.D., Duke University) is the Taylor Professor of Biblical Theology and History at Andover Newton Theological Seminary. A leader in feminist biblical scholarship, she has served on the editorial boards of the *Journal of Biblical Literature*, *Women in Judaism*, and the *Catholic Biblical Quarterly*. Her books include *Smooth Words: Women, Proverbs, and Performance in Biblical Wisdom* and the forthcoming *Eyes of Flesh: The Bible, Gender, and Human Rights*.

Thomas Hentrich (Ph.D., Université de Montréal) has served as a post-doctoral fellow at Kyoto University. With expertise in the Old Testament in relation to ancient Near Eastern literature, his current interdisciplinary research project examines ancient medicine, especially questions of disability and purity laws in ancient Israel. It is intended to be expanded into a theological examination of the relationship between disabilities and religion during the early Christian period.

Nicole Kelley (Ph.D., Harvard University) is an Assistant Professor of Religion at Florida State University. She is the author of *Knowledge and Religious Authority in the Pseudo-Clementines* (2006), as well as several articles on ancient Christianity and Judaism. She is currently working on a monograph about late antique Christian attitudes toward deformed and disabled persons.

Janet Lees, an ordained minister of the United Reformed Church and a speech therapist, currently works as a Research Associate in the Department of Sociological Studies at the University of Sheffield, where she is also an Honorary Lecturer at the Department of Human Communication Sciences and a member of the Centre of Applied Disability Studies.

Sarah J. Melcher is Associate Professor of Hebrew Scriptures at Xavier University in Cincinnati. She received her Ph.D. in Hebrew Bible from Emory University in 2000. Sarah has published numerous articles on kinship and sexuality in the Pentateuch, disability in the Bible, Jewish-Christian dialogue, and African American biblical interpretation. Currently, Sarah is working on the edited volume *Discerning the Body: Metaphors of the Body in the Bible*.

David Mitchell is Associate Professor in the Disability Studies program at the University of Illinois, Chicago. To date he has published three books on disability culture and history including *The Body and Physical Difference* (1997), *Narrative Prosthesis* (2000), and *Cultural Locations of Disability* (2006). He has also served as senior editor on the five-volume *Encyclopedia of Disability* (2006). David has served as president of the Society for Disability Studies and as a founding member of both the Committee on Disability and the Disability Studies Discussion Group for the Modern Languages Association. In 2006, he served as a principal organizer of the Chicago Festival of Disability Arts and Culture for which he curated the Chicago Disability History exhibit and co-organized Chicago's first international disability and deaf film festival.

Jeremy Schipper (Ph.D., Princeton Theological Seminary) is a lecturer in Hebrew Bible at Temple University in Philadelphia. He is the author of *Disability Studies and the Hebrew Bible: Figuring Mephibosheth in the David Story* (2006) as well as several articles on disability in the Hebrew Bible, which have appeared in the *Journal of Biblical Literature, Catholic Biblical Quarterly,* and *Vetus Testamentum.* He serves as co-chair of the SBL program unit "Disability Studies and Healthcare in the Bible and Near East."

Sharon Snyder is Assistant Professor in the Department of Disability and Human Development at the University of Illinois, Chicago, where she is also Program Director of the Disability and Cultural Studies Unit. As well as being a coauthor of *Cultural Locations of Disability* (2006) and *Narrative Prosthesis: Disability and the Dependencies of Discourse* (2001), coeditor of *Disability Studies: Enabling the Humanities* (2002) and *The Body and Physical Difference: Discourses of Disability* (1997), she is the author of numerous essays on disability theory, culture, and representational history that have been published widely and translated for many professional journals. The founder of Brace Yourselves Productions, she is also an award-winning filmmaker whose work includes *Self-Preservation: The Art of Riva Lehrer* (2004), *Disability Takes On the Arts* (2005), *A World without Bodies* (2002), and *Vital Signs: Crip Culture Talks Back* (1996). She is a founding member of the MLA's Committee on Disability Issues, a key organizer of the MLA's Disability Studies Discussion Group, and has served as director for the Society for Disability Studies.

Holly Toensing (Ph.D., Vanderbilt University) is an Assistant Professor at Xavier University in Cincinnati. Her research interests include New Testament, biblical narrative criticism, and feminist criticism. She serves as the chairperson of the SBL program unit "LGBT/Queer Hermeneutics Consultation."

Neal H. Walls (Ph.D., Johns Hopkins University) is an Associate Professor of Old Testament Interpretation at the Wake Forest University Divinity School. He is the author of *The Goddess Anat in Ugaritic Myth* and *Desire, Discord, and Death: Approaches to Ancient Near Eastern Myth.* He is the editor of *Cult Image and Divine Representation in the Ancient Near East.*

Kerry H. Wynn teaches biblical literature at Southeast Missouri State University. He has served as chair of the American Academy of Religion's Religion and Disabilities Task Force and co-chair of the AAR's Religion and Disability Studies Group. He has written articles on the Bible and disability for *Prospectives in Religious Studies* and *The Bible Translator.*

Index of Subjects

Aaron, 82, 83, 84, 85, 126
Abraham, 79, 84, 94, 100, 156
Adad-guppi, 23, 24, 109, 111
Adam, 74, 76, 77, 147, 148, 208
Ahijah, 53, 59, 113
Akhenaten, 69
American Academy of Religion (AAR),
    vii, viii, 3, 209, 218, 221
Americans with Disabilities Act, 15,
    186, 188
anthropomorphism,
Apollodorus, 35, 36, 41, 44
Aristophanes, 41
Aristotle, 32, 37, 42, 44, 48, 93, 205, 213,
    217
Asa, 2
Athena, 35, 36, 41, 43
audiocentric(ity), v, 7, 47, 48, 50, 51, 52,
    53, 54

Baal, 54, 215
Babylonian(s), 2, 14, 15, 16, 18, 21, 24,
    25, 26, 29, 54, 112, 201, 204, 207, 210,
    213, 215
bias, 72, 92, 94, 95, 98, 101, 112
Bible, remembered, 162, 163, 164, 167,
    168, 170, 171
blemish, 26, 38, 83, 84, 86, 199, 205
bless(ing), 1, 36, 37, 39, 93, 94, 95, 96,
    98, 99, 100, 101, 105, 109, 188, 193
blind, 3, 5, 14, 15, 16, 17, 23, 27, 28, 31,
    32, 34, 41, 43, 44, 45, 70, 71, 76, 79,
    81, 82, 87, 92, 93, 94, 105, 107, 108,
    120, 121, 122, 123, 125, 126, 166, 186,
    193, 205, 206, 208, 210, 211, 213
blindness, 28, 30, 32, 34, 41, 42, 43, 44,
    45, 55, 82, 93, 94, 95, 96, 100, 103,

105, 108, 110, 113, 153, 177, 180, 193,
    203, 216
blood, 17, 71, 106, 107, 125, 146, 148,
    149
body, v, vi, 1, 4, 6, 8, 9, 13, 16, 17, 18,
    26, 29, 37, 47, 48, 58, 61, 62, 63, 69,
    70, 71, 74, 77, 83, 87, 92, 99, 103, 104,
    106, 107, 111, 113, 116, 124, 133, 134,
    140, 145, 146, 148, 149, 152, 155, 156,
    161, 162, 167, 174, 175, 176, 178, 180,
    183, 189, 193, 197, 198, 199, 200, 201,
    202, 204, 205, 210, 211, 212, 213, 214,
    215, 216, 217, 220, 221

Cain, 194
Callimachus, 41, 43
canon, 63, 64, 65, 70, 154, 181, 204
castration, 18
Christianity, 76, 176, 178, 181, 198, 202,
    205, 213, 219, 220
Christian(s), vii, viii, 9, 70, 87, 97, 131,
    133, 169, 171, 179, 180, 181, 182, 183,
    195, 201, 203, 205, 208, 211, 214, 219,
    220
Cicero, 38, 39
circumcision, 84, 85, 100
cognitive disability, 1, 4, 13, 15, 18, 28,
    30, 105, 107, 111, 116, 118, 120, 123,
    127, 128, 176, 177, 199, 200
community model, 6, 15, 19, 29, 30,
    177, 189
congenital abnormality, 7, 28, 31, 32,
    35, 36, 37, 38, 39, 41, 45, 70, 116, 175
corporeal criticism, 47, 58, 198
corporeality, 180, 202
cripple, 15, 16, 28, 35, 36, 38, 39, 80, 91,
    96, 97, 98, 99, 100, 108, 154, 179, 180

Index of Modern Authors

Index of Ancient Sources

Index of Selected Foreign Terms and Phrases

Printed in the United States
200257BV00004B/1-117/A